JULES FLANDRIN

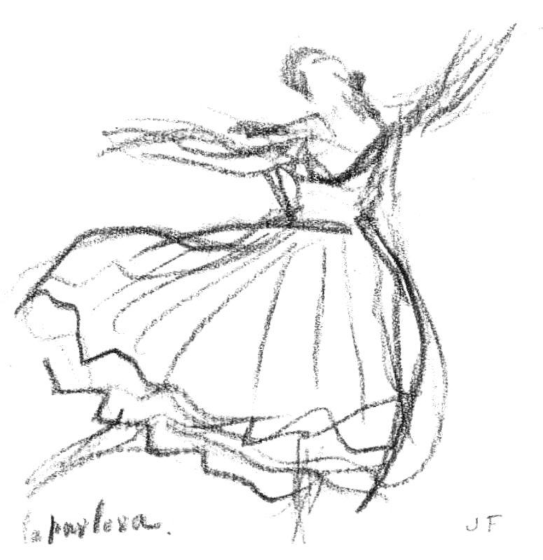

JULES FLANDRIN, *La Pavlova*, c.1910–11.
Pencil, private collection, Grenoble.

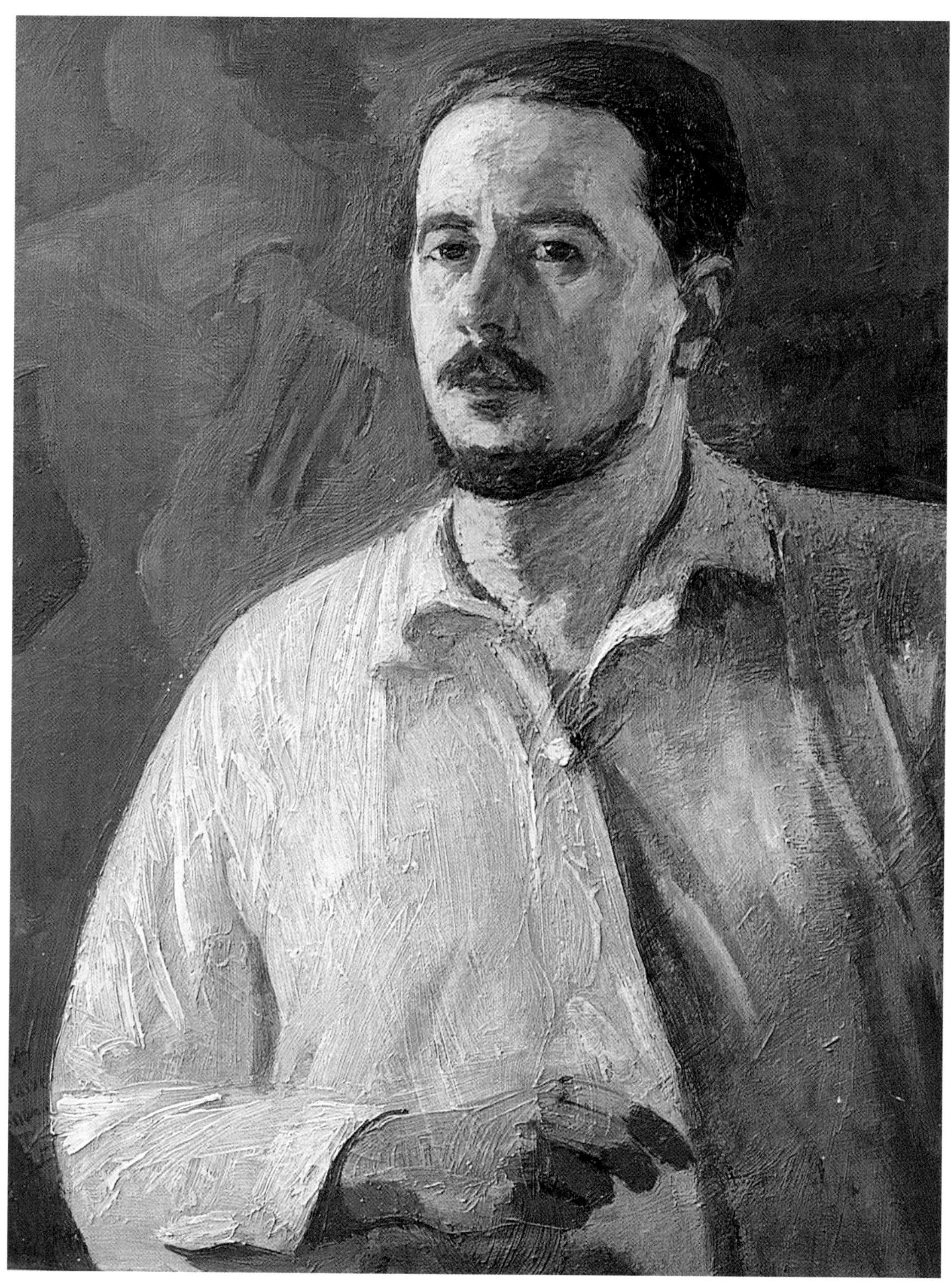

JULES FLANDRIN, *Portrait of the Artist*, 1924. Oil on canvas, 55 × 46 cms, private collection, Grenoble
(Cat. 70).

JULES FLANDRIN

1871–1947
THE OTHER FIN DE SIÈCLE

Juliet Simpson

With essays by
Georges Flandrin, Geneviève Lacambre and Jon Whiteley

Edited by Juliet Simpson
with editorial assistance from Tim Farrant

Ashmolean Museum, Oxford, 2001

Catalogue published in association with

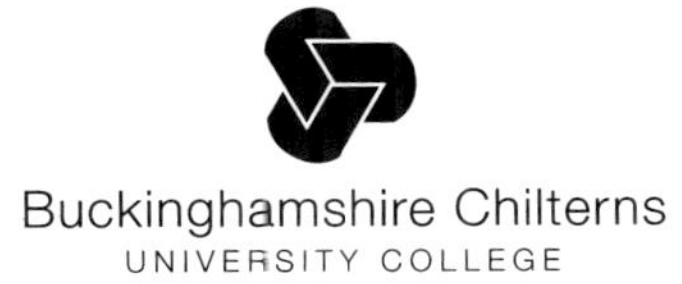

Buckinghamshire Chilterns
UNIVERSITY COLLEGE

This catalogue was first published on the occasion of the exhibition,
JULES FLANDRIN (1871–1947): THE OTHER FIN DE SIÈCLE,
Ashmolean Museum, Oxford, 17 April–24 June 2001

British Library Cataloguing in Publication Data

A Catalogue record for this book is available from the British Library

ISBN 1 85444 143 4 (paperback)
ISBN 1 85444 151 5 (hardback)

Cover illustrations:
(front) JULES FLANDRIN, *The Toilet (Marval)*, 1897. Oil on canvas, 92 × 60 cms,
private collection, Grenoble (cat. 19).
(back) JULES FLANDRIN, *Portrait of the Artist*, 1924. Oil on canvas, 55 × 46 cms,
private collection, Grenoble (cat. 70).

CATALOGUE DESIGNED BY BEHRAM KAPADIA
Typeset in Monotype Photina

Printed and bound in Belgium by Snoeck-Ducaju & Zoon, Gent, 2001

Contents

Foreword

There are many good reasons for holding an exhibition of the work of Jules Flandrin but the best is that he was a talented and important artist. We are pleased to think that the first major selection of his work seen outside France since his death in 1947 should be shown at the Ashmolean Museum. He is an appropriate artist to honour here as he was born and worked for many years in Grenoble, a city which Oxford counts among its 'twins'. We are glad to be able to honour an eminent *Grenoblois* and hope that there may be other occasions to build upon this opening. Our warmest thanks go to Dr Juliet Simpson, Reader in Art History at Buckinghamshire Chilterns University College, who conceived and curated this exhibition and has written the catalogue; and to our sponsors, Buckinghamshire Chilterns University College. In particular, we should like to thank the Director, Professor Bryan Mogford, and Mr John Oram, Dean of the Faculty of Applied Social Sciences and Humanities, Buckinghamshire Chilterns University College, and his colleagues at the College whose generosity and enthusiasm have made the exhibition possible. We are also most grateful to the artist's son, M. Jules Flandrin, to his nephew Dr Georges Flandrin, and to other members of Flandrin's family who have generously lent us works from their collections. We are equally grateful to many other lenders in France who have responded positively and readily to requests for loans. Without them, there would be no exhibition. Dr Georges Flandrin, in particular, has given unstinting help in many ways and on many occasions. The tribute to his uncle which he has written for the catalogue forms an eloquent introduction to Flandrin and his family. We are also very grateful to Mme Geneviève Lacambre, *conservateur en chef* at the Musée d'Orsay and curator of the Musée Gustave Moreau, for contributing an illuminating essay on the role of Moreau as a teacher.

DR CHRISTOPHER BROWN
Director, Ashmolean Museum

Preface

The exhibition of the work of Jules Flandrin has created a unique opportunity for the University College to help bring to the attention of a wider public the work of an artist who, as we can now appreciate, played a significant role in the development of modern painting. This has been conceived, developed and curated by the enthusiasm and diligence of my colleague, Dr Juliet Simpson, Reader in Art History at the University College. We would like to thank colleagues and staff at the Ashmolean Museum, in particular, the Director, Dr Christopher Brown, and his colleague, Dr Jon Whiteley, Senior Assistant Keeper of Western Art, for their support and guidance in helping the project to be realized. Above all, we are indebted to the Flandrin family and the many private lenders who have generously allowed the artist's work to be made available for exhibition. Special thanks are due to the artist's son, M. Jules Flandrin, and to his nephew, Dr Georges Flandrin who have given so unstintingly of their time in order to bring the works together, and who have provided insight into the artist's life. It is they who have made the exhibition possible. I am aware, however, that projects such as this can only be successfully realized through the efforts of many colleagues here and in France, for which we are most grateful. I am delighted to see our commitment to an international collaboration expressed in this unique cultural event.

PROFESSOR BRYAN MOGFORD
Director, Buckinghamshire Chilterns University College

Acknowledgements

This is the first British retrospective exhibition of Jules Flandrin, an artist who contributed to some of the most significant developments in late nineteenth- and early twentieth-century French art. It would not have been possible without the immense generosity of the Flandrin family, and of the many other private lenders to whom I owe an enormous debt of gratitude.

I am particularly grateful to Dr Georges Flandrin and to his wife Monique for their unstinting advice and help on all aspects of the exhibition's genesis; for allowing me access to the *Flandrin Family Archives*, and for their most generous hospitality in Paris. My deepest thanks are also due to the son of the artist, M. Jules Flandrin, for his support for and cooperation with the project from Corenc.

The exhibition has been mounted with the sponsorship of Buckinghamshire Chilterns University College, and the Arts and Humanities Research Board of Great Britain. I am deeply grateful for the generosity of the College, to the Director, Professor Bryan Mogford and, in particular, to Mr John Oram, Dean of the Faculty of Applied Social Sciences and Humanities, for making the project possible; to the Arts and Humanities Research Board for a Research Leave Award to complete it; and, on behalf of both myself and the College, to the Director, Dr Christopher Brown and staff of the Ashmolean Museum for hosting the exhibition, and for their practical help at every stage.

Dr Georges Flandrin, Mme Geneviève Lacambre, *conservateur en chef*, Musée d'Orsay, Paris, and Dr Jon Whiteley, Ashmolean Museum, Oxford, have most generously written essays in this catalogue while extremely busy with other professional duties. Dr Tim Farrant, Brian and Susan Taylor Fellow in French, Pembroke College, Oxford, has translated Dr Georges Flandrin's essay, and has provided invaluable assistance with the exhibition's overall conception and editorial support. I am immensely indebted to all of their inspiring and painstaking efforts on my behalf. At all stages in the mounting of this exhibition, Dr Jon Whiteley has offered wise guidance, reassurance and practical help. The project would not have been launched without the initial suggestion of Professor David Mason, Pembroke College, Oxford, and the support of Professor Alan W. Raitt, University of Oxford, and Mr Christopher Lloyd, Surveyor of the Queen's Pictures, whose advice and encouragement over a period of three years has underpinned the whole enterprise. My warmest thanks are also due to the following: Dr Jean-Claude Vatin, CNRS, Paris; Dr Jean-Claude Sergeant, Maison Française, Oxford and CNRS, Paris; Dr MaryAnne Stevens, Royal Academy of Arts; Professor Richard Thomson, University of Edinburgh; Professor Neil McWilliam, University of Warwick; Dr Paul Smith, University of Bristol; Dr Neil Cox, University of Essex; Dr M. Sonenscher, King's College, Cambridge; Mlle Agnès Muller, Université de Paris X, Nanterre, and

M. Jean-Louis Flandrin for generous translation advice; and to colleagues in the Department of Arts and Media and Faculty of Design at Buckinghamshire Chilterns University College, for all their help both academic and practical in bringing the exhibition to fruition. Photography has been arranged by Dr Georges Flandrin and the Ashmolean Museum photographic studio. For their enormous practical assistance, I am immensely grateful.

My greatest debt is to my family, to their encouragement in every detail of the exhibition's development; and to the late Dr Vera Daniel, Fellow of St. Hugh's College, Oxford and *Chevalier des Palmes Académiques*, whose warm friendship and immense knowledge of French culture has helped to shape my path.

Photographic acknowledgements: I. F. O. T. (Grenoble); M. Jacquet, Atelier 7 (Paris); A2C (Grenoble); Pierre Fillioley (Grenoble); Photo Cité (Grenoble); Photo J. Janisson (Paris); J. Klossa, ICG-Tribvn (Paris); Dr G. Flandrin (Paris); Ashmolean Museum (Oxford); RMN (Paris).

DR JULIET SIMPSON
Buckinghamshire Chilterns University College

Editor's Note

For the essays and catalogue, the following abbreviations have been used:

Flandrin and Roussier: Georges Flandrin and François Roussier, *Jules Flandrin (1871–1974): Un élève de Gustave Moreau témoin de son temps*, La Tronche, 1992.

Copier Créer: Jean-Pierre Cuzin, *et al., Copier Créer: De Turner à Picasso, 300 oeuvres inspirées par les maîtres du Louvre*, exh. cat., Musée du Louvre, Paris, 26 April–26 July, 1993.

Spurling: Hilary Spurling, *The Unknown Matisse: Man of the North, 1869–1908*, London, 1998.

The presentation of French titles in the essays follows the standard conventions of the Bibliothèque Nationale, Paris. Essays in English include translations of all quotations in French in the main text; the original citations are given in the references at the end of each essay. Dr Georges Flandrin's essay in French is also given in full English translation (by Dr Tim Farrant); Mme Geneviève Lacambre's is followed by a short summary in English (by Dr Jon Whiteley). I am immensely grateful to Dr Tim Farrant and to Dr Jon Whiteley for their translations from the originals.

The catalogue is divided into four sections which include works on paper as well as paintings: *Flandrin and Moreau: Copy and Creation, The Eclectic Eye, Expressing Modernity* and *Towards a New Classicism*. The works within each section are arranged chronologically.

Colour illustrations for the individual essays (between pages 64 and 65) are identified in each case by the author's name followed by the illustration number as it appears in the essay text, e.g. 'Juliet Simpson 7' and in the essay texts as 'col. ill. 7' (in Georges Flandrin's essay this is given as 'ill. coul. 7'); colour illustrations for catalogue entries are simply identified by catalogue number, followed by the title of the work in English, e.g. '19 *The Toilet (Marval)*, 1897', and denoted by an asterisk* after each title in the catalogue text.

Titles in the catalogue are given in English, followed in all cases by the French original.

All paintings are in oil on canvas unless otherwise stated; drawings and prints are on paper unless otherwise stated, their medium is always specified.

Dimensions of all works are given in centimetres (cm), height preceding width.

Some works executed by Jules Flandrin in the period covered by the exhibition (1886–1931) cannot be firmly dated. Where external evidence exists to permit a firm date within a given year, the date is given without qualification, e.g. '1892'. Where stylistic and/or external evidence suggest that the work was probably executed within a given year, the date is preceded by '*c.*', e.g. '*c.*1895'. Where stylistic and/or external evidence suggest that the work was executed within a longer period, the extent of the period is denoted as follows: '*c.*1906–8'.

When the history of a painting is uncertain, an ellipsis indicates the name of the collection or the sale through which the painting may have passed, e.g. '...'.

Exhibition references for works are listed chronologically. The titles of all exhibitions have been abbreviated as follows: location, institution and date, e.g. 'Paris, Louvre, 1993'. Full details of exhibitions are given in the *List of Exhibitions* at the end of the catalogue, following the *Select Bibliography*.

Bibliographical references for paintings are given in chronological order under 'LIT.:'. Primary source references have been abbreviated to author's surname, title and date of publication, e.g. Alexandre, *Le Figaro*, April 1898. In addition, where a reference occurs frequently in the catalogue as well as the essays, it has been abbreviated to the author's surname(s) followed, where necessary by date of publication and page reference(s), e.g. Marval (1913), p.160. Full bibliographical details are given in the *Select Bibliography*.

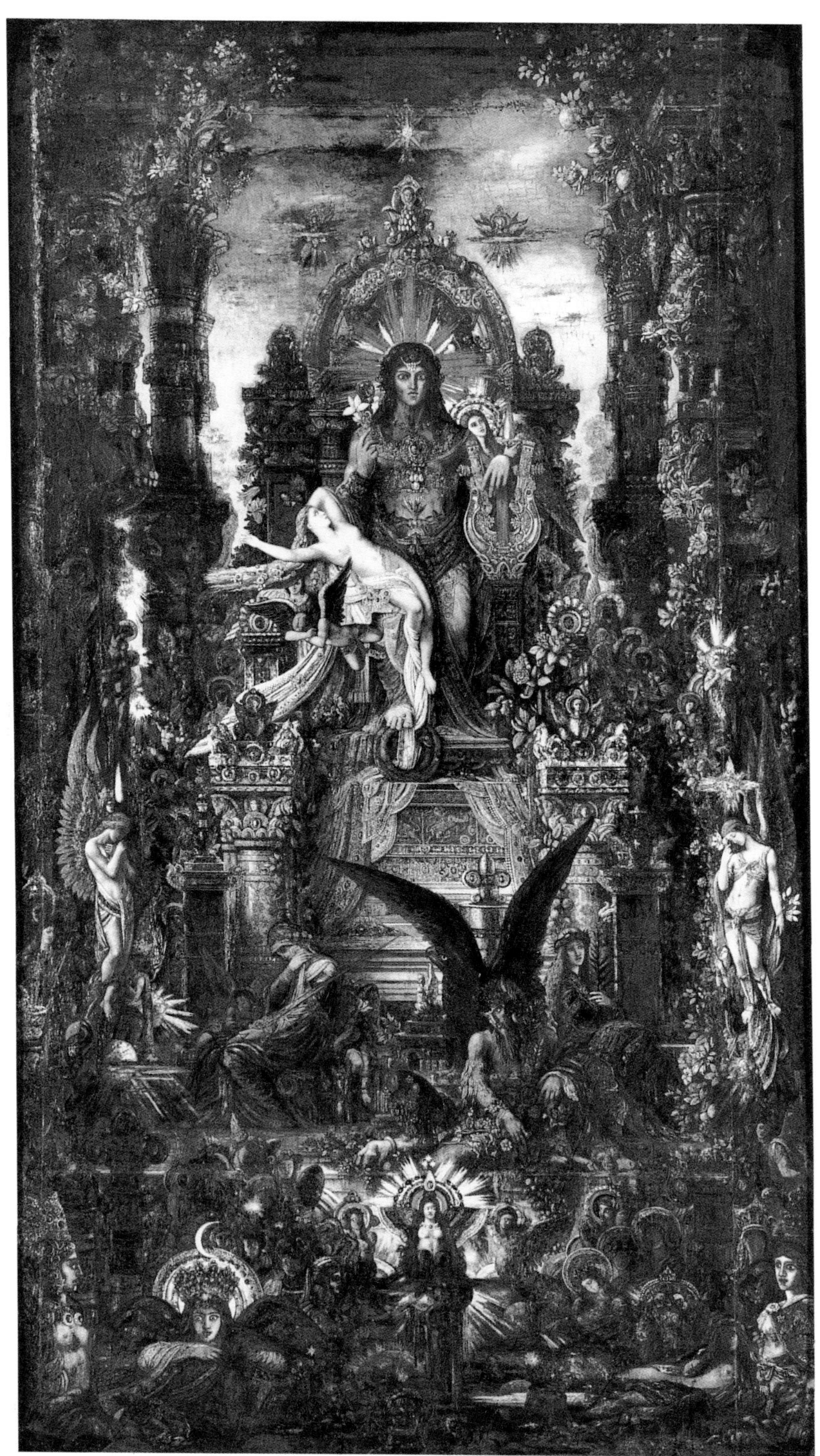

Illustration 1:
GUSTAVE MOREAU,
Jupiter and Semele,
1889–95.
Oil on canvas,
212 × 118 cms,
Musée Gustave
Moreau, Paris.
Photo: ©RMN, Paris.

Jules Flandrin: Between Two Centuries

Juliet Simpson

Do not be afraid to depend on the Masters. You will always find what you are after.[1]

All artists bear the imprint of their time but great artists are those in which this stamp is most deeply impressed.[2]

'Jules Flandrin is a whole epoch': in Lucien Mainssieux's 1948 tribute, Flandrin is the consummate embodiment of his period. And what a period this is: 'that which goes from the end of the nineteenth century with Bonnard, via the Fauves, to our own time.'[3] Flandrin has rarely featured in histories of the pioneering spirits of modern art. Yet his name crops up constantly in the company of Matisse, Albert Marquet, Georges Rouault, Kees Van Dongen, Othon Friesz:[4] that gifted generation of young artists who saw out the last years of the nineteenth century under the tutelage of Gustave Moreau, and who went on to form the nucleus of the Fauvist and Expressionist tendencies in the first decade of the twentieth century. The poet and defender of Cubism André Salmon dubbed Flandrin a trailblazer for the new 'art vivant' in 1912:[5] an idea which may not seem so far-fetched if we consider that this was a period of enormous transition not only for artists themselves, but for art institutions, for the art-going public, and indeed for the whole apparatus which determined how artistic reputations were made. The canons of today were neither defined nor certain in the heady and often confusing years of the century's turn. Flandrin was part of a ferment of new artists' groups still struggling to come to terms with Impressionism and Symbolism; assimilating the lessons of Courbet and Manet alongside those of Gauguin and Van Gogh, and persistently preoccupied by Cézanne's 'instinctual classicism'.[6] As well as these 'traditions' of the modern, the members of the group which came together under Moreau were also busy interpreting and translating the traditions of the past: traditions which acquired new resonance in response to a widespread need for durable forms and durable ideas within the ceaseless flux of modern life. Flandrin's art strikingly embodies these contradictions. Deeply involved with the innovations of his contemporaries, his example also shows the extent to which tradition and modernity were inseparably entwined goals of early twentieth-century avant-garde art.

Flandrin and Moreau: Copy and Creation

Flandrin entered Gustave Moreau's official studio at the École des Beaux-Arts in May 1895, following his arrival in Paris in 1893, and a brief period spent at the École des Arts Décoratifs in 1894.[7] Having begun his artistic career working as a capable but humble apprentice-printmaker in Grenoble for the Allier printers, contact with Moreau drew him rapidly into a new world that would profoundly shape his future work. From 1892 to 1898, Moreau's studio acted as a magnet for young artists struggling to make a name for themselves in the restrictive art environment of 1890s Paris. In 1895, Flandrin joined the ranks of Moreau's most favoured pupils: Georges Rouault, René Piot, Henri Matisse, Albert Marquet, Henri Manguin, Charles Guérin, the Belgian Henri Evenepoël, Simon Bussy, Georges Desvallières, swollen in 1897–8 by François-Joseph Girot and Charles Camoin;[8] they emerged as a loose-knit but clearly identifiable group between 1895 and Moreau's death in 1898. In Matisse's resonant words, these were the artists who found 'communion in Moreau';[9] who assimilated Moreau's teaching but were also encouraged, as Matisse later reflected, to step outside the confines of received histories and traditions in pursuit of their individual aesthetic ideals. 'He didn't set his pupils on the right road, he took them off it', quipped Matisse, 'he made them uneasy'.[10]

Moreau was seen by Flandrin's generation very much as a father of late nineteenth-century French art. Indeed, he was something of a colossus in the art world of the period; straddling two camps, he was both a respected academic, and held to be a precursor of the Symbolist movement. Along with Puvis de Chavannes, he appeared to stand apart from his establishment contemporaries, assuming instead the role of heroic 'moderniser' for the generation of the 1880s and 1890s.[11] What was so special about Moreau's studio for Flandrin and his contemporaries? And how did an artist steeped in the traditions of nineteenth-century history painting inspire the spiritedly modern work of his pupils which appears to be the very antithesis of Moreau's dense, symbol-laden allegories as epitomized by the monumental late *Jupiter and Semele* (1889–95: ill. 1)? Moreau's appeal was in part bound up with his debts to the past, but also with his deliberate individuality in the face of academic tradition. This flexibility of approach was unusual amongst his immediate academic counterparts, notably William-Adolphe Bouguereau, Jean-Léon Gérôme, Léon Bonnat and Jules Lefebvre. All holders of state honours, these were the figureheads of the French Academy, whose ideas dominated the teaching progamme at the prestigious École des Beaux-Arts in the rue Bonaparte, and at many of the respected private *ateliers* of the period, such as the Académie Julian where Bouguereau was in charge. Moreau was very much part of this establishment; in 1892, following the death of Jules-Élie Delaunay, he was elected to join Bonnat and Gérôme as one of the three professors who oversaw the curriculum at the École des Beaux-Arts. Yet his studio differed markedly from those of his academic contemporaries in that Moreau acted as both patron as well as teacher of his pupils, guiding them by an astute combination of instruction and inspiration.

Rouault recalls how Moreau's fierce but kind lessons galvanized his students' imagination, especially those which took place in the Louvre. As Matisse recalled: 'He didn't show us how to paint; he roused our imaginations in front of the life he found in those paintings.'[12]

The atmosphere in Moreau's studio was worlds away from the often tedious repetitiveness of the training in Bouguereau's, Bonnat's, Gérôme's and Lefebvre's, where students were habitually required to repeat sterile academic exercises to perfect their drawing techniques from the study of antique casts. There was little opportunity to learn about colour or form, and almost no direct training for specifically painterly concerns, as the young Henri Evenepoël's frustrations attest: 'Faced with the *antique*, I'm off ... I'll return to the studio in the hope of finding some living flesh!'[13] Moreau, in striking contrast, constantly encouraged his students to copy and learn intelligently from the Masters (as well as from real models). It is Evenepoël who gives us the most detailed and vivid insight into what it was actually like to be taught by Moreau during this period:

> He wants you to work simply and to put 'style' into your drawing as much as possible. He's an admirer of the 'Old Masters'. One can observe a little of this in his pupils, all of whom, without exception, copy not the tone of the model, but turn it into a sort of monochrome with the tones one sees in the Titians and the Veroneses in the Louvre.[14]

Indeed, Moreau saw copying in the Louvre as an essential aspect of any young artist's training. But here he urged his students to think of copying as a process of 'interpretation' rather than mere imitation, stimulating them to study a wide range of Masters, including those of the High Renaissance, sixteenth- and seventeenth-century Venetian art; the Florentine 'Primitives', and works by seventeenth-century Dutch masters, notably Rembrandt and Frans Hals. The models Moreau suggested emphasized the importance he assigned to the role of imagination and colour in art, and to decoration, as well as drawing: his advice to Evenepoël: 'You must copy nature with imagination. Colour should be thought, dreamed and imagined.'[15] Matisse recollects Moreau's fascination with texture which inspired him with a similar passion;[16] while Flandrin praises Moreau's particular method of mining a work for its secrets: 'After this progress, another, another, and I believe that we will all have a reason later to thank him from our hearts.'[17] Moreau's assiduous critiques of his young pupils' work also gave a sense of his direct engagement with their artistic discoveries. Daunting and memorable at the same time, Matisse recalls how in their early experiments with colour he and Flandrin were frequently given a tongue-lashing by the 'père Moreau' in ways which provoked them to probe more deeply into the traditions which they were only just beginning to grasp and exploit.[18]

In their different ways, Evenepoël's, Matisse's and Flandrin's comments all draw attention to the wider significance of Moreau's patronage for their contemporaries.

In promoting his own tastes over those of convention, Moreau perceptibly shifted the 'canons' of the past from the emulation of mainly High Renaissance Italian art (which formed the core of the Academic tradition),[19] towards a more eclectic understanding of tradition as represented by the Venetians, Titian and Veronese, the Dutch seventeenth-century school, and eighteenth-century French masters, chiefly Chardin and Watteau. What is more, Moreau's example encouraged students to engage with tradition as a living concern; as a 'hands-on' process of direct transmission between masters and students. In turn, this prompted in Moreau's pupils an interpretative response to the past which was to have major implications for the status of copying and its relation to the originality prized by the early twentieth-century avant-garde.[20] Finally, as a beacon of the Symbolist movement, Moreau was also a bridging figure between the old and new. As he himself prophesied: 'I am the bridge over which some of you will pass.'[21] Although ostensibly removed during the 1890s from currents in modern art, notably Impressionism and Neo-Impressionism, Moreau's eclectic use of tradition, his rich jewel-like colourism, and intensely decorative compositions linked his conception of art with the preeminence given to colour and form as languages in their own right advocated by the major exponents of Symbolism in the late 1880s and early 1890s: Redon, Bernard, Gauguin, Maurice Denis and the young Nabis group. Closely related was Moreau's emphasis on expressing interiority and emotions which were not merely stimulated by external sensations alone: an interiority created from a synthesis of traditional and contemporary artistic concerns. But here again, as Evenepoël reminds us, Moreau encouraged his students to look to those qualities in the art of the Old Masters which transcended rules and limiting generic categories: '*style, substance*, the *expressive arabesque* and the *imaginary transformism* of colour [Evenepoël's emphases].'[22] For Moreau, in other words, the innovations of the present should bear the stamp of those universal characteristics which are the hallmarks of all great art.

Such ideas played a formative role in Flandrin's developing artistic sensibility. In June 1895, unlike Matisse or Evenepoël, he finally gained full admission to the École des Beaux-Arts. But his expectations were soon to be dashed by what the critic Gustave Coquiot later described as the 'odious little farm at the rue Bonaparte'.[23] At this time, then, and in the immediate aftermath of Moreau's death, it was Moreau rather than the École, who provided the guiding inspiration for Flandrin. During the period 1895–1900, we see him responding to Moreau's influence in two distinct, yet related ways: in copies which attempt to interpret past traditions in the light of more contemporary artistic theories of colour and form; and in works concerned mainly with themes of interiority and states of self. Prior to arriving in Paris, Flandrin had already produced a number of paintings (cat. 1, 2 and 4) based on the scenery of his native Corenc, which, even at this early stage, show a mind constantly eager to assimilate new techniques and ideas. The small, atmospheric *Sunset* (1892: cat. 4), one of a series of oil landscape studies from the same period,[24] represents a move away from his more topographical compositions of the 1880s, such as *The Massif of the Chartreuse, the Pinéa seen from Saint-Egrève* (1889: cat. 2). Similarly, the Corotesque 1890 *Avenue of Blackberry Bushes* (cat. 3), with its remarkably free brushwork and expressively worked surface, suggests the style of Moreau's landscape studies *avant la lettre*, as well as anticipating the Impressionist tendencies in Flandrin's works of the early 1900s (see cat. 8, 22 and 33). Although Flandrin's subject-matter was to change considerably during his apprenticeship with Moreau, landscape painting remained his touchstone throughout his artistic career. 'It is the soul of Flandrin', remarked Joachim Gasquet.[25] It was to nature via the Masters that Flandrin turned when he wished to renew and nourish his aims as an artist; landscape was to be both his solace and his crucible for innovation.

Under Moreau we see Flandrin beginning to experiment with a huge variety of new sources and influences – an eclecticism which was to be a marked feature of his later work. Following Moreau's advice, he spent long periods in the Louvre, often in the company of Matisse, Marquet and Charles Camoin (see cat. 12), making copies of Moreau's favoured masters, notably, of Titian, Rembrandt, Veronese, Rubens and Watteau, as well as of the Florentine Primitives, Fra Angelico and Mantegna (see cat. 5, 6, 13, 14 and 15). It is clear from Flandrin's letters at this time that he saw Moreau's 'Louvre path' as being central to the development of his own style.[26] Some of the copies, especially his *Gilles* after Watteau, are exercises in the art of skilled imitation. But others, after Rubens's *The Coronation of Maria de' Medici* (1897: cat. 15), Veronese's *Wedding Feast at Cana* (1897),[27] and Rembrandt (1894–6: cat. 6 and 13), show him absorbing lessons in the creation of decorative effects through colour, and in the independently expressive power of colour and line. Several of Flandrin's copies earned him Moreau's approval, and at the state *Salon de la Société Nationale* at the Champ-de-Mars, where he exhibited work for the first time in 1896:

> Has M. Jules Flandrin really been able to put to good use the lessons of his illustrious teacher without thinking himself compelled to pastiche him? To find this surprising, one would need to have have forgotten how far the teaching of Gustave Moreau rose above simple studio recipes and how he was able to break with the traditions which before him had thwarted the development of individual temperaments

commented one critic, praising Flandrin's 'admirable reproduction' of Watteau's *Gilles*.[28] The idea of copying as the expression of individuality, here, is revealing. Of even more significance is Flandrin's parallel effort to transform his copying activities into new works which synthesize the techniques and spirit of past traditions with contemporary subjects and themes.

Two works from the period 1896–8 are particularly illuminating: *The Toilet (Marval)* (1897: ill.2, cat. 19) and the *Portrait of François Flandrin Reading* (1898: cat. 24). *The Toilet* is – revealingly, one may feel – one of his first studies of Marval (Marie Vallet), the Grenoblois seamstress whom he met in 1895, and who was to influence

Illustration 2:
JULES FLANDRIN, *The Toilet (Marval)*,
1897.
Oil on canvas, 92 × 60 cms,
private collection, Grenoble.

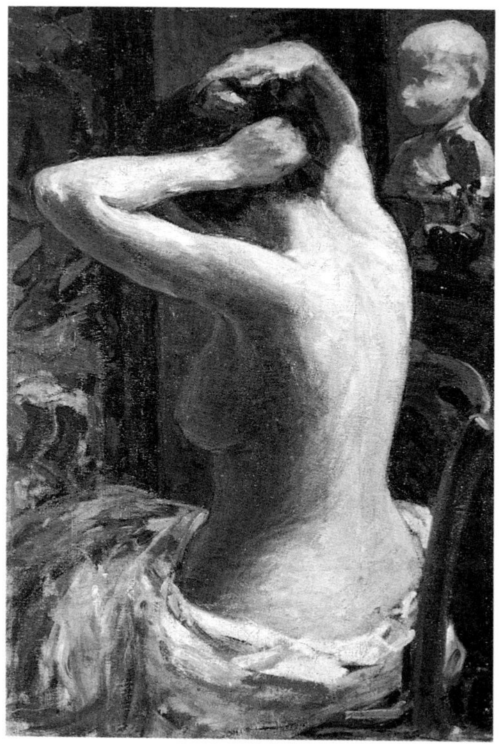

the future path of his art as his mistress, model and artist-partner for more than three decades. One of only two nudes painted by Flandrin,[29] its solid plasticity and sensuous rendering of flesh shows his debt to the sixteenth- and seventeenth-century Venetian school and Rubens; while the charcoal study of *François Flandrin Reading* derives its inwardness in part from the artist's use of Rembrandtesque *chiaroscuro* to create subtle effects of light and dark. Similar tendencies are evident in Matisse's work at this time, notably in his *Woman Reading* (1895: ill. 3): one of several rear-view figures and portraits painted in the manner of seventeenth-century Dutch and eighteenth-century French masters, especially Chardin. Yet the intensely meditative quality of Flandrin's paintings, with their expressive treatment of colour and form, also suggests contact with newer influences deriving from contemporary Symbolist use of form to evoke the inner world of emotions and psychological states. Moreau was doubtless the main route for these ideas. But we know that Flandrin was also voraciously absorbing directly from other sources which offered alternatives to those advocated by the École: Puvis de Chavannes, whose work he saw at the annual *Salon du Champ-de-Mars* and who crops up constantly in his letters; Pierre Bonnard, Maurice Denis; and the graphic work of Toulouse-Lautrec and Jules Chéret. In *The Toilet*, for example, the nude's treatment, which forms part of and is bounded by the red interior, recalls Bonnard's decorative 'intimism' where figure and setting are fused together in tense and synthetic

Illustration 3:
HENRI MATISSE, *Woman Reading*,
1895.
Oil on wooden panel, 61.5 × 48 cms,
Musée nationale d'Art moderne,
Paris. Photo: ©RMN, Paris.

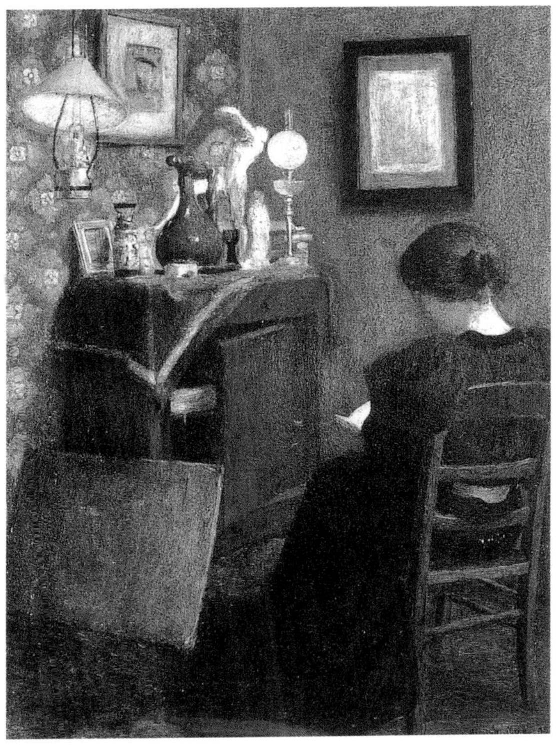

designs. Flandrin would have been familiar with Bonnard's and Denis' work through the regular *Peintres impressionnistes et symbolistes* exhibitions at Le Barc de Boutteville's gallery, and at Ambroise Vollard's in the rue Lafitte from 1897. As Georges Flandrin observes, his work of 1896–8 with its decorative treatment of form and space, certainly shows a marked debt to Nabi art.[30] Bold simplification, combined with an intimate quality of atmosphere and mood are also key characteristics of the small jewel-like *Shady Street, Paris* (c.1895: cat. 8), *Marval Reading* (1895: cat. 9), *Woman with a Bouquet in front of Le Moucherotte (Marval)* (c. 1897: cat. 20), and the introspective *Portrait of François Flandrin in Blue* (1897: cat. 17).

In this, Flandrin's most overtly Symbolist painting, there is a clear attempt to evoke a psychological 'portrait' of the subject's mood through suggestive colour harmonies and the unreal, dream-like landscape. At the same time, as in *François Flandrin Reading*, the stylized forms with their strong outlines and colour patterns have the graphic immediacy of a poster. We see Flandrin here attempting to combine his artisanal roots and his experience as a printmaker and illustrator (see cat. 11) with lessons in how to arrest the eye with a type of visual shorthand learned directly from poster art. Flandrin's elder brother Joseph had thoughtfully supplied examples by Lautrec and Chéret in order to make his studio a 'sympathetic environment'.[31]

To a large extent, Flandrin's experiments reflect those of Moreau's other 'fidèles' in this period. Evenepoël's accounts of his time spent with Moreau attest a constant exchange of new ideas amongst Moreau's devotees, especially about the Old Masters, copying techniques, colour and its effects, and painting 'en plein air'.[32] Flandrin's letters of the late 1890s reveal that he was working closely with Matisse, Marquet and Camoin, at a point when each artist had begun to explore the past as a way of getting to grips with the present. There are also striking similarities in theme and style between Flandrin's art and Evenepoël's, particularly in their interpretations of family and childhood. Flandrin's *Grandmother Giving Soup to her Grand-daughter* (1898: cat. 21) shows him working in a lyrical, realist tradition close in spirit to Evenepoël's early work;[33] whilst in the series of colour studies of Flandrin's niece, Dédé (see cat. 25 and 26), impressionistic colour effects and the fluid, open brushwork capture child-like innocence and spontaneity in a manner which recalls the easy informality of Evenepoël's portraits of children.[34] But what is perhaps most distinctive about Flandrin's early work is its embodiment of the broader struggles facing his contemporaries at the century's turn: of fusing Moreau's legacy with Puvis's; combining a classical sense of form and structure with a modern and decorative intimacy; allying the painterly (a love of colour) with the expressive immediacy of the graphic arts. Such concerns were clearly foremost in Flandrin's mind when in 1898, after visiting the newly-opened Gustave Moreau Museum, he wrote admiringly of his master's 'love of colour allied to an absolute feeling for drawing'.[35] A long letter to his father the following year expands on Moreau's example, emphasizing the importance of beauty, of 'intelligent drawing' and of the necessary simplification of details which Flandrin sees as characteristic of the great works of the past. The idea is taken up again in a letter of 1900 which includes a genealogy of artists, with Puvis and Moreau at the head of an inheritance which unites via Ingres and Delacroix, the great Masters of classicism and of colour.[36] Above all, the past must be a beacon for future innovation. 'I believe that progress will consist of making a larger number of men capable of learning and applying what is good, but not necessarily of finding a new kind of the good': in his own words, Flandrin describes what will become the animating concerns in the following decade.[37]

The Eclectic Eye

The deaths of Moreau and Puvis in 1898 left a gaping hole in the world of *fin-de-siècle* Paris. For Flandrin's generation, which had come to see them as links between the present and past, the double loss was especially acute. Over the following years, bereft of Moreau's guidance but fiercely loyal to his ideals, his pupils faced an identity crisis which persisted into the early 1900s.[38] Matisse turned his back on Paris and went south in 1898; Evenepoël died young in 1899; Marquet and Rouault both withdrew from public life for a time – Rouault more or less permanently. Flandrin continued to haunt the galleries of the Louvre, furious at Fernand Cormon,

Moreau's inept replacement at the École ('an empty head' as he called him[39]) and wistfully invoking the mastery of Moreau and Puvis.[40]

Added to these tensions was a broader and profound questioning of artistic and cultural aims and directions as the new century approached. The years around 1900, like those of our own *fin de siècle*, were very much characterized by the sense of an age and its *mentalité* in transition, with its identity still undefined; its reference points still rooted in late nineteenth-century values and conflicts. Despite the public triumph of the 1900 *Exposition Universelle*, the celebrations which accompanied the dawning of the twentieth century seemed to many to be concocted and confused in a France smarting from the aftermath of the Dreyfus Affair. 'The motley show that this hour of an ending century offered', is the way in which the Belgian poet Émile Verhaeren described the 1900 Exhibition.[41] The political and social turmoil of the late 1890s was everywhere marked: in the riots and skirmishes on the streets, mirrored by the restlessness and fighting in cafés and artists' *ateliers* (including Moreau's)[42] across the capital. 'Paris is toppling' wrote Evenepoël in his final days, 'politics is becoming indecipherable [...] there is an enormous rise in anarchy [...] there is something rotten going on here'.[43] Similar upheavals were being felt in the sphere of art, as older institutions for public display and acclaim, such as the *Salon des Champs-Élysées*, were being eclipsed by the newer, more cosmopolitan state-run *Salon de la Société Nationale des Beaux-Arts* and the ever-expanding *Société des Artistes Indépendants*, which itself was soon to be upstaged by the *Salon d'Automne* from 1903.[44] Then there was the proliferation of entrepreneurial private dealer-galleries and networks – Berthe Weill, Ambroise Vollard, Daniel-Henry Kahnweiler, the Bernheim-Jeune family – which built on the efforts of Le Barc de Boutteville and Père Tanguy in the last decade of the nineteenth-century in establishing new ways of both viewing and purchasing modern art. As Gérard Monnier has argued: 'Paris shone with the resources given by an exclusive concentration of the art market and a large, cosmopolitan artistic population.'[45] Modern art, too, was shifting ground. Impressionism, still a force to be reckoned with, was becoming 'institutionalized' and (in the minds of many critics) conflated with a diversifying Symbolism. Indeed, former definitions of modern and of modern art, were increasingly open to question.

So far from being isolated, Moreau's pupils found themselves at the epicentre of these changes. Caught in a period of transition – both private and public – their efforts would soon bear fruit in works which, in many ways, epitomize that process of transition itself. A major stimulus was the emergence, in the early 1900s, of specific group identities defined by small galleries and dealers rather than by 'artists' societies' or the State; and by an artistic climate that was increasingly receptive to the expression of individuality.[46] Described as loosely 'Impressionist', the artists who came together in the first exhibition at the new Berthe Weill Gallery in February 1902, included Flandrin, Matisse, Marquet and Marval in a conscious attempt to promote a group ethos.[47] For Flandrin, like Matisse and Marquet, the early 1900s were lean years. Yet despite his failure to sell, his work was already attracting critical attention in the official exhibition world: at the Salons of the *Société Nationale* to which he had been elected as a *sociétaire* in 1898.[48] The response, though, was not all favourable; while his early portraits, interiors and copies had met with praise,[49] the ten new paintings, including *The Toilet* (1897), and seven drawings exhibited in 1899 earned him the epithet 'outsider and Symbolist' for works which appeared to travesty tradition and celebrate ugliness by their 'brutal' colours and stylized forms.[50] Published in the mainstream *Écho de Paris*, the negative publicity, however, worked to Flandrin's advantage both aesthetically and politically: by highlighting differences between his modern traditionalism and Academicism; by categorizing him as an 'Independent' and therefore as an 'innovator'; and by implicitly linking the two.

The image of Flandrin as an 'Independent' was further bolstered by his inclusion amongst the 'Indépendants' at the 1900 *Exposition Universelle*, even though he continued to seek recognition at the state *Société Nationale*. This was not – as it may seem – a conflict of interests: it was, rather, symptomatic of a tendency fostered by the *Société Nationale* itself, in which distinctions between 'Salon' artists and 'Independents' had become blurred. By the early 1900s, the *Société des Artistes Indépendants* witnessed a similar process of diversification, which meant that it could hardly claim to represent a minority avant-garde.[51] For Flandrin and fellow disciples of Moreau, the problem of finding an identity or a voice, of defining their aims in relation to the legacies of Naturalism, Impressionism and Symbolism was becoming a central preoccupation, especially in the context of a baffling array of new avant-garde tendencies. It is this situation which in part explains the initiative of the Weill gallery exhibition in 1902. The aim was to mark out a new territory which in some sense would stand apart from the indistinct ranks of former and contemporary avant-gardes: '[this] would be a new dawn for me' as Flandrin hoped in 1900[52] – although, in reality, it represented an effort that would remain transitional for several years. The prophetic words of the veteran Symbolist, Charles Morice, sum up the bigger picture in 1905:

> It is clear that at the present time, the plastic arts are hesitating between memories and desires, the former weighing heavily on the latter and impeding their ascent. There is, in consequence, above all amongst the younger generation, a profound disquiet, which the annual exhibitions have betrayed for some time. We are in the aftermath of *something*. Are we also on the eve of *something else*? [Morice's emphases][53]

Morice's pregnant question aptly links the idea of homage to a call for renewal, for perhaps of more importance to Moreau's disciples at this period than labels of 'independent' or 'avant-garde', was a concern to take the implications of Moreau's guidance further: to study the life on the streets *outside* the museum as well as the Masters inside.

For Flandrin, the opportunity to develop these ideas came in 1901 when he set his mind on earning his living as a professional artist. He had begun to sell work through the Fénoglio Gallery in Grenoble – an association which was to serve him well throughout his life. But the major impetus to his career came from his close contact with Matisse and Marquet, and from his mistress Marie Vallet. She and Flandrin had been living together at 9 rue Campagne Première since 1895, and around 1900, under his influence, she began to paint in earnest, restyling herself as an artist under the pseudonym Jacqueline Marval. The large apartment block, near the Luxembourg gardens and a warren of studios including Flandrin's, was a short walk from 19 Quai St. Michel – another veritable artist's colony, home to Matisse and his wife since 1899[54] and eventually to Flandrin and Marval in 1919.[55] The many comings and goings between studios sparked a rich exchange of ideas and inspiration, fired especially by Marval's forceful and flamboyant personality. From 1901, Matisse and Marquet were regular visitors to rue Campagne Première, where they set up easels alongside Flandrin and Marval in their studio, painting views of the Luxembourg gardens and the nearby suburbs at Arcueil in colours which would soon provoke outcry.[56] It was, as an interview with Marquet later recorded,[57] an ambience conducive to a special kind of *ménage*; the cradle of the Weill 'Jeune peinture' exhibition in 1902, it was also the wellspring whence Flandrin's new ideas sprang.

Two quite marked innovations in Flandrin's work of the early 1900s attest his shared interests with Matisse and Marquet in this period: his developing concern with the structural as well as the expressive properties of colour; and his search for inspiration drawn from the street, taken *sur le vif* (see ill. 4). In addition, Flandrin was giving greater emphasis to his graphic work, as is shown by a series of improvisatory studies of Marval, now his constant muse (see cat. 32 and 53), of family and friends music-making and at play (see cat. 31), and in numerous summary sketches of boats and harbour captured on a visit to Le Havre with Marval in 1903. His early training at the École des Arts Décoratifs had also imbued him with a strongly decorative tendency – a marked feature of his early drawings and lithographs (see cat. 11). This, combined with the newer influences of the Nabis, and Chéret and Lautrec – whom he continued to admire – was to remain a developing and constant feature of his art in the two following decades. Whereas Matisse was much preoccupied with painterly problems in the early 1900s, yet was still struggling with his drawings, Flandrin's have a fluid and almost calligraphic boldness with close affinities to Marquet's and Camoin's.[58] Not only does this suggest a reciprocal dependence on each other's ideas, with Flandrin and Marquet pushing back boundaries ahead of Matisse in some cases,[59] it indicates that the graphic was increasingly serving as a vehicle for working through larger problems about expression, structure and form. Paring a subject down to the essentials of shape and line was to become a way of seizing both the fleeting impression of a sensation and its durable aspect; of conveying what is permanent in the instant.

These graphic concerns are integrally connected with painterly innovations of the period, which show Flandrin, along with Matisse and Marquet, attempting to

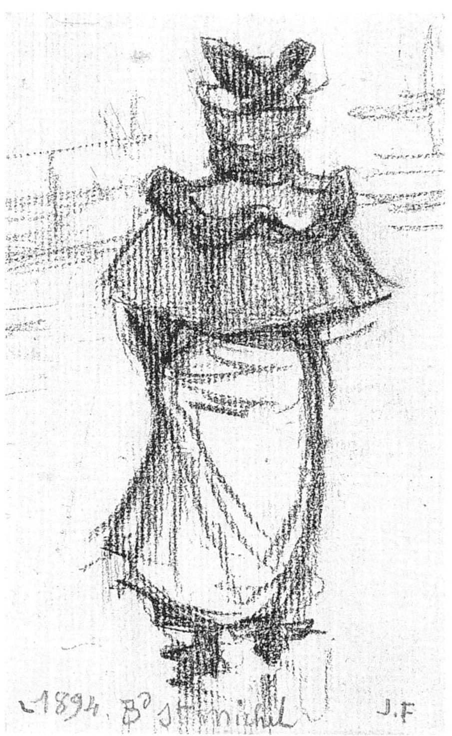

Illustration 4:
JULES FLANDRIN, *On the Boulevard*, 1894.
Pencil, 13.5 × 8.5 cms,
private collection, Grenoble.

assimilate and transform the Impressionist inheritance. For Flandrin, the break-through into colour had come in the late 1890s in the portraits of Dédé (cat. 25, 26 and 30) where we see his direct response to Matisse's example, particularly to the glowing landscapes painted in Corsica and Toulouse in 1898. Matisse, 'the Ravier of sunlight', as Flandrin describes him in a letter to his father, 'recalls our sunny Corenc, and gives me real joy'.[60] The comparison indicates a new point of depar-ture. Like Matisse, Flandrin starts to abandon the earthy tones associated with Flemish and Dutch traditions of painting, for high-keyed Impressionist colour, as shown in his Corenc landscapes, *The Alps at Twilight, Corenc* (1898: cat. 23), and in family portraits, notably, *Dédé in Blue* (1899: cat. 26). But his tendency to use colour non-naturalistically to create decorative effects as well as light, as in *The Toilet, Shady Street*, and in an early self-portrait of 1897 (cat. 16), already looks ahead to future interests. The early 1900s see Flandrin, Matisse, Marquet and Camoin turn-ing variously to Paris streetscapes, landmarks, and views of the Seine, all revisiting the subjects of Impressionism, in the light of Moreau's advice that 'colour should be dreamed and imagined',[61] and the innovations of Gauguin, Van Gogh and Cézanne.

Flandrin's atmospheric *The Seine at Sunrise* (1902: cat. 33) shows a clear debt to Sisley's and Monet's late work, as well as making a passing nod in the direction of Signac and Neo-Impressionism. But the heightened yellow tonalities and decorative effects of sky and sunset also attest the more recent influence of Symbolism. It is significant that in his letters of the period Flandrin was frequently referring to Impressionism either in connection with the past – with the art of Corot, Millet and Courbet – or through the lens of Puvis and Moreau. The two concerns are visible in *The Seine at Sunrise*, where colour is deployed as a luminous, expressive and structural element in a way similar to Matisse's and Marquet's efforts to translate light and atmosphere in terms of simple. flat and intense colour planes in their views of Notre-Dame and the Quai St. Michel, notably, Matisse's *Notre-Dame with a Violet Wall* (1902: private collection), and Marquet's *Notre-Dame, Sun* (1904: Musée des Beaux-Arts, Pau). What is at issue is the larger problem of combining sensation and abstraction, vision and the visionary; as Matisse put it, 'of giving to reality a more lasting interpretation' – making time stand still.[62] From this point onwards, as in *Horsewoman and Horseman, boulevard Montparnasse* (1899, redated 1900: cat. 28), we begin to see Flandrin subsuming both Impressionist and overtly Symbolist interests in works which marry expressive and intense colour to solidity of form and composition; which unite the modern, the decorative and the durable.

Whilst Flandrin's latest paintings of Paris were being met with incomprehension in Grenoble, his increasingly daring approach to colour was putting him on the Paris dealer-gallery circuit. The Weill exhibition marked the point of closest intimacy for the Flandrin–Marval and Matisse–Marquet partnerships. A modest event in itself, it sparked a rise in each artist's fortunes, setting a precedent by which reputations were championed through small group identities that highlighted both group and individual innovations. Although short-lived, the unity of the Weill group exhibition left its imprint on Flandrin in both practical and artistic terms. In 1903, he exhibited at the first *Salon d'Automne* organized by the enterprising Frantz Jourdain; and he continued to be represented at the *Indépendants* for the rest of the decade. In 1905 he was taken up by Eugène Druet, the dealer who mounted Flandrin's first one-man show in January 1906 at his newly-opened gallery on the rue du Faubourg Saint-Honoré, and oversaw his Paris career thereafter.[63] The paintings of the 1904–5 period are also marked by the experimentalism of the previous years. Flandrin's close affiliation with Fauvism at this point is highlighted in his efforts to capture the transience of sensations, and to communicate their intensity. In the extraordinarily expressive *The Little School Boy* (c.1904: ill. 5, cat. 34) and perhaps less strikingly in *The Masquerade* (c.1904: cat. 35), portraits are abbreviated in vigorous daubs and hatchings of unmixed pigment, so boldly applied that patches of bare canvas are visible between the individual strokes. The cursory forms, flying colours and sheer energy of the brushwork have much in common with Matisse's and Marquet's boldly simplified landscapes of 1901–2, such as Matisse's vibrantly-hued *The Luxembourg Gardens* (1900–2: The Hermitage Museum, St. Petersburg) and the later series of Fauvist portraits by Matisse and André Derain, where colour has been liberated from naturalistic description. This is painting for another world, a new age. *The Little School Boy* may not deploy pure colour as does much of Matisse's contemporary work, but its sense of raw energy conveyed in the forceful painterly notations is strikingly 'fauve' in character. Colour and form, unleashed as independently evocative elements in their own right, are accentuated and simplified to convey the idea of rapid, almost aggressive improvisation. This, together with the powerfully visible texture, 'the coarse materiality', as the critic Camille Mauclair described it, bears all the hallmarks of Fauve modernity.[64] In *The Little School Boy*, the very paint becomes a translation of its subject, transposing into an expressive language of colour, form and texture, the feeling of a child's world: its liveliness and fragility.[65]

To his mingled chagrin and relief, Flandrin was left out of the celebrated 'fauve' débâcle in 1905,[66] despite being dubbed by Morice – along with Rouault, Matisse, Maillol, Desvallières and Kees Van Dongen – as an instigator of the art of the future.[67] Of the famous 1905 article in *L'Illustration* (4 November) which featured a double-page spread with examples of the offending art, Flandrin complained to his mother: 'Luckily at least you can see what my pictures represent since they didn't think me fit to appear there, but out of ten artists, eight are friends of mine and I know the other two!'[68] The mixture of philosophical tone and palpable disappointment reflects Flandrin's contemporary ambivalence about his own artistic aims. From 1906 onwards, he parted ways with the group around Matisse. Although he continued to use colour in the spirit of the Fauvist effort, the work from 1906 to 1910 places greater emphasis on decorative, classicizing tendencies, expressed in his preoccupation with pastoral subjects: landscapes and still-lifes. Here, Flandrin's art can also be seen as a barometer of more general artistic currents of the period: a Janus-faced period which saw, as well as an explosion of avant-garde 'petites-révolutions' as Morice put it in 1905,[69] a panoply of retrospectives – Gauguin in 1903; Puvis, Redon, Renoir, Cézanne and Lautrec in 1904 (at the *Salon d'Automne*); Ingres, Cézanne, Seurat and Van Gogh in 1905 (at the *Salon d'Automne*); Cézanne in 1907 – as *hommages*, and in response to the turning of an age.[70] These, along with the State bequests of great private collections – Étienne Moreau-Nélaton's in 1906 and 1907[71]; Isaac de Camondo's in 1914: both to the Louvre – gave Flandrin's generation an almost unprecedented opportunity to view works by past and modern masters side-by-side with the latest trends in contemporary art. In short, this was an historical encounter with traditions in formation, whose implications no young artist of the time could ignore. 'In my eyes it pushed back the boundaries of art', records Flandrin, thrilled by his visit to Moreau-Nélaton's celebrated *hôtel-musée* in 1904, especially by the Corots.[72] The 1904 *Salon d'Automne*, with its individual *hommages* to Cézanne, Puvis, Renoir, Redon and Lautrec, inspires in him a similar response: 'It's a sort of *coup d'état* by the young school of Independents and its Masters.'[73]

New perspectives on modern art, combined with Flandrin's continuing debt to Moreau's ideas, were to shape his artistic development from now on. His eclecticism also becomes symptomatic of the bigger and continuing problem of how to take Impressionism and Symbolism forward, identified by Morice as the main challenge facing the avant-garde in his extensive 'Enquête sur les tendances actuelles des arts

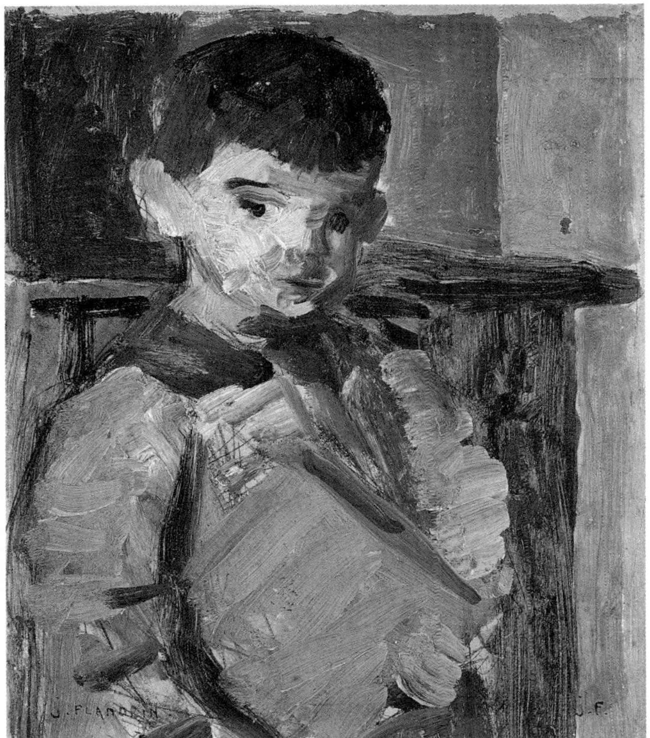

Illustration 5:
JULES FLANDRIN,
The Little School Boy,
c. 1904.
Oil on board,
27.5 × 23.5 cms,
private collection, Paris

plastiques' of 1905.[74] It is not surprising, therefore, that we find him preoccupied in his letters of the period with a familiar and insistent theme: how to use tradition as a stimulus for innovation, now framed by concerns emerging from his contact with Matisse at the start of the decade. 'What you will find there', as he had written in 1902 to his old army compatriot, Lucien Mainssieux in the context of the Old Masters, 'is the secret of forms, which is so hidden in nature, even though it is always there'.[75] Finding the 'secret of forms', or suggesting what is lasting in nature by simplifying the tumult of sensations, defined the underpinning goals of the Fauvist effort in 1905. But Flandrin takes up this idea in response to newer influences deriving from Puvis and especially Denis, with whom he was on close terms from 1904.

The work of the 1906–1910 period is markedly indebted to these sources, particularly to Maurice Denis's religiosity and naïve stylizations – 'the language of the soul of an artist', as Flandrin describes it following a visit to Denis in 1905.[76] The two interests are united in the monumental *Homage to Handel* (*The Blue Angel*) (1905: see cat. 36) intended as a decoration for the church at Corenc. This, Flandrin's first major religious project, displays his affinities with Denis in his attempt to create a modern, decorative and monumental art, close in spirit as well as style, to the great fresco cycles of early Renaissance art. Yet the vibrant use of colour, and robustly simplified forms link *Homage to Handel* directly to the experimental works of 1904: a major reason for its hostile reception at the *Société Nationale* – 'a horror and one of considerable dimensions', as one reviewer indignantly put it in 1905.[77] A similar fusion of tendencies characterizes the series of still-lifes, including the magisterial *Glass Fruit Bowl* (1910: cat. 43) admired by André Salmon, and the idyllic landscapes and children at Corenc, painted between 1908 and 1910. In the series of studies of small girls: *Seated Girl, Corenc (Pierrette)* (1908: cat. 40), *Juliette in a Hat* (1910: cat. 44), and notably *Two Young Girls, September Afternoon* (1908, redated 1913: cat. 42), we see Flandrin simplifying and synthesizing form and colour so as both to render his composition intelligible, in a manner similar to Matisse's ideas in his 'Notes of a painter' of 1908; and to convey a harmony and balance within nature, related to Puvis's pastoralism and to Denis's decorative ornamentalism. The willed search for order and permanence would lead him inevitably towards 'The sacred soil of Italy' (as he prophesied to his brother Joseph in 1909)[78] – to the combination of intimacy and monumentality we see in his portrait the *Young Italian Woman* (1912: cat. 59). At the same time, Flandrin was also absorbed with turning tradition into a dynamic, vital impulse, animating even the most contemporary manifestions of the modern.

Expressing Modernity

With the dawning of a new century, Flandrin had found himself plunged into an artistic milieu caught up in the fever of the contemporary, as well as in the immediate past. This was a time of intense and rapid innovation, which no young artist like Flandrin could ignore. Light and power were transforming city streets; the pace of life had quickened. The motorcar, telephone and camera were changing the very way in which reality was being perceived. For Flandrin, as for many of his contemporaries, the sheer novelty of the age was both bewildering and inspiring. In 1900, the coming of electricity transformed his working life: 'It's thanks to my electricity that I was able to do what I wanted', he wrote to his mother;[79] the new industrial architecture of the 1900 *Exposition Universelle* enthralled him.[80] By mid-decade, he had become passionately keen on photography, and was teaching the photography-enthusiast Druet about the Lumière brothers and their pioneering experiments in the field of colour transparency.[81] His own work of the period was inescapably marked by these innovations. Although landscape and nature remained persistent interests up to and beyond the Great War, Flandrin was also responding to the stimulus of the modern, drawing inspiration, along with Matisse, Marquet, Camoin and Van Dongen, from the city and its entertainments: from its kaleidoscope of change.

Modern life was hardly a new theme for the artists of Flandrin's generation. But what was different for Flandrin and his contemporaries was the increased technology for and the speed of change. For artists, the dynamism of the age was also giving rise to a palpably new aesthetic: an *esthétique de la rue*, as the writer Gustave

Kahn termed it, in a provocative study published in 1901. This was expressed especially in what Kahn characterizes as the 'polychromy' of the urban space, now illuminated by bright, electric light, by its 'festival of scientific illuminations',[82] and splashed everywhere with coloured posters – quintessential emblems of modernity. Posters, products of the new industrial process of chromolithography, were adverts for the times – key elements in what Kahn calls the 'décor' of streets, and ablaze with images, forms and colours that were shaping a whole attitude to, and more vitally, mentality of the modern.[83] An article published in the *Mercure de France* in 1905 expanded on Kahn's ideas, suggesting that posters are, indeed, the *musée ambulant* of the urban world. These, the mobile masterpieces of the streets, symbolize the very spirit of the time: of 'an era in love with vulgarity and avid for change'.[84] Linked to this is the idea that the ceaseless movement of modern forms was also tapping into the fundamental flow of life itself. A major exponent of such notions was the poet Jules Romains who, in *La Vie unanime* (1908), tries to seize the pulse of urban life, and expose the hidden physical and psychological rhythms which underpin and unify its multiple changing surfaces.

The vitalism and energy of modernity is a key theme in Flandrin's graphic work from the early 1900s, and explains his captivation with theatre and ballet subjects after 1905. But while Flandrin, like Matisse, Marquet and Camoin, was concerned with capturing a new, modern and dynamic reality, this is combined with his attempts to express its essential qualities: a fusion emblematic of his outlook in general, and of the future path of his art. From his youth, Flandrin had filled notebooks with drawings and sketches, noting and recording passing impressions; like countless earlier artists, using drawing as a way of seeing and apprehending life around him – its manifold variety. But contacts with Matisse and Marquet in the first years of the decade had given his drawing a new and urgent significance in relation to his artistic development as a whole. For Flandrin, as for Moreau's other students, drawing was a means of understanding the principles of the work of the Masters; yet like Matisse and Marquet, it was also to become a distillation of his art – the zero-point at which expression is born. The vital stimulus for this process was the ever-changing world of modern forms. The modern city, in Romains's characterization, is a place without limits, of fluid, open contours: a place where the flow of humans and streets mingles and combines.[85] It is this sense of a new energy and rhythm of modernity that begins to shape the forms of Flandrin's work. Modernity was exciting Flandrin, as with his contemporaries to see, and more importantly, to feel differently.

Flandrin's response to modernity is expressed in his work in two quite specific ways: in numerous sketches and lithographs inspired by modern subjects, observed *sur le vif*; and in his general concern with the animation and colours of modern forms, as shown in the summary figures, described in gaudy splashes of colour in *The Folk Dance* (*La Danse populaire*, 1909: col. ill. 6), and in the later improvisatory, *Vaison, Market Day* (1923: ill. 8, cat. 68). In his early graphic work, as in Marquet's and Camoin's, we see Flandrin increasingly experimenting with ways of capturing both an impression and a feeling of an instant (see ill. 4). His numerous sketches of Paris streets, concerts, café scenes and friends – these, often drawn directly on to concert and theatre programmes (see cat. 52) – are expressed with sketch-like rapidity, which combine journalistic illustration and the comparative instantaneity of the photograph with the simplifying concision of the modern poster. Unlike his immediate contemporaries, notably Matisse and Marquet, Flandrin was not so interested in depicting the imagery or brashness of posters themselves, even though Toulouse-Lautrec's work had become and remained one of his enduring passions. But Flandrin's vision of modernity, as with his art in general, was influenced as much by poster art's simplifying visual language and techniques as by other sources. This is apparent in copious drawings and lithographs, including the many sketches of Marval (see cat. 32 and 53), and horse-and-rider subjects (see cat. 45, 47 and 57) which Flandrin produced up to and after the First World War. Here, the boldly-refined forms, incisive silhouettes and fluid contours, reminiscent of Chéret's and Lautrec's poster stylizations, also share similarities with the calligraphic abbreviations of Marquet's and Camoin's graphic work of the period, where fluidity draws attention to the idea of speed of execution.[86] It is this sense of swiftness, as in Flandrin's dramatically improvised *The Smoker* (1912: cat. 52), where image turns into sign, which draws attention to the act of capturing itself. A similar process is at work, as we have seen, in *The Little School Boy* (ill. 5, cat. 34): a tendency which continues to be manifest in the Corenc portraits of 1907–1910, where Flandrin was also using photography as an aid to apprehend and fix his motifs. Photography and graphic art become linked, therefore, as ways of conveying the movement and vitality of modernity: of accentuating, yet arresting it; making it seem more vivid, but at the same time, more intelligible.

The opportunity to develop these notions came with Flandrin's 'discovery' of dance and ballet with Marval in 1905; married to his interest in music, the ballet would remain a vital source of inspiration for Flandrin throughout his career. What captivated him about dance, and about ballet in particular, was its seeming embodiment of ideas dear to his own evolving artistic vision: unity of rhythm, movement and formal precision. As Marval attested in 1913, for Flandrin, ballet symbolized both the poetry of movement and repose; both vitality and structure, life and order: 'It's perhaps going too far to find repose in a movement and I do not know if I am making myself clear; yet that is the impression that I have.'[87] Marval here highlights tendencies detectable in Flandrin's earliest ballet subjects, but which become especially marked in his depictions of the *Ballets russes* between 1910–1913. Passionate about music and an avid concert-goer, Flandrin's first contact with ballet and dance opened a new world for him. Enraptured by seeing the *première* of Gluck's *Armide* with Marval at the Paris Opéra in July 1906, he had already begun work on a series of drawings inspired by the ballet's pastoral themes, and culminating in the monumental *Berger d'Armide* (1905) shown at the *Salon d'Automne* in 1906. This, a curious synthesis of classicism and extreme stylization – reminiscent of Van Dongen's doll-like mannequins (he had first encountered Van Dongen in

1904) – was criticized for its 'artificial naïveté', lacking in grace.[88] But it was Flandrin's first real attempt to match form to theme; to suggest, in his decorative fresco-like arrangements of figures the nature of the balletic *mise-en-scène* itself: its unity of music, movement and décor.

In 1909, the European début of the *Ballets russes* took Paris by storm. Astounded by the arrival of a sensational new concept in ballet, Flandrin turned aside from the pastoral and mythological fantasies of *Armide* for fresh subjects taken directly from the repertoire of the *Ballets russes* in 1909: *Cléopâtre* and *Les Sylphides*. Like so many of his contemporaries, what fired Flandrin's enthusiasm was the novelty of the *Ballets russes* combined with its startling modernity. Directed by the impresario, Sergei Diaghilev, with choreography by Fokine, designs by Léon Bakst, and featuring as its lead dancers Pavlova and Nijinsky, the *Ballets russes* brought to Paris by Diaghilev were pioneering an approach to dance using a vocabulary of modern forms and ideas, designed, as Fokine himself puts it, to achieve 'a complete unity of expression – [of] music, painting and plastic art'.[89] It represented the acme of modernity, for the *Ballets russes* signified the latest, and most striking, expression of the Symbolist ideal of a Wagnerian *Gesamtkunstwerk* or 'total art', fusing not just the sister arts (dance, music and painting) but art and life itself. Even more importantly, the revolutionary treatment of *mise-en-scène* as integral to theme and subject, gave a new prominence to elements of rhythm and form, thereby echoing contemporary associations between 'primitive' and modern art, epitomized in Matisse's now-celebrated *Music* and *Dance* of 1909–10.

These innovations were not lost on Flandrin. 'It's a real artistic treat', he exclaims to Joseph Flandrin, describing his first experience of the *Ballets russes* in June 1909, 'music, songs and dances, drawing and colour [...] You can imagine what a field day painting will have with it'.[90] The fruits of his enthusiasm were revealed the following year, in his second one-man show at Druet's gallery in February 1910, where a whole section was devoted to Flandrin's paintings of *Ballets russes* subjects from the 1909 repertoire: *Cléopâtre*, *L'Oiseau de feu* and famously, *Les Sylphides*. Numerous individual studies of Nijinsky, Pavlova and Karsavina were to ensue,[91] culminating in the series of large-scale *tableaux* depicting Nijinsky and Karsavina dancing the ethereal *Spectre de la rose* in 1913 (see cat. 54). In Marval's view, Flandrin's absorption with the *Ballets russes* was in part due to its sensuality, its almost 'primitive' physical appeal, which came as a heady tonic to Paris audiences used to the rather more sober fare of the *Ballets de l'Opéra*. Flandrin was certainly bowled over by the exoticism, costumes and sheer colour of the *Ballets russes* spectacles, as is shown in *The Folk Dance* (1910: col. ill. 6). 'The brio and rude health of these dances is truly admirable', as he writes to his mother in 1909.[92] But, once again, what strikes him most is 'the total fusion of music and dance [...] the feeling in what they do'.[93]

It is precisely in this modernity – in the expressive synthesis of music, rhythm and colour – that Flandrin perceives new possibilities for his art. The *Ballets russes* embodied a vital, even elemental, concept of dance, concerned, above all, with the pulse that is life itself. In his scenes from *Cléopâtre*, *L'Oiseau de feu* (1909: cat. 49) and *Les Sylphides* (see cat. 50), we see Flandrin translating both his studies of the Masters, and the energy and rhythm of his contemporary graphic work, into supple forms, contours and flowing decorative colours which suggest painterly equivalents to musical compositions: into 'the melodic and harmonic element in the art of dance'.[94] For Flandrin – echoing Bakst's original ideas for the *Ballets russes* designs, especially for *Cléopâtre* – colour is the primary agent of synthesis, unifying linear and plastic elements, creating the invisible music – 'coloured rhythm', as he calls it[95] – which balances and binds them together. But, as with his other work of the period, Flandrin also uses colour in his dance subjects in a decorative and structural manner to evoke what he sees as the complete 'architecture' of the form of the *Ballets russes*, not just its plastic effects. In his series inspired by *Le Spectre de la rose* (see cat. 54), Nijinsky and Karsavina are rendered in broad, flat planes of heightened unnatural colour against simplified backdrops, their bodies stylized and monumentalized to suggest both the rhythms and symmetries of their *pas de deux*.

These interpretations of the *Ballets russes* bring Flandrin in the period 1910–1913 close in spirit, if not in style or appearance, to an abstract conception of art. Contemporary critics were certainly struck by their originality – by their innovative compositions, colours and light, by '[the] vivid line of the light which animates [the painting] and idealizes it' as one commentator remarked.[96] What Flandrin took principally from the *Ballet russes*, however, was its emphasis on movement and rhythm within structure, expression within form. Here, Flandrin's art comes remarkably close to Matisse's notion of expression as being part of the total composition of a painting, not just linked to its separate elements – 'the art of arranging in a decorative manner the various elements at the painter's disposal for the expression of his feelings', as he writes in 1908.[97] Indeed, Flandrin was greatly struck by Matisse's *Dance* and *Music* – the two panels destined for the Russian Sergei Shchukin's collection – exhibited at the *Salon d'Automne* in 1910. While Flandrin may have rejected Matisse's means, the 'primitivist' style, he was clearly seduced by its underlying principles. 'Larger than life, Music and Dance', as he reflects in a letter to Joseph in 1910, alongside his free renditions of the two works (see cat. 51).[98] It is this idea of a concentrated expressivity which we see him exploring though the vehicle of the *Ballets russes*. But if Flandrin was interested in abstraction, unlike contemporary Cubist and Futurist innovations, the latter of which he rejected out of hand, this was firmly linked to recognizable subjects; to his attempts to combine a perceived and felt reality. Whereas Flandrin saw Cubism – and Futurism, in particular – as presenting a fragmented concept of modernity, his own reponse is a fundamentally unifying one. His distillations of modernity may have taken him towards abstraction, but they also led to order, discipline and tradition: tradition conceived not as an empty gesture to the past, but as a union of past and immediate concerns.

Towards a New Classicism

The years immediately prior to the First World War witnessed an explosion of avant-garde activity in Paris, with the genesis of Cubism, Futurism, and a host of other 'isms' – all individually vaunting their claims to originality over each other. For Flandrin, this was a period of both intense renewal and of consolidation. Following his adoption by Druet, and his first one-man show in 1906, his reputation and his fortunes had begun to prosper. As well as regular contributions to the *Société Nationale*, the *Indépendants*, and the *Salon d'Automne* (from 1905), in 1908, his work was featuring, along with Marval's, Marquet's, Van Dongen's, Henri Manguin's and Othon Friesz's, in Druet's series of exhibitions devoted to Moreau's former pupils, and to the latest exponents of modern art. From 1909, Flandrin was exhibiting paintings at the independent *La Libre esthétique* in Brussels; in April 1910, he was represented at the celebrated *D'après les Maîtres* show at the Galerie Bernheim-Jeune, and in a Post-Impressionist exhibition at the Stafford Gallery in London in November of the same year. He held three further solo exhibitions at Druet's in 1910, 1912 and 1913, following his initial two in 1906 and 1908; and in February 1913, his work was included in the international art event of the century – the 'Armory' show in New York. Partly as a result of Fénoglio's efforts in Grenoble, and partly due to Druet's astute patronage and entrepreneurial flair, Flandrin's paintings had also started to sell. Amongst Druet's core band of collectors were the future purchasers of Flandrin's work: the industrialists, Kapferer and Pacquement; the Marquis de Magallon; and Cézanne's patron, Joachim Gasquet. Although Flandrin's fortunes would eventually rest with this small group, by 1913 he was hopeful of greater acclaim, as State negotiations were well underway to buy one of his works for the showcase of living art: the Musée du Luxembourg collection.[99]

Druet's support and patronage meant that, increasingly, Flandrin's art was being linked with some of the most prominent artistic tendencies of the period. His work was now starting to excite attention from leading critics of the time, including the young poet-critics, Guillaume Apollinaire and André Salmon – defenders of the new avant-garde, especially the Cubists – as the response generated by his solo 1910 exhibition revealed. A major event, featuring over eighty works, it included, alongside *Ballets russes* subjects and still-lifes, a selection of views inspired by Flandrin's visit to Italy in 1909 (see cat. 58), and numerous landscapes based on the scenery of his beloved Corenc. What it offered his contemporaries was a summary of his artistic evolution to date: a combination of intimacy, lyricism and grandeur, as embodied in the monumental *The Wooded Gorge* (*Le Vallon boisé*, 1910: col. ill. 7) – praised by Apollinaire at the 1910 *Salon du Champ-de-Mars* for its antique character – and expressive of the emphasis he was now placing on nature, harmony, and order.[100] Whilst a few critics inevitably found fault with Flandrin's energetic treatment of forms, perceived lack of modelling and hasty brushwork, the general reaction to the 1910 works was favourable, particularly to their simplifying boldness and decorative bias: qualities now being sought as requisites of modern, but durable art. 'An ordering joy and an edifying wisdom, are the two great virtues of this robust but lucid artist', comments Salmon, anticipating the themes of his account of contemporary art, *La Jeune peinture française* in 1912.[101] A number of commentators drew comparisons with Puvis and notably Cézanne, acclaiming Flandrin's 'Virgilian charm'; his 'works in a fine style and freely executed';[102] and 'still-lifes which have the virile brilliance of Cézanne'.[103] Morice, in a long review of the Druet show, goes further, applauding Flandrin's 'grandes réalisations', in which 'the dual counsel of nature and (true) tradition'[104] conjoin in a Baudelairean synthesis: in 'a tenebrous and profound unity.'[105]

The 1910 show, indeed, was a watershed for Flandrin. For nature and tradition – nature linked with tradition – were to be the two themes which would dominate his art from this point on. Here, Flandrin's visit to Milan, Venice and Florence in September of the previous year, was undoubtedly the stimulus. Filling sketch-books with impressions of the wonders of the Uffizi, the architecture, the colours, above all, of the radiant light – it was the Italian brilliance which had inspired him to think and model in terms of broad tonal contrasts of light and dark – more importantly, to distil his initial observations and to simplify nature, as in the 1910 *Square in Venice* (cat. 58). Directly related to his experiments with Matisse and Marquet, the emphasis on simplification and the suppression of unnecessary details shows Flandrin refining and sharpening his sensations in his concern to give them a more lasting form. Yet simplification is increasingly a route to the past. For Flandrin, following in the spirit of Puvis and Cézanne, it becomes a means of understanding and translating the 'Masters' in modern terms: of reconciling expression with structure, or, in Cézanne's resonant words, giving 'concrete shape to sensations and perceptions'.[106] If this is a process which can be detected at an earlier stage in Flandrin's artistic development, what is striking about the work of the immediate pre-war period is his marked effort to now marry past and present interests. In his Corenc landscapes and rider subjects, as in the *Riders in the Bois* (c.1909–11: cat. 47) and the later *Riders on the Corenc Road* (1913: cat. 61), we see him combining intense colourism and a bold, decorative treatment of forms, with a weighty massing of shape and volumes, echoing the principles of classical art, especially Poussin's, with which he was being frequently linked by critics of the period.[107] Many of the Corenc landscapes such as *Two Young Girls* (1908, redated 1913: cat. 42) and notably, *The Wooded Gorge* (1910: col. ill. 7) include figures whose meditative inwardness recall his previous, Symbolist-inspired portraits, merging dream and reality, a person or a place both experienced and imagined. But introspection and intimacy have also become fused with the grand and the monumental. The vast scale of *The Wooded Gorge*, in part conceived to impress at the *Société Nationale*, like that of the later portraits, notably the *Girl in a Large Hat* (1913: cat. 60), expresses Flandrin's aspiration towards the creation of the 'grand-oeuvre' synthesizing the modern and the traditional. 'A painting is a harmony', intones Flandrin to his friend Mainssieux in 1913, in the words of Gauguin and then Matisse.[108] Uniting observation, a direct encounter with modernity and a concentrated intensity of feeling, with a sense of an underlying accord within nature, this would be Flandrin's effort to forge a tradition for the present.

Yet, here, once again, Flandrin's art can be seen as emblematic of the larger concerns of his generation. Consistently allied with Marquet, Marval, Lebasque, Laprade and Guérin, by Apollinaire and Salmon amongst others,[109] his form of traditionalism was emerging as expressive of a group of 'moderns' who fell between Matisse and Cézanne in the pre-war years, pursuing what Bernard Dorival later called 'their persistent attachment to life' in their refusal of 'the unreality of pure painting'.[110] This was not so much a compromise of innovation, but a middle path between the goals which Cézanne defined and to which Matisse, increasingly, in a similar way but in a different context, aspired: to unite the fragmented and the temporal with the structured and the whole in a synergy evocative also of modern vision and experience. There was a connection, too, between these ideas, and the efforts of the Cubists – as both Apollinaire and Salmon, champions of the 'new' art perceived. Vilified at their *début* at the *Indépendants* in 1911 for their fragmented and incoherent 'distortions' of reality, the Cubists – those following Picasso's and Braque's lead – were, as two of their major exponents, Gleizes and Metzinger, insisted actually refashioning the aims of art in their quest for a 'profounder reality' than that of the senses or the compass.[111] Apollinaire goes further, seeing in Cubism – which he now relates to a whole range of avant-garde innovations in 1913 – a reconceptualization of the very notion of tradition itself, which will, accordingly, subsume the past in the suggestiveness of '[what] will be pure painting'.[112]

But it is precisely this ostensibly dissociated modernity that Flandrin rejects. His pursuit, instead, of a recognizable tradition was also becoming part of a larger concern with creating a stable artistic identity in the face of an apparently incessant and chaotic cult of the new. Repeated criticisms of Cubism, and its spin-offs – Orphism and Futurism – sparked by the Futurist exhibition at Bernheim-Jeune in February 1912, attest his growing frustations with a form of *peinture mentale,* as he sees it, which, by having internalized nature has also, in a sense, abjured it. 'That sneaky little Metzinger!', mocks Flandrin, in defence of his own aims and those of Marval's, 'that's where he got the carafe which blends into a plate'.[113] Of the Futurists' vaunting of 'dynamisme plastique', he is even warier, as he confides to Joseph in 1912: 'In their imagining, only someone living in Paris can look at the problem in an amusing way, an immense coloured mosaic whose pieces have been a little muddled up.'[114] It is this fragmenting of reality which serves to intensify Flandrin's concern with its alternative: with a return to what he conceives as nature's original simplicity and harmony. But such a vision is also to be expressed in modern terms – terms inspired by those artists whose work continued to enthuse him, and in whom he found a meeting of modernity, nature and tradition: Bonnard, Matisse, Marquet, Van Dongen, Marval, Le Douanier Rousseau, Valloton and, not least, the 'pères' Puvis, Moreau, Corot and Ingres. *Young Horsemen by a Spring* (1913, reworked 1923: cat. 62), in many ways, can be seen as the culmination of these ideals, and the high-point of Flandrin's artistic development on the eve of the First World War. His last work to be shown at the *Société Nationale*, the *Young Horsemen* was also of talismanic significance for Flandrin in the context of his wider artistic aspirations. 'I have been able, in my quite large canvas', explains Flandrin to his mother, 'to make them almost life-size, as large as nature, and very naturally under the beautiful Corenc sun'.[115] If the monumental scale and arcadian theme hark back to Puvis's vestigial classicism, and to the example of earlier masters (to the Italian Primitives), the work is also a synthesis of many traditions of the old and the new. As with Puvis's loosely antique *rêveries*, the self-absorbed, static figures in their pastoral idyll, suggest an almost dream-like fusion of the real and ideal: a 'grand manner' fusion, developing that of *The Wooded Gorge*, of lyrical and Symbolist tendencies. In a fashion analogous to Matisse's *Danse* and *Music*, Flandrin also expresses the harmony of nature though the clarity of his formal stylizations and decoration, but without returning to a 'primitivist' *tabula rasa*. The simplifying vocabulary, a distillation of tradition, fuses the visionary with the directly contemporary, at the same time as anticipating the modern classicism of Derain's work following the war. What is striking about the *Young Horsemen* is that it looks both ways at once. But from eclecticism has sprung unity of vision; unlike the fragmenting one of Cubism, a conception of modern art as intelligible, continuous and human.

This was to be the case even following the cataclysmic ruptures of the First World War. Just prior to 1914, Flandrin had found himself on the crest of a wave. New dealers and entrepreneurs – Weill, Druet, Vollard, Bernheim-Jeune – had admitted him to their inner circles of artists and collectors. Hailed in 1912 by Salmon, now one of the most influential critics of his generation as a 'torchbearer' of 'l'art vivant', his work was making a critical *éclat* at Druet's, the *Indépendants* and the *Salon d'Automne*. In the same year, at the *Nationale*, his great personal statement of the period, the *Young Horsemen*, was being widely praised for its 'rare and eloquent beauty', its combination of 'taste for the style and cadence of classical art' and 'rigorously modern execution'.[116] There were high hopes, too, with keen State interest, that this was to be the work that would soon grace the walls of the Luxembourg, fulfilling Salmon's prophecy that 'a day will come when Flandrin's landscapes will find their place in the Louvre'.[117] In Grenoble, Flandrin's reputation was flourishing as well. In 1912, with Marval, and the Grenoblois collector, Andry-Farcy, he had embarked on a bold scheme to improve the collections of the Musée de Grenoble with some of the latest examples of Parisian avant-garde art. A logical outgrowth of his interest in decorative art, he had even turned his attention to tapestry, with plans for a works well underway, negotiated through his growing circle of Parisian and Dauphinois contacts.

Inevitably and relentlessly, war intervened. As with his whole generation, Flandrin's future, henceforth, would be irrevocably shaped by the experience and wider effects of the conflict. Recruited to the territorial army in 1914, and billeted permanently in Seine-et-Oise from 1915, he spent much of his time when not on duty recording, in a series of vivid drawings, sites, battles, the intimate, small rituals of life at the Front, many of which were later shown at the 1917 War Salon: the *Salon des Armées de la République*. The war years would claim some of Flandrin's closest friends: his old Moreau *atelier* companion, Girot, his dealer, Druet who died in 1916. But despite its horrors, and his view that 'gentle painting' could never convey such grim realities, his drawings show him attempting to wrest a poignancy, even a beauty from his experiences. Even under siege, he is able to visualize a charm in the landscape and villages of the Seine-et-Oise, with their 'houses [...] like small temples to the divinities of the fields'.[118] Colours are noted with a painter's eye – morning *reveille* is accompanied by 'the first rays of the sun which dusts red gold over everything'.[119] Off-duty camaraderie, drinking, eating, smoking, as well as soldiers' travails, are evoked by Flandrin's characteristic swiftness and economy of means (see cat. 63). In all of this, Flandrin still continues to learn about 'the secret of colour and of form'.[120] Recalling the terrors of battle in 1917, he forgets momentarily the carnage before him, seeing only a vision of Gauguin's 'Tahitians' scything the bushes, where the advancing troops should have been.

Returning to Paris in 1919, and to his old haunts, Flandrin began to pick up the threads of his life from the pre-war years. But nothing would be quite the same, either in his personal or his artistic fortunes. Settling with Marval for a time in the location of Matisse's former home at 19 Quai St. Michel alongside Marquet, relations became increasingly stormy. War and absence had left their mark; and in 1921, Flandrin struck up a friendship with Henriette Deloras, the young Grenoblois artist who was later to become his wife. The State purchase for the Luxembourg had fallen through, and with it, some of Flandrin's hope for acclaim amongst the ranks of the (recognized) innovators of his generation. Resuming his exhibiting activities – at the Druet gallery, the *Salon d'Automne*, and, from 1923, at the new *Salon des Tuileries* where he was elected as a juror for the decorative arts – Flandrin found himself busier than ever. But although still inextricably linked with his former companions, including Marval, Matisse, Marquet, Camoin, Friesz and Van Dongen,[121] he now found himself classed as an 'ancient', out of the cutting-edge avant-garde. With this maturity had also come a subtle shift in critical reaction to his work. Widely praised for his landscapes, and increasingly for his decorative projects of the period, his bold colours and simplified forms no longer allied him directly to the controversies of the pre-war years. Former supporters, and leading champions of the avant-garde, notably Salmon, had become sceptical of Flandrin's ability to capture anew 'the movement of the modern street according to the modern sentiment', as Salmon puts it in 1920.[122] Instead, with the critical and artistic realignments of the post-war period,[123] Flandrin's art was gradually subsumed into the centre-ground of an acceptable and essentially conservative modernism. Dissociated from the experimental vigour of his youthful years, in Salmon's words, 'already at the doors of the museum',[124] he was now being firmly placed within a genealogy of landscape painting – stemming from Corot – seen to combine both tradition and nationalism.

To a large extent, these views aptly reflected the path of Flandrin's art in the years following the war. A major public commission for a large-scale composition on patriotic themes for the restaurant des Tourelles in the boulevard Delessert in 1919, had given Flandrin the opportunity to develop his interests of the pre-war period, now in the context of a monumental, decorative art. The same year saw the opening of his tapestry *atelier* in Grenoble, and the start of a grand project to translate into a modern, tapestry form, his own paintings, including the *Young Horsemen* as well as celebrated works by nineteenth- and early twentieth-century artists, including Ingres, Delacroix, Corot, Puvis and Gauguin. His concern with the decorative and patriotic was also mirrored in an increasingly prolific production of works of a pastoral nature: abundant still-lifes, flowers, and the omnipresent sun-drenched landscapes peopled by riders and children, of his youth. If this subject-matter indicates a certain repetitiveness and lack of direction in Flandrin's art during the early 1920s, it also suggests a longing for an Edenic quietism – a form of *rappel à l'ordre* as an antidote to the pain of war, and representative of a broader contemporary concern with ostensibly 'neutral' themes: still-lifes, portraits and decorative interiors (by Vuillard, Bonnard and Matisse) redolent of the comfort, harmony and sensuality of a former 'belle époque' ideal. Yet the concern with the energy of the street and modern life in general which Flandrin had shared with artists now as diverse as Marval, Marquet, Matisse, Van Dongen and Camoin in the early years of the century, was not so much abandoned as displaced and channelled into new forms. The nature of modern reality and the return of the 'grand subject' (to which Picasso amongst others was increasingly drawn) now became acutely urgent preoccupations for a generation sundered from their past by war. For Flandrin's contemporaries, unlike the moderns – Dadaists, Surrealists – of the new avant-gardes too young to remember the pre-war years, the *rappel à l'ordre* was, therefore, indispensable in their coming to grips with an irrevocably changing world. But this was not a traditionalism in any merely imitative sense; nor was it a retreat from, but rather a deeply-felt response to the trauma of the historical transition of which they were part.

Flandrin's efforts to create a coexistence of modernism and classicism in his work of the 1920s is strikingly indicative of these larger tendencies, perhaps most clearly embodied in Derain's work of the period.[125] As Salmon recognized, Flandrin attempts to recover a movement, even a gaiety, combined with a harmony in the reality after war, which brings his work close in spirit to the contemporary human-ists' dream of a liberal, but fraternal and cohesive modernity.[126] Although Flandrin did not espouse any overtly political viewpoint, it is this idealistic, but at the same time, intensely human quality which characterizes his work of the earlier part of the decade. Profiting from his renewed contacts with Marquet and Matisse follow-ing the move to 19 Quai St. Michel, and from those brought by his new friend, the old *Salon d'Automne* veteran, Frantz Jourdain, his work between 1919–1925 shows him attempting to recapture the inspiration of the early 1900s in paintings which unite expressive and decorative elements, colourism and monumentality. While

Reading (Pierre Flandrin Reading in the Studio) (1922: cat. 67), a portrait of Flandrin's nephew reading Morice's 1920 monograph on Gauguin, attempts to recreate a Gauguinesque manner, with its exotic colours and simplified forms, the series of views of Notre-Dame (see cat. 65 and 66) and the Seine based on those from Flandrin's studio windows, show him working in the spirit of Matisse and especially Marquet. If these are experiments in how to translate luminosity into colour effects, the Seine views, as in the wintry *Pont-Neuf, Winter Afternoon* (1924: cat. 69), also demonstrate Flandrin's clear preoccupation with clarity and structure now synthesized with a still vibrant fluidity of touch. With their planar geometries of bridges, buildings and trees, the two majestic visions of Notre-Dame at different times of day (cat. 65 and 66) can be seen, too, as a reminder of the simplifying, expressive abstractions of the 1900–1904 period, of Marquet's pared-down language of forms as signs. Yet the presence of a latter-day modernity is visible everywhere: in the people, cars, trams and buses that animate Flandrin's scenes; most of all in the way in which, like a photograph, their distilled and frozen images make us acutely aware of the passage of time.

The theme of both recovery and rediscovery permeates Flandrin's work prior to and following his permanent return to Grenoble in 1931. Summers spent at Biarritz with Marval between 1923 and 1926 in the dying days of their love had reacquainted him with the wonders of light and sun: 'the fresh colours and the brilliant tones on a light gold sand and this silver sea are truly a lesson in painting,' as he writes to his mother in August 1923.[127] Vaison, the location of the war years, is recaptured again, not as a village under siege, but in the cursory forms of *Vaison, Market Day* (1923: ill. 8, cat. 68), as a vibrant, bustling, place of colour and life. But after 1926, the search for a connectedness between past and present takes Flandrin towards another and inevitable 'rediscovery' – to Italy, and to his dream of

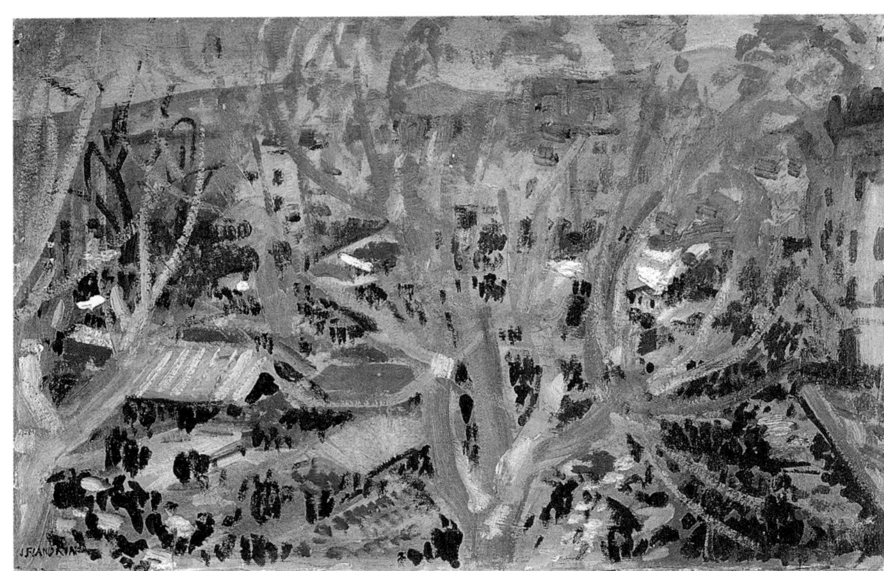

Illustration 8:
JULES FLANDRIN,
Vaison, Market Day, 1923.
Oil on board,
34 × 52 cms,
private collection,
Paris.

Romanized landscapes, renconciling, as Flandrin sees it, the eternal battle 'between nature and artist'; between harmony and vision.[128] 'Italy is where I've got to finish', as Flandrin prophetically announces in 1927.[129] Italy was now to become the dominant inspiration for Flandrin's art, as his repeated visits between 1926 to 1930 and his numerous paintings of its cities (see cat. 75) and the Roman *campagna* attest. The presence of Italy would continue to be manifest in the late Paris views and the scenery of Corenc and Grenoble: in the classicizing, albeit sometimes contrived clarity of light; and in the solid and monumentalized landscape forms – enduring reminders of the balance and order of the classical tradition. With the lure of Italy, and of Henriette Deloras, Paris – 'so far from the sun'[130] – was soon to be displaced from Flandrin's affections by a stronger force. In 1931, he turned his back on Paris for Corenc, his new wife and soon his only child, Jules; and henceforth until his death in 1947, for the visions of Dauphiné and his 'pays natal'.

'An embodiment of living art: Jules Flandrin': so wrote the art critic Yves Farge in 1938, in homage to the artist during the last years of his life[131] – a touching echo of the very words of Salmon which fired Flandrin's hopes at the height of his success. Left out of the Fauve group in 1905, and dropped from his place amongst the vanguard of modern art after the Great War, Flandrin's particular contribution to his period has almost disappeared from view. But that Flandrin may not have subsequently achieved the fame and recognition of his now-celebrated contemporaries – Matisse, Derain, Marquet, Rouault, to name but a few – does not dimish his significance as a bearer of 'l'art vivant'. Unlike the work of those artists who appear to stand apart from their age by virtue of their now legendary individuality – Matisse, Picasso, Braque – Flandrin's art is deeply emblematic of it. Profoundly human, not a probing intellectual tussling with cerebral aesthetic problems, Flandrin nonetheless presents the picture of an artist intimately caught up with the wider artistic struggles of his time. During a period of unprecedented upheaval, renewal and transition, Flandrin's art vividly embodies that constant dialogue between various notions of tradition, different identities of the modern, which generated the creative forces that shaped the art of the early twentieth century. Indeed, Flandrin's example sheds light on a history of modernism, of 'avant-gardism', which was never written. As Salmon wrote: 'Tomorrow we will not have that pleasure of studying a Jules Flandrin, recognized as a master by the most discerning, and whose mastery will be publicly proclaimed.'[132] In hindsight, it may seem extraordinary that, in 1912, when Salmon's reputation as a critic was indissoluably linked with Cubism and its subsequent mythology, that he should have included Flandrin amongst the bearers of a new spirit in contemporary French art. But this only serves to highlight an essential instability and fluidity in conceptions of avant-gardism in the pre-war years: an avant-gardism in which Flandrin's traditionalism coexists with the radical innovations of Picasso, Braque and their followers. As Flandrin's case suggests, it is perhaps time, at the dawn of another century, to shift the focus away from avant-garde art and its polarities, and to look anew at the representatives of tradition and continuity: at those who reflected as well as bore the torches of their age.

REFERENCES

1. 'Ne craignez pas de vous appuyer sur les Maîtres, vous vous y retrouverez toujours', Gustave Moreau, cited in Pierre Schneider, *Matisse* (Paris, 1984), p. 57.

2. Henri Matisse, 'Notes of a Painter' (1908), transl. Alfred H. Barr Jr., in Herschel B. Chipp, *Theories of Modern Art. A Source Book by Artists and Critics* (Berkeley, Los Angeles and London, 1968), pp. 136–7.

3. 'Jules Flandrin, c'est toute une époque [...] celle qui va de la fin du XIXème avec Bonnard, en passant par les Fauves, jusqu' à notre temps.' Cited in Georges Flandrin and François Roussier, *Jules Flandrin (1871–1947): Un élève de Gustave Moreau témoin de son temps* (La Tronche, 1992), p. 10 (hereafter abbreviated as Flandrin and Roussier).

4. See, for example, Alfred H. Barr Jr., *Matisse: His Art and His Public* (New York, 1951, repr. 1966), p. 16; Pierre Schneider, *Matisse*, transl. Michael Taylor and Bridget Strevens Romer (London, 1984), p. 54; Jack D. Flam, *Matisse: The Man and his Art, 1869-1918* (London, 1986), p. 33; and Hilary Spurling, *The Unknown Matisse: Man of the North, 1869–1908* (London, 1998), esp. pp. 142–3, 225–6 (hereafter abbreviated as Spurling). In recent literature on Matisse and his circle, only Spurling has accorded Flandrin more than a passing mention.

5. André Salmon, *La Jeune peinture française* (Paris, 1912), pp. 63–4.

6. The critic Charles Morice's expression ('classique instinctif'), see: 'Le XXIème Salon des Indépendants', *Mercure de France*, vol. LIV, nc.188 (April 1905), p. 551.

7. He was officially registered for temporary study (inscription no.887) under the guidance of Moreau at the École des Beaux–Arts on 2 May 1895: certificate of inscription, *Flandrin Archives*, Paris.

8. For a full list of Moreau's students and their dates of entry to his studio, see *Gustave Moreau et ses élèves* (exh. cat., Musée Cantini, Marseille, 1962).

9. Cited in Schneider, *Matisse* (1984), p. 56.

10. 'Moreau a mis ses élèves non pas dans un chemin, mais hors des chemins. Il leur a donné l'inquiétude.' Cited in Jean-Pierre Cuzin, *et al.*, *Copier Créer: De Turner à Picasso* (exh. cat., Louvre, Paris, 1993), p. 35 (hereafter abbreviated as *Copier Créer*).

11. On Moreau's influence on late nineteenth-century art, see Douglas W. Druick, 'Gustave Moreau and the Symbolist Ideal', in Lacambre, *et al.*, *Gustave Moreau 1826–1898: Between Epic and Dream* (exh. cat., Grand Palais, Paris, 1998–9; Art Institute of Chicago, Chicago; Metropolitan Museum of Art, New York, 1999), pp. 33–9.

12. See Spurling, pp. 84–5.

13. 'Devant l'*antique* ... je me suis enfui. J'y retourne [...] pour y retrouver de la chair!', cited in Francis E. Hyslop (ed.), *Henri Evenepoël à Paris: Lettres choisies, 1893–1899* (Brussels, 1971), p. 15.

14. 'Il veut qu'on fasse simple et qu'on mette du 'style' dans son dessin autant que possible. C'est un admirateur des "Maîtres anciens". On le remarque par exemple un peu à ses élèves, qui *tous*, sans exception, ne copient pas le ton du modèle, mais font en quelque sorte un camaïeu avec les tons qu'on voit au Louvre dans les Titien et Véronèse.' Evenepoël to his father (18 March 1893), in *Lettres choisies*, p. 47.

15. 'Il faut copier la nature avec de l'imagination [...] la couleur doit être pensée, rêvée et imaginée. Quoted in Evenepoël, letter to his father (27 July 1891), in *Lettres choisies*, p. 59.

16. See Spurling, p. 85.

17. 'après ce progrès-là, un autre, un autre, et je crois que nous aurons tous à l'en remercier intérieurement plus tard', cited in Flandrin and Roussier, p. 32.

18. Confronted with one of Flandrin's landscapes painted during the summer of 1896 at Corenc depicting a pavilion and valley at sunset, Moreau is reputed to have exclaimed: 'Ah Flandrin, non, je ne vous suis pas jusque là!' ('Ah Flandrin, I cannot go along with you that far!'), cited in Flandrin and Roussier, pp. 34–5. Cf. on Matisse and Moreau's disfavour, Spurling, p. 143.

19. On Moreau's particular response to Italian High Renaissance art, see Larry J. Feinberg,

'Gustave Moreau and the Italian Renaissance', in *Gustave Moreau* (Paris, Princeton, 1998), pp. 5–13.

20. On this theme, see especially, Roger Benjamin, 'Recovering Authors: the Modern Copy, Copy Exhibitions and Matisse', *Art History*, 12 (June 1989), pp. 176–201. Cf. on the wider context of the Louvre and modern art, Pierre Schneider, *Les Dialogues du Louvre* (Paris, 1967, repr. 1972), pp. 9–37, and *Copier Créer*, *passim*.

21. Cited in Schneider, *Matisse* (1984), p. 56.

22. 'le *style*, la *matière*, l'*arabesque*, et le *transformisme imaginaire* de la couleur', Evenepoël, letter to his father (8 November 1895), *Lettres choisies*, p. 121.

23. 'cette odieuse métairie de la rue Bonaparte', cited in Flandrin and Roussier, p. 31.

24. *Flandrin Archives*, Corenc and Paris. I am very grateful to Georges Flandrin for drawing these to my attention.

25. Cited in Flandrin and Roussier, p. 10.

26. 'chemin du Louvre', see *Ibid.*, p. 34.

27. Reproduced in *Copier Créer*, p. 225, fig.150f.

28. 'M. Jules Flandrin a su mettre à profit les leçons de son illustre professeur sans se croire obligé de le pasticher? pour s'en étonner, il faudrait avoir oublié combien l'enseignement de Gustave Moreau s'élevait au-dessus des recettes d'atelier et comment il sut rompre avec les traditions qui avaient jusqu'à lui, sévi l'expansion des individualités', Revel, cited in Flandrin and Roussier, pp. 31–2. A number of Flandrin's copies were eventually acquired by the State, including: a copy after Fra Angelico acquired by the Musée de Rouen in 1895, *Archives nationales*, F/21/4909B; dossier 10; pièce 98 [série cahiers des musées]; a copy after Ingres's *Grande odalisque* (c.1903–4), now thought to be mistakenly attributed to Hippolyte Flandrin, in the Musée de Montauban (see Daniel Ternois, *Ingres et son temps*, Paris, 1965, p. 124: I am very grateful to Mme Lacambre for drawing this to my attention): AN, F/21/4909B; dossier 10; pièce 22; a copy after Raphael's *Balthazar Castiglione*, acquired by the Musée de Mont-de-Marsan (Landes), AN, F/21/4909B; dossier 10; pièce 20 (attribution uncertain); a copy after Poussin, acquired by the Musée des Andelys in 1903, AN, F/21/4500B; dossier 2; pièce 14 (attribution uncertain).

29. The other nude, of which only a photograph survives (*Flandrin Archives*, Paris) is now thought to be lost: see cat. 19, and accompanying note.

30. Flandrin and Roussier, p. 43.

31. *Ibid.*, p. 32.

32. See, for example, Evenepoël's letter to his father (8 November 1895), in *Lettres choisies*, pp. 120–2.

33. For an overview of Evenepoël's work, see Francis E. Hyslop, *Henri Evenepoël: Belgian Painter in Paris 1892-1899* (Unversity Park, 1975), *passim*.

34. Cf. Evenepoël's *Girl with a Doll*, 1894: reproduced in Hyslop (1971), pp. 38–9.

35. 'amour de la couleur allié à une conscience toujours absolue du dessin', Flandrin, letter to his father (31 December 1898), cited in Flandrin and Roussier, p. 45.

36. Flandrin, letter to André Lizambert (4 March 1900), cited *ibid.*, p. 57.

37. 'Je crois que le progrès consisterait à rendre le plus grand nombre d'hommes capables de comprendre et d'appliquer le bien, mais non a en trouver un d'un nouveau genre', Flandrin, letter to his father (10 June 1899), cited *Ibid.*, p. 47.

38. For André Gide, Matisse, Rouault, Bussy and Moreau's other students pursued a form of secular sainthood, approaching their art with an austerity and harshness as if were a high priesthood, see Philippe Loisel, *et al.*, *Simon Bussy (1870–1954): L'Esprit du trait, du zoo à la gentry* (exh. cat., Musée Départementale de l'Oise, Beauvais; Paris, 1996), p. 130.

39. Flandrin, letter to his mother (10 December 1899), cited in Flandrin and Roussier, p. 51.

40. 'dans chacune j'ai rétrouvé cette assistance sincèrement émue où jeunes et vieux, illustres et inconnus songent côte à côte', Flandrin, letter to his mother (17 November 1898), cited *ibid.*, p. 44.

41. Cited in Eugene Weber, *France Fin de Siècle* (Cambridge, Mass., and London, 1986), p. 105.

42. See Spurling, pp. 74–5.

43. '[...] l'état politique ici devient indéchiffrable [...] il y a une poussée d'anarchie formidable! [...] il y quelque chose de bien pourri ici!!' Evenepoël, letter to Charles Didisheim (18 September 1899), in *Lettres choisies*, pp. 192–3.

44. On these institutions in the wake of the 1900 Exhibition, see Robert Jensen, *Marketing Modernism in Fin-de-Siècle Europe* (Princeton, 1994), pp. 135–7.

45. 'Paris brille des ressources que donnent une concentration du marché d'art exclusive et une population artistique nombreuse et cosmopolite', Monnier, *L'Art et ses institutions en France: de la Révolution à nos jours* (Paris, 1995), p. 212 (on this theme generally, see pp. 207–16).

46. See Francis Carco, *L'Ami des peintres* (Paris, 1953), pp. 194–5.

47. Called the 'Exposition de Groupe', the exhibition also included Henri Petitjean and the Russian, Krouglicoff, see Flandrin and Roussier, p. 69.

48. See *ibid.*, p. 43.

49. Amongst the early favourable reactions to his work were extended reviews by Thiébault-Sisson (*Le Petit temps*, 23 April 1897) and Arsène Alexandre ('Supplément du vernissage', *Le Figaro*, 30 April 1898): cited *ibid.*, pp. 37 and 41–2.

50. 'outrancier et symboliste', Octave Uzanne, 'Outranciers et symbolistes', *L'Écho de Paris*, 1 May 1899.

51. Although it did gain in prestige after 1901 when the exhibition venue moved to the Grand Palais: see Robert Jensen, *Marketing Modernism* (1994), pp. 135–6.

52. '[ce] pourrait être pour moi une bonne aubaine', Flandrin letter to André Lizambert (17 May 1900), cited in Flandrin and Roussier, p. 57.

53. 'Il est manifeste qu'à l'époque présente les arts plastiques hésitent entre des souvenirs et des désirs, ceux-là pesant lourdement sur ceux-ci et les gênant dans leur essor. Il en résulte, surtout chez les jeunes, un trouble profond, que les expositions annuelles avouent depuis longtemps déjà. Nous sommes au lendemain de *quelque chose*. Sommes-nous à la veille de *quelque chose?*' [Morice's emphases], Morice, 'Enquête sur les tendances actuelles des arts plastiques', *Mercure de France*, vol. LVI, no.195 (August 1905), p. 346.

54. See Spurling, p. 184.

55. See Flandrin and Roussier, pp. 16–7 and p. 23, n.20.

56. On Matisse's visits to rue Campagne Première, see Spurling, pp. 225–6.

57. Georges Besson, *Marquet* (1920), cited in Flandrin and Roussier, p. 21.

58. Camoin was one of the group in whose company Flandrin frequented the Louvre (see cat. 12). He was in close regular contact with Marquet in the early 1900s, although only sporadically in Paris, participating in a group exhibition with Matisse, Marquet, Manguin and Puy at the Berthe Weill Gallery in April 1904. On his graphic work, see Véronique Serrano, *et al.*, *Charles Camoin: rétrospective, 1879-1965* (exh. cat., Lausanne, 1997; Marseille, 1997–8, Paris, 1997), pp. 147–8.

59. Indeed, Schneider contends that at this time 'Matisse's drawing was still groping in search of itself, while Marquet's had already achieved assurance': *Matisse* (1984), p. 124. It is notable that Flandrin remained closer to Marquet than Matisse, suggesting a greater affinity between Flandrin and Marquet, rather than between Matisse and Marquet even during their period of partnership in the early 1900s.

60. 'Ravier de plein soleil [...] m'ont rappelé notre soleil de Corenc [...] m'ont vraiment fait plaisir', Flandrin letter to his father (29 June 1898), cited in Flandrin and Roussier, p. 43. The comparison here is to the pre-Impressionist artist François-Auguste Ravier (1814–1895), greatly admired by Flandrin for the luminosity of his work.

61. See n.15 above.

62. Cited in Schneider, *Matisse* (1984), p. 102.

63. Druet was the first dealer following Berthe Weill to specialize in the art of Matisse's circle; Matisse showed with him from 1906, and he became Marquet's dealer in 1907: see Spurling, pp. 340–1.

64. 'la grossièreté matérielle', Camille Mauclair, *La Farce de l'art vivant* (Paris, 1929), p. 165. On this point, see Jean-Claude Lebensztejn, 'Tournant', in Suzanne Pagé, *et al.*, *Le Fauvisme ou 'l'épreuve du feu': Éruption de la modernité en Europe* (exh. cat., Musée d'Art Moderne de la Ville de Paris, 1999–2000, Paris, 1999), esp. pp. 27–31.

65. Cf. Matisse's portraits of his children, especially *Marguerite* (1901, formerly dated 1906: whereabouts unknown), painted in the aftermath of an emergency operation on her larynx; and *Pierre Matisse with Bidouille* (1904: private collection).

66. Given the violence associated with the Fauves, Flandrin may simply have wished to remain out of the fray. Even so, his lack of prominence amongst the group at this point may have contributed to his invisibility in later critical accounts of Fauvism. Despite the range of artists featured in the recent Fauvism retrospective at the Musée d'art moderne de la ville de Paris (1999–2000), Flandrin's name is still strikingly absent.

67. Morice, 'Le Salon d'Automne', *Mercure de France*, vol. LVIII, no.203 (December 1905), pp. 379–80.

68. 'heureusement que l'on voit au moins ce que mes tableaux représentent puisqu'ils ne m'ont pas jugé digne d'y figurer, mais sur dix artistes, j'y ai huit amis qui y sont et deux que je connais!!', Flandrin, letter to his mother (5 November 1905), cited in Flandrin and Roussier, p. 84.

69. Morice, 'Le Salon d'Automne', *Mercure de France* (December 1905), p. 379.

70. Indeed, retrospectives were part of the organizing intentions of the *Salon d'Automne* as Roger-Marx made clear in 1904: see Robert Jensen (1994), pp. 136–7 and n.100.

71. See Françoise Cachin, Pierre Rosenberg, *et al.*, *De Corot aux Impressionnistes, donations Moreau-Nélaton* (exh. cat., Grand Palais, Paris, 1991), *passim*.

72. 'Cela [...] a élargi à mes yeux les limites de l'Art', Flandrin to Adèle Lizambert (25 January 1905), cited in Flandrin and Roussier, p. 77.

73. 'c'est une manifestation un peu en coup d'état de la jeune école des Indépendants et ses Maîtres', Flandrin, letter to his mother (5 November 1905), cited *ibid.*, p. 79.

74. Published in the *Mercure de France* (vols LVI and LVII), in three instalments: 1 and 15 August; 1 September 1905, pp. 346–59; 538–55 and 61–85 (Marval was included, but not Flandrin).

75. 'Ce que vous y trouverez, c'est le secret des formes, si caché dans la nature, quoiqu'il y soit toujours', Flandrin, letter to Mainssieux (26 December 1902), cited in Flandrin and Roussier, p. 69.

76. 'langage d'une âme d'artiste', Flandrin, letter to André Lizambert (25 January 1905), cited *ibid.*, p. 80.

77. 'une horreur et de dimension considérable', Henri Bernard, cited *ibid.*, p. 81.

78. 'le sol sacré de l'Italie', Flandrin, letter to Joseph Flandrin (19 April 1909), cited *ibid.*, p. 96.

79. 'c'est grâce à mon électricité que j'ai pu faire ce que je voulais', Flandrin, letter to his mother (23 January 1900), cited *ibid.*, p. 53.

80. Flandrin, *ibid.*

81. Flandrin started using 'autochromes' (a method of colour photography invented by the Lumière brothers) in the early 1900s for taking views of Paris, Corenc and its surrounding landscape, and for his portraits: *Flandrin Archives*, Paris.

82. 'fête aux lanternes scientifiques', Kahn, *L'Esthétique de la rue* (Paris, 1901), p. 241.

83. See *ibid.*, esp. pp. 206–25.

84. 'une époque éprise de vulgarisation et avide de changement', Émile Magne, 'L'Esthétique de la rue', *Mercure de France*, vol. LVI (July 1905), p. 181.

85. As characterized in his *Puissances de Paris* (Paris, 1911; repr. 2000): see esp. pp. 121–9.

86. Schneider compares the script-like nature of Marquet's drawings to that of Chinese and Japanese prints: see *Matisse* (1984), pp. 124–32; on Camoin and drawing, see Serrano, *et al.*, *Charles Camoin* (1997), pp. 147–8.

87. 'c'est peut-être exagéré de trouver du repos dans un mouvement et je ne sais si je me fais comprendre: pourtant c'est l'impression que je ressens', Jacqueline Marval, 'Les Danseuses de Flandrin', *L'Art décoratif*, no.190 (April 1913), p. 167: article repr. in *Les Ballets russes par Jules Flandrin 1871–1947* (exh. cat., Galerie Thomire, Paris, 1990), pref. by Georges Flandrin.

88. 'naïveté artificielle', Henri Bernard, cited in Flandrin and Roussier, p. 82.

89. Fokine, cited in Janet Kennedy, *The 'Mir Iskusstva' Group and Russian Art* (New York, 1977), p. 354.

90. 'C'est une joie d'art [...] [c'est] musique, chants et danses, et dessin et couleur. Tu penses si la peinture s'en donne', Flandrin, letter to Joseph Flandrin (1 June 1909), cited in Flandrin and Roussier, p. 100.

91. See, for example, Martine Kahane, *et al.*, *Nijinsky 1889-1950* (exh. cat., Musée d'Orsay, Paris, 2000–2001), p. 142, cat. no.95.

92. 'L'entrain et la belle santé de ces dances sont vraiment admirables', Flandrin, letter to his mother (9 June 1909), cited in Flandrin and Roussier, p. 100.

93. 'la fusion complète [...] de la musique, et de la danse [...] l'émotion de ce qu'ils font', Flandrin, *ibid.*.

94. 'l'élément mélodique et harmonique dans l'art de la dance', Madeleine Vincent, cited *ibid.*, p. 113.

95. 'le rythme coloré': see *ibid.*, p. 112.

96. '[le] trait vif de la lumière qui anime [le tableau] et l'idéalise', Édmond Epardaud, cited *ibid.*, p. 111.

97. Matisse, 'Notes of a Painter' (1908), transl. Alfred H. Barr Jr., in Herschel B. Chipp, *Theories of Modern Art: A Source Book by Artists and Critics* (Berkeley, Los Angeles and London, 1968), p. 132.

98. 'Plus grands que nature, la Musique et la Danse', Flandrin, letter to Joseph Flandrin (2 November 1910), cited in Flandrin and Roussier, p. 120; see also cat. 51. and notes.

99. Via Druet with Léon Bérard, under-secretary for the Ministry of Fine Arts. Negotiations apparently reached the paper stage, but were never completed: *Flandrin Archives*, Paris; Flandrin and Roussier, p. 144.

100. Apollinaire, 'Avant le vernissage du Salon de la Société Nationale des Beaux-Arts' (1910), *Chroniques d'art* (Paris, 1960), p. 87.

101. 'La joie qui ordonne, la sagesse qui édifie sont les deux grands vertus de cet artiste, assez robuste, assez lucide', André Salmon, 'Les Expositions de peinture: Jules Flandrin (Galerie Druet)', *Paris-Journal*, 9 February 1910.

102. 'ouvrages d'un beau style et d'une large exécution', R.M. Ferry, cited in Flandrin and Roussier, pp. 110–11.

103. 'natures mortes [qui] ont le mâle éclat des Cézanne', Édmond Epardaud, cited *ibid.*, p. 111.

104. 'le double conseil de la nature et de la (vraie) tradition', Morice, cited *ibid.*, p. 110.

105. 'une ténébreuse et profonde unité', *ibid.*

106. Cézanne, letter to Émile Bernard (26 May 1904), transl. Marguerite Kay, repr. in Chipp, *Theories of Modern Art* (1968), p. 20.

107. Notably by Louis Vauxcelles and Réne-Jean: cited in Flandrin and Roussier, pp. 128–9.

108. 'Un tableau est un accord', Flandrin, letter to Mainssieux (12 July 1913), cited *ibid.*, p. 139.

109. See Apollinaire, 'Au Salon, avant le vernissage de la "Nationale"'(1912), in *Chroniques d'art*, p. 240.

110. 'l'irréalisme de la peinture pure', Bernard Dorival, cited in Flandrin and Roussier, p. 87.

111. See Albert Gleizes's and Jean Metzinger's *Du Cubisme* (Paris, 1912), repr. in extracts (transl. Unwin) in Chipp (1968), pp. 207–16.

112. '[que] sera de la peinture pure', Apollinaire, *Méditations esthétiques: Les Peintres cubistes* (1913), ed. Leroy C. Breunig and Jean-Claude Chevalier (Paris, 1965), p. 50.

113. 'Ce petit cachotier de Metzinger! voilà où il avait pris la carafe qui se continue en assiette', the context for this remark was an exhibition of Marval's work at the Galerie Druet in February 1912: cited in Flandrin and Roussier, p. 133.

114. 'Dans leur fantaisie, seul celui qui habite Paris, tourne de façon amusante le problème, une immense mosaïque colorée où on aurait un peu embrouillé les morceaux', Flandrin, letter to Joseph (5 February 1912), cited *ibid.*, p. 134.

115. 'J'ai pu, dans ma toile assez grande (plus de deux mètres), les mettre presque grandeur de la nature, et bien au naturel sous le beau soleil de Corenc', Flandrin, letter to his mother (8 March 1913), cited *ibid.*, p. 136.

116. 'goût du style et de la cadence classique [...] exécution rigoureusement moderne', Louis Vauxcelles, cited *ibid.*, p. 137.

117. 'un jour viendra où les paysages de Flandrin trouveront leur place au Louvre', Salmon, 'Le Salon de la Nationale', *Paris-Journal*, 15 April 1911.

118. 'maisons [...] comme des petits temples aux divinités champêtres', Flandrin, letter to Angèle Flandrin (22 December 1915), cited *ibid.*, p. 178.

119. 'un avant-lever de soleil qui pose de l'or rouge sur tout', Flandrin, letter to François (6 January 1916), *ibid.*

120. 'le secret de la couleur et de la forme', Flandrin, letter to Joseph (6 September 1917), cited *ibid.*, p. 188, attested in Flandrin's numerous sketches of his war locations and life as a soldier, *Flandrin Archives*, Paris.

121. The group that Élie Faure, indeed, linked as 'décorateurs', *Histoire de l'art moderne* (Paris, 1924), pp. 497–9.

122. 'le mouvement de la rue moderne selon le sentiment moderne', Salmon, cited *ibid.*, p. 211.

123. For an overview, see Monnier, *L'Art et ses institutions en France* (1995), pp. 290–304.

124. 'déjà aux portes du Musée', Salmon, cited in Flandrin and Roussier, p. 211.

125. On Derain and tradition, see Jane Lee, *Derain* (Oxford, 1990), pp. 47–9 and 54–61.

126. See Micheline Tison-Braun, *La Crise de l'humanisme* (Paris, 1967), vol. II (1914–1939), pp. 219–20.

127. 'les couleurs fraîches et les notes éclatantes sur un sable d'or clair et cette mer d'argent sont vraiment une leçon en peinture', Flandrin, letter to his mother (23 August 1923), cited in Flandrin and Roussier, p. 221.

128. 'entre la nature et l'artiste', Flandrin, letter to François Flandrin (26 January 1927), cited *ibid.*, p. 229.

129. 'C'est l'Italie qu'il me faut terminer', Flandrin, *ibid.*

130. 'si loin du soleil', Flandrin, letter to his mother (25 September 1925), cited *ibid.*, p. 226.

131. 'Une personnification de l'art vivant: Jules Flandrin', cited *ibid.*, p. 256.

132. 'Demain cette joie nous échapperait d'étudier un Jules Flandrin, reconnu maître par les plus avertis, et dont la maîtrise va être publiquement proclamée', *La Jeune peinture française* (1912), p. 63.

Flandrin avant Flandrin: Une Tradition Picturale en Dauphiné

GEORGES FLANDRIN

C'est surtout après son arrivée à Paris, et comme élève de Gustave Moreau, que Flandrin commença à se faire une réputation d'artiste. Mais il n'est pas parvenu à la peinture sans suivre d'autres chemins qui lui étaient plus familiers. La nature fastueuse de la Vallée du Grésivaudan qui s'offrait en spectacle à ses regards d'enfant et qui l'inspira si souvent, ne fit que s'ajouter à une atmosphère familiale propice. Bien que la profession de son père, pharmacien, ne puisse le laisser supposer, c'est dans une ambiance d'étonnante préoccupation picturale que se déroula son enfance.[1]

Son père avait épousé une lointaine cousine, Louise Ricard, et du fait de ce mariage, les enfants descendaient par leur père et par leur mère de deux frères Flandrin, François et Antoine, issus d'une vieille famille du Pont-de-Beauvoisin.[2] Au XVIIIème siècle ils avaient tous deux occupé des fonctions dans leur Province, le Dauphiné de l'Ancien Régime. L'ancêtre du père, François, né en 1729, avait eu la fonction de Capitaine-Général des Fermes ; le cadet né en 1732 (ill. coul. 1), ancêtre de la mère, avait été Officier-de-Bouche du Lieutenant-Général de la Province, le Comte de Clermont-Tonnerre, puis, fortune faite avait acheté le café sis en face du Parlement et plus tard une propriété de campagne à Corenc. Antoine Flandrin avait marié sa fille aînée à Joseph Mollard, représentant d'une lignée d'orfèvres et d'horlogers grenoblois.[3]

Les deux fils d'Antoine Flandrin et deux des enfants Mollard avaient été les élèves de J.-A. Treillard, peintre originaire de Valence, qui après s'être illustré à la Cour de Parme, était venu à Grenoble en 1763 créer une école de Peinture.[4] Cette école, encouragée par les notables et particulièrement le Lieutenant-Général qui y avait inscrit son fils, était largement ouverte et les artisans entre autres y envoyèrent leurs enfants.[5] Influence atavique ou histoires de famille ressassées, toujours est-il que les enfants Flandrin avaient présent à l'esprit ces vieilles racines d'une ancienne tradition de l'artisanat.[6] Peu était matériellement conservé de ce passé lorsque Jules était enfant, mais un dessin académique signé *'fait par Flandrin en 1786'*, sans doute chez Treillard, était encore montré aux enfants par leur père (ill. 2).[7]

Sur les six garçons Flandrin issus des deux frères, cinq furent fauchés par les guerres Révolutionnaires et du Consulat, avant même l'Empire. Le seul qui échappa à l'hécatombe pour transmettre le nom, François-Eustache, l'aîné du Capitaine des Fermes et qui avait reçu l'enseignement envié du Collège Royal Dauphin, traversa la Révolution, l'Empire et la Restauration comme responsable politique au

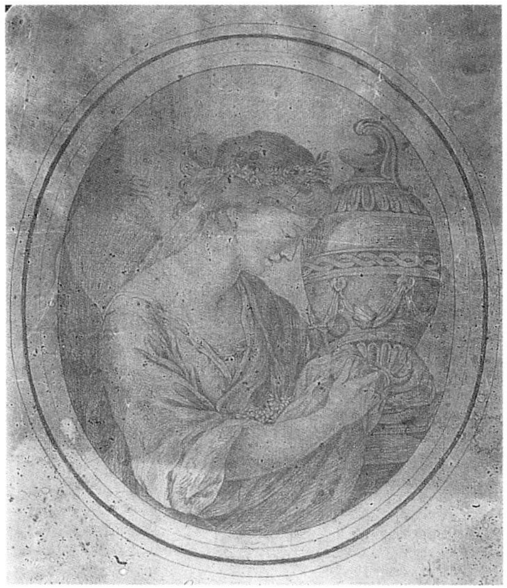

Illustration 2: *Dessin académique, signé
Flandrin*, 1786. Sanguine, collection privé,
Paris.

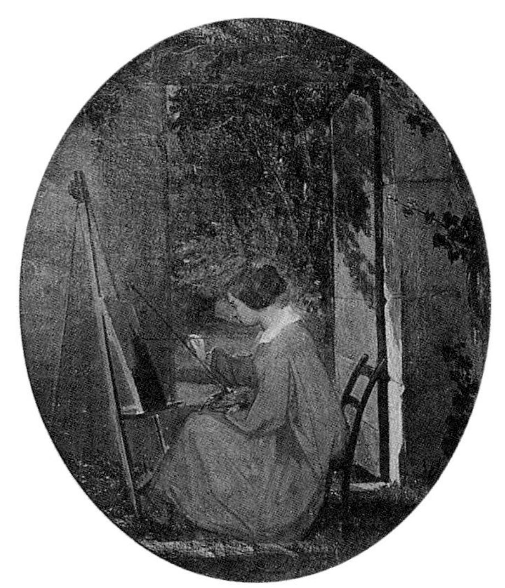

Illustration 4:
FONTAINE, *Adèle Gamel peignant*, 1840.
Huile sur toile, 39 × 31.5 cms,
collection privé, Paris.

Pont-de-Beauvoisin,[8] mais ne transmit rien du monde des artisans, bien qu'il eût
envoyé son fils – le grand-père de Jules – suivre les cours de peinture des nouveaux
professeurs, Jay et Couturier.[9] Le lien à la peinture et à l'artisanat se maintint cependant par les Mollard et par plusieurs détours dont les enfants Flandrin de la génération de Jules avaient les exemples encore tout proches. La fille aînée de Joseph
Mollard, horloger à Grenoble, avait épousé le confiseur Alexandre Gamel, qui avait
sa confiserie dans le Couvent des Minimes au lieu-dit 'la Plaine' touchant à
Grenoble. Là, dans les années 1830, il tenait table ouverte et les jeunes gens, cousins
ou amis de la famille Mollard, se préparant au métier de peintre, avaient coutume
de venir 'peindre les bonbons', et 'peindre sur sucre' selon une pratique du temps,
et courtiser les jeunes filles Gamel.[10] Ces demoiselles, elles-mêmes peintres aussi
talentueuses que méconnues, fréquentèrent l'atelier de Fantin père, se prenant
pour modèles les unes les autres (ill. coul. 3 et 4).[11] Passèrent ainsi par 'la Plaine' des
peintres qui eurent leur célébrité dauphinoise, le cousin Henri-Blanc-Fontaine (le
parrain de la sœur de Jules),[12] et Diodore Rahoult (fils de confiseur lui aussi, comme
Ravier)[13] – l'illustrateur de la complainte de Grenoble inondé 'Grenoblo Malherou'.[14]
Lorsque les enfants Flandrin parlaient du talent qui n'avait pas besoin de gloire,
'Voyez les cousines de la Plaine !' était l'expression de leur préoccupation d'indépen-
dance.[15]

Un des neveux de Joseph Mollard, Horace Mollard, peintre et professeur de
dessin à Grenoble, avait laissé dans la famille des souvenirs de cette époque:

Illustration 6:
Jules Flandrin,
Chemin sous les arbres, 1886.
Huile sur panneau,
23.5 × 14.5 cms,
collection privé, Paris
(cat. 1).

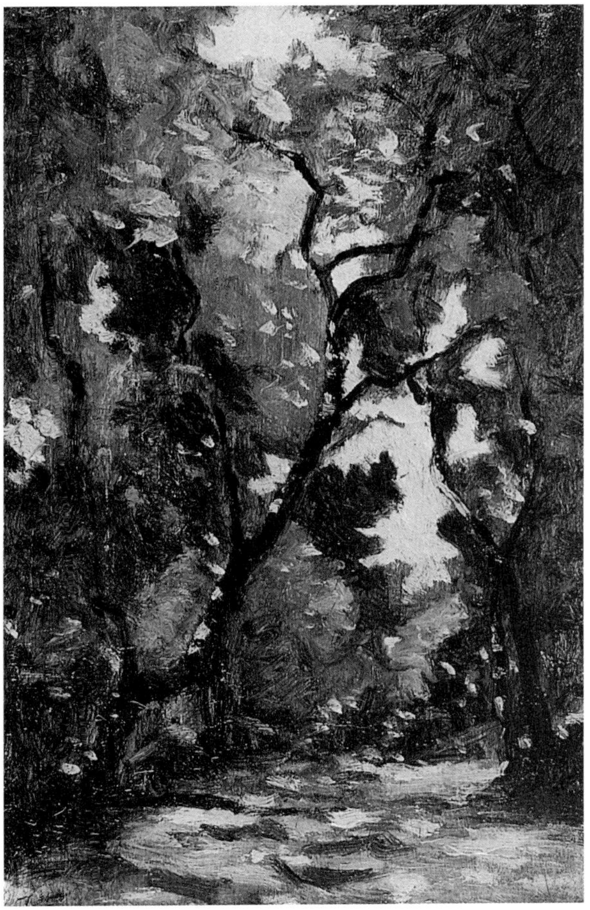

Grenoble et la Citadelle en 1830 (ill. coul. 5), et une vue de la 'Grande Maison' de Corenc. Corenc avait été acquis par Antoine Flandrin et son gendre Joseph Mollard en 1791, par suite à la Vente des Biens de l'Église. Il s'agissait de biens du Clergé, sous la forme du presbytère de l'église et de ses dépendances sur la butte du village. Depuis lors, Corenc n'avait cessé d'être le mot symbole du bonheur des Flandrin, génération après génération ; le petit Jules y avait son cœur ancré à jamais. Diodore Rahoult et Henri Blanc-Fontaine, à chaque naissance écrivaient pour féliciter Louise de l'arrivée de ces enfants qui paraissaient à la famille être venus au monde pour la relève du sang des artistes. Blanc-Fontaine avait repéré le petit Jules à son jeune talent et l'appelait 'mon petit Fragonard' (ill. 6). Etre peintre avait été le désir rentré du père, Joseph Flandrin le pharmacien, qui était lié d'amitié avec le peintre Jean Achard,[16] et c'est sans trop d'obstacles que fut progressivement admise dans la famille la destinée que Jules se forgeait petit à petit. Ce troisième fils n'avait pas précisément été un bon élève au Lycée de Grenoble, mais il participait à tout ce qui se présentait comme cours et concours municipaux de dessin ou de sculpture, se vieillissant parfois de trois ans sur les formulaires pour pouvoir s'y inscrire. En 1889 il fut décidé qu'il quitterait le Lycée avant le terme pour être mis en apprentissage chez les imprimeurs Allier à Grenoble. Il y resta trois ans de 1889 à 1893. Durant cette période Jules Flandrin continue à dessiner et à peindre sur les conseils de son père et ayant sous les yeux la leçon des Maîtres du lieu, Auguste Ravier,[17] Diodore Rahoult, Jean Achard, Théodore Ravanat[18] (cat. 4), multipliant aussi les visites au Musée de Grenoble[19] et se plongeant dans la lecture des vieux 'Magasins Pittoresques'. Il se forgeait ainsi une culture ésotérique et singulière qu'il ne reniera cependant jamais, mais il en sentait les limites. Ayant atteint le niveau que lui proposait son ambiance locale (cat. 3), refusant de s'en contenter et impatient de secouer une tutelle paternelle trop pesante,[20] il part à Paris en octobre 1893 avec en poche une bourse de la Municipalité de Grenoble pour s'inscrire à l'École des Arts Décoratifs et pour préparer son entrée à l'École des Beaux-Arts. Il est admis dans son Atelier par Gustave Moreau en 1895, entrant dans ce lieu privilégié à la même période que de futurs camarades qui marqueront leur époque, Matisse et Marquet entre autres.

RÉFÉRENCES

1. Voir Flandrin et Roussier, *Jules Flandrin* (1992), *passim*.

2. Abbé H.-J. Perrin, *Histoire du Pont-de-Beauvoisin* (Paris, 1897), p. 307.

3. *Archives familiales Flandrin*, Paris; voir aussi Flandrin et Roussier, p. 13–4, et Édmond Maignien, *Les Artistes Grenoblois* (Grenoble, 1887), p. 181 et 246.

4. Voir Marianne Clerc, *Jacques-André Treillard, 1712–1794, peintre Dauphinois* (Grenoble, 1995), p. 134, 151 et 164.

5. *Archives familiales Flandrin*, Paris.

6. *Archives familiales Flandrin*, Paris.

7. *Archives familiales Flandrin*, Paris.

8. *Archives familiales Flandrin*, Paris; aussi, Perrin, *Histoire du Pont-de-Beauvoisin*, p. 307.

9. *Archives familiales Flandrin*, Paris. Cf. Maignien, *op.cit.*, p. 181 et 246, et Clerc, *op.cit.*, p. 134, 151 et 164.

10. *Journal de Diodore Rahoult, 1837–1838, Archives familiales Flandrin*, Paris.

11. *Ibid.*

12. Voir Aristide Albert, *Le Peintre Blanc-Fontaine*, Grenoble, 1902.

13. Diodore Rahoult, 'Grenoblo Malhérou', *Les Alps pittoresques*, 31 décembre 1907 – 1er janvier 1908.

14. Par Blanc dit 'la Goutte': *Poésies en patois du Dauphiné*, préface de George Sand, Grenoble, 1864. Cf. G. Vellein, *Le Poète Blanc-la-Goutte*, Grenoble, 1907.

15. *Archives familiales Flandrin*, Paris.

16. Marcel Raymond, *Jean Achard (1807–1884), peintre paysagiste*, Paris, 1887.

17. Voir Paul Jamot, *Auguste Ravier (1814–1895)*, Lyon, 1911.

18. Voir Marcel Reymond, *Étude sur le Musée de Tableaux de Grenoble*, Grenoble, 1879.

19. *Catalogue des tableaux* (ville de Grenoble), Grenoble, 1901.

20. Flandrin et Roussier, p. 14–5.

Flandrin before Flandrin: a Pictorial Tradition in the Dauphiné

TRANSLATED FROM THE FRENCH BY TIM FARRANT

It was above all after his arrival in Paris, and as a pupil of Gustave Moreau, that Flandrin began to make his reputation as an artist. But he did not come to painting without first following other, more familiar paths. The luxuriant natural surroundings of the Grésivaudan valley, which formed a pageant before his childhood gaze, did but supplement the propitious atmosphere at home. Although his father's profession as a pharmacist might not lead us to suppose as much, it was in an ambience of extraordinary interest in the pictorial that his childhood was spent.[1]

Jules's father had married a distant cousin, Louise Ricard, and, in consequence, their children descended on both the paternal and the distaff sides from two Flandrin brothers, François and Antoine, who came from an old Pont-de-Beauvoisin family.[2] In the eighteenth century, both these brothers had held offices in their province, the Dauphiné of the Ancien Régime. Jules's father's ancestor, François, born in 1729, had been *Capitaine-Général des Fermes*, a local official of the Farmers-General; his mother's forebear the younger brother, Antoine, born in 1732 (col. ill. 1), had served as *Officier-de-Bouche* (in approximate terms, butler and manciple) to the Province's Lord Lieutenant, the Count of Clermont-Tonnerre. Having made his fortune, Antoine had bought the café situated opposite its *Parlement* and, in due course, a country house at Corenc. Antoine Flandrin had married his eldest daughter to Joseph Mollard, one of a line of Grenoblois goldsmiths and clockmakers.[3]

The two sons of Antoine Flandrin and two of the Mollard children had been pupils of J.-A. Treillard, an artist from Valence who, having distinguished himself at the Court of the Duchy of Parma, had come to Grenoble in 1763 to establish a school of painting.[4] This school, encouraged by the local notabilities and particularly by the Lord Lieutenant, who had enrolled his son there, offered largely unrestricted access, and local artisans, amongst others, sent their own male offspring to it.[5] Be it by dint of some atavistic influence or the simple retelling of family stories, the roots of a longstanding artisan tradition were deeply established in the Flandrin children's minds.[6] By the time of Jules Flandrin's childhood, little physical vestige of this tradition had actually survived, but an academic drawing, signed 'by Flandrin in 1786', and no doubt done in Treillard's school, was still shown to the children by their father (ill. 2).[7]

Of the six Flandrin children who were descended from the two brothers, five fell in the wars of the Revolution and the Consulate, before even the beginning of the first Napoleonic Empire. The only one to escape this immolation and carry on the name, François-Eustache, the eldest son of the *Capitaine-Général*, who had received a privileged education at the Collège Royal Dauphin, went through the Revolution, the Empire and the Restoration as a political official at Pont-de-Beauvoisin,[8] but did not pass on anything of the artisan milieu, even though he had sent his son – the grandfather of Jules – to pursue an artistic training with two new professors, Jay and Couturier.[9] The link with painting and with the artisan world was maintained via the Mollards, as well as in various roundabout ways of which the Flandrin children of Jules's generation could still see examples at close hand. The eldest daughter of Joseph Mollard, the Grenoblois clockmaker, had married the confectioner Alexandre Gamel, whose business was in the Convent of the Minimes at the place called 'La Plaine' on the outskirts of Grenoble. There, during the 1830s, he held open house, and the youngsters, cousins or friends of the Mollard family who were training to be painters were in the habit of coming 'to paint the sweets', according to a custom of the time, and pay court to the young Gamel daughters.[10] These young ladies, who were themselves painters as talented as they were unrecognized, regularly worked in the studio of Fantin-Latour the elder, using each other as models (col. ill. 3 and 4).[11] Thus there passed through 'La Plaine' a number of painters who had their hour of glory in Grenoble: Henri Blanc-Fontaine, who was a cousin and Jules's godfather,[12] and Diodore Rahoult,[13] the illustrator of the lament for the flooding of Grenoble 'Grenoblo Malhérou'.[14] When the Flandrin children talked of those talents which had no need of fame, 'look at the La Plaine cousins!' was their way of showing how seriously they took their independence.[15]

One of Joseph Mollard's nephews, Horace Mollard, a painter and drawing-master at Grenoble, had left in the family mementoes of this period: *Grenoble and the Citadel in 1830* (col. ill. 5), and a view of the 'Grande Maison' at Corenc. Corenc had been acquired by Antoine Flandrin and his son-in-law Joseph Mollard in 1791, subsequent to the sale of Church lands. It had been the property of the clergy, consisting of the presbytery of the church, together with its associated buildings on the hill in the village. Since that time, Corenc had been the name which symbolized happiness for successive generations of Flandrins, and little Jules had set his heart there for ever. At each new birth, Diodore Rahoult and Henri Blanc-Fontaine would write to congratulate Louise on the arrival of the children who, to the family, seemed to have come into the world to take up the baton of this race of artists. Blanc-Fontaine had spotted the young Jules's talent early on, calling him 'my little Fragonard' (ill. 6).

To be an artist had been the suppressed desire of Jules's father, the pharmacist Joseph Flandrin, who had formed a friendship with the painter Jean Achard,[16] and it was without putting too many obstacles in his path that the family gradually accepted the destiny which, little by little, Jules was shaping for himself. This third son of the family had not been exactly a good pupil at the Lycée de Grenoble, but he took part in any and every municipal drawing- and sculpture-class or competition, sometimes increasing his age by three years in order to enrol. In 1889 it was decided that he would quit the Lycée before the leaving-age in order to become an apprentice to the printers Allier in Grenoble. He remained there for three years, from 1889 to 1893. During this period, Jules Flandrin followed his father's advice to continue to draw and paint, with the examples of the local masters Auguste Ravier[17] (cat. 4), Diodore Rahoult, Jean Achard and Théodore Ravanat[18] constantly before his eyes, making many visits to the Musée de Grenoble[19] and immersing himself in the perusal of old copies of the illustrated journal *Le Magasin pittoresque*. He thus acquired a singular and rather esoteric kind of culture which he would never disown, but whose limitations he nonetheless felt. Having got as far as possible in his local milieu (cat. 3), but refusing to stop there, and impatient to shake off over-heavy paternal tutelage,[20] in October 1893 he left for Paris with a bursary from the Municipality of Grenoble to enrol at the École des Arts Décoratifs and prepare for entry to the École des Beaux-Arts. In 1895 he was admitted to Gustave Moreau's studio, entering its privileged confines at the same time as fellow pupils who would leave their mark on their era, amongst them Marquet and Matisse.

REFERENCES

1. See Flandrin and Roussier, *Jules Flandrin* (1992), *passim*.

2. Abbé H.-J. Perrin, *Histoire du Pont-de-Beauvoisin* (Paris, 1897), p. 307.

3. *Flandrin Archives*, Paris; see also, Flandrin and Roussier, pp. 13–4, and Édmond Maignien, *Les Artistes Grenoblois* (Grenoble, 1887), pp. 181 and 246.

4. See Marianne Clerc, *Jacques-André Treillard, 1712–1794, peintre Dauphinois* (Grenoble, 1995), pp. 134, 151 and 164.

5. Details furnished by *Flandrin Archives*, Paris.

6. *Flandrin Archives*, Paris.

7. *Flandrin Archives*, Paris.

8. *Flandrin Archives*, Paris; see also Perrin, *Histoire du Pont-de-Beauvoisin* (1897), p. 307.

9. *Flandrin Archives*, Paris. Cf. Édmond Maignien, *Les Artistes Grenoblois*, pp. 181 and 246, and Clerc, *op. cit.*, pp. 134, 151 and 164.

10. In the *Journal de Diodore Rahoult, 1837–1838, Flandrin Archives*, Paris.

11. *Ibid.*

12. See Aristide Albert, *Le Peintre Blanc-Fontaine*, Grenoble, 1902.

13. Diodore Rahoult, 'Grenoblo Malhérou', *Les Alpes pittoresques*, 31 December 1907 – 1 January 1908.

14. By Blanc called 'la Goutte': *Poésies en patois du Dauphiné*, preface by George Sand, Grenoble, 1864. Cf. G. Vellein, *Le Poète Blanc-la-Goutte*, Grenoble, 1907.

15. *Flandrin Archives*, Paris.

16. In Marcel Raymond, *Jean Achard (1807–1884), peintre paysagiste*, Paris, 1887.

17. See Paul Jamot, *Auguste Ravier (1814–1895)*, Lyon, 1911.

18. See Marcel Reymond, *Étude sur le Musée de Tableaux de Grenoble*, Grenoble, 1879.

19. *Catalogue des tableaux* (ville de Grenoble), Grenoble, 1901.

20. Flandrin and Roussier, pp. 14–5.

Gustave Moreau et son atelier

Geneviève Lacambre

Malgré la création d'un musée pour son œuvre dans sa maison agrandie du 14 rue de La Rochefoucauld à Paris, qui devait conserver 'ce caractère d'ensemble qui permette toujours de constater la somme de travail et d'efforts de l'artiste pendant sa vie',[1] Gustave Moreau (1826–1898), dans la tourmente des novations du début du XXème siècle, fut rapidement un peintre oublié et incompris. La fidélité indéfectible de ses élèves, et en premier lieu de Georges Rouault, Georges Desvallières et Henri Matisse, a même contribué à créer l'image d'un excellent professeur qui n'aurait été qu'un peintre médiocre.

Aussi tout le XXème siècle a-t-il été jalonné de manifestations mettant à l'honneur cette alchimie difficile à décrire qu'était le discours – notamment ces conversations admirables devant les Maîtres, selon Rouault[2] – d'un homme âgé, le 'père Moreau', petit, le front dégarni et la barbe imposante, qui restait secret sur son art et sur sa vie, puisqu'il avait, croyait-on, toujours refusé de se faire photographier. Cela n'était vrai que depuis 1876 et le Musée Gustave Moreau conserve de nombreux portraits photographiques du peintre jusqu'à l'âge de cinquante ans (ill. 1), arborant alors fièrement sa décoration de la Légion d'honneur. Une seule photographie le montre plus âgé, peut-être vers 1896,[3] dans la foule d'une sortie de cimetière (ill. 2). Elle inspira à Rouault une des deux belles lithographies qu'il fit de la tête de Moreau en 1926.

C'est alors le temps de l'exposition consacrée à Gustave Moreau et quelques-uns de ses élèves en avril 1926 à la galerie Georges Petit, à Paris. Après la modeste Exposition des élèves de Gustave Moreau, à la Galerie Hessèle en 1910, cette nouvelle manifestation nécessitait quelques explications, Gustave Moreau n'étant alors plus guère à la mode. Certes, il s'agissait de marquer d'un événement le centenaire de sa naissance. Le peintre Georges Desvallières se chargea, dans la préface, d'expliquer la fascination que Moreau avait exercée sur ceux qui avaient suivi son enseignement. Il rapporte notamment:

Son esprit, c'est là ce qui attirait toute la jeunesse des ateliers, son esprit nous gagnait, amenant des discussions très vives entre les purs naturalistes et ceux qui croyaient à l'expression plus précise de la pensée en art. Le sens critique de tous s'aiguisait ainsi et nos besoins s'affirmaient, s'éclairaient. Faut-il avouer que même devant son cercueil, réunis pour la veillée mortuaire, le plus clair de nos prières fut une longue controverse sur le rôle de la pensée dans l'art? Le jour parut que les arguments surgissaient encore pour soutenir l'une ou l'autre thèse. Ainsi devant le corps inanimé de notre maître, sa pensée nous animait encore, s'exaltait même; est-ce présomption de croire que son âme put sentir quelque douceur à voir que la graine qu'il avait posée en nous n'était pas morte avec le semeur ...[4]

Plus tard, les œuvres des élèves sont de nouveau groupées autour de celles du maître dans des expositions à Marseille en 1962,[5] au Japon en 1974 et en 1984, à Marcq-en-Barœul en 1990, à Mexico en 1994, tandis que l'artiste 'redécouvert' par André Breton et les surréalistes, faisait l'objet, à partir de 1961,[6] d'expositions monographiques qui allaient progressivement le réhabiliter comme peintre majeur.[7]

Gustave Moreau s'était éteint le 18 avril 1898 à soixante-douze ans. Georges Desvallières – un élève particulier – et René Piot – inscrit officiellement à l'atelier Moreau à l'École des Beaux-Arts le 9 novembre 1891 – qui signèrent l'acte de décès du peintre à la mairie du IXème arrondissement de Paris, étaient-ils les seuls à participer à la veillée mortuaire évoquée ci-dessus? Ni l'un, ni l'autre ne durent défendre la thèse du naturalisme. Mais Gustave Moreau, on le sait, suggérait plutôt à ses élèves d'être sincères avec eux-mêmes et de développer leur personnalité.

Gustave Moreau était, depuis novembre 1888, membre de l'Académie des Beaux-Arts. Il avait d'abord refusé de participer à l'enseignement de l'École des Beaux-Arts, lorsqu'on lui proposait de remplacer Bonnat, l'un des huit professeurs – dont quatre peintres – du 'Cours de dessin et de sculpture de l'école du soir' – sans doute en raison de soucis personnels – la maladie et la mort le 28 mars 1890 d'Alexandrine Dureux, sa 'meilleure et unique amie'. Mais après la mort de son vieil

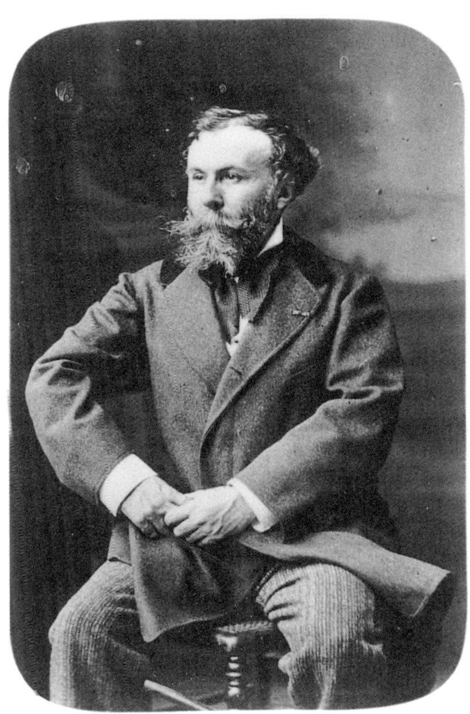

Illustration 1:
Portrait de Gustave Moreau assis,
Octobre 1876.
Photo: ©RMN, Paris.

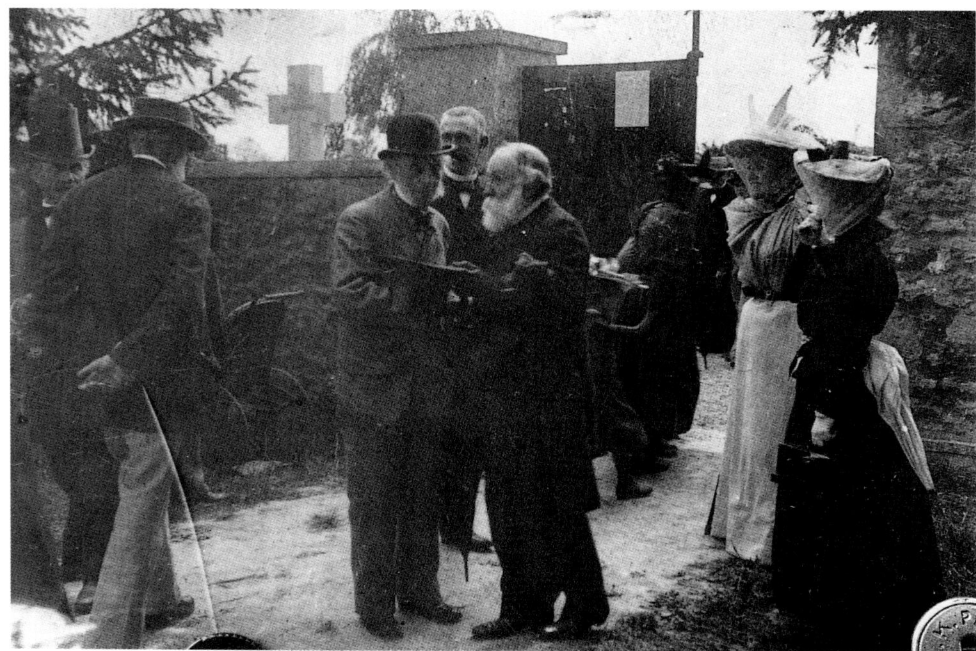

Illustration 2: *Georges Rouault, c.* 1896. Photo: ©Musée Gustave Moreau, Paris.

ami Jules-Élie Delaunay le 5 septembre 1891, il accepta de le remplacer dès la rentrée d'octobre comme professeur d'un des trois ateliers de peinture et fut nommé officiellement à ce poste le 1er janvier 1892. Ses deux collègues, également membres de l'Institut, étaient Léon Bonnat, professeur dès 1881 et promu chef d'atelier en 1888, et Jean-Léon Gérôme, en place depuis près de quarante ans, tandis que l'École du soir était assurée par quatre autres membres de l'Institut, Jules Lenepveu, William Bouguereau, Jean-Paul Laurens et Luc-Olivier Merson.

Léon Bonnat (1833–1922) était une vieille connaissance. S'il n'avait obtenu qu'un second prix au concours pour Rome en 1857, il s'était rendu en Italie, grâce à une bourse de sa ville natale, Bayonne; il s'y trouvait en même temps que Gustave Moreau qui, d'octobre 1857 à septembre 1859, fit un long voyage d'étude grâce à l'aide financière de ses parents. Ils firent, en compagnie du Prix de Rome de sculpture, Henri Chapu (1833–1891), l'ascension du Vésuve en août 1859. Le souvenir nous en est gardé grâce à un dessin de Bonnat, longtemps conservé plié avec les lettres de Bonnat dans les Archives du Musée Gustave Moreau[8] (ill. 3). D'amusantes légendes ont été apposées sur cette véritable bande dessinée en trois épisodes dont le héros, un certain Landry, n'est autre que Gustave Moreau en personne: 'Mr Landry monte au Vésuve précédé et suivi de ses deux meilleurs élèves', puis 'Landry au sommet du Vésuve n'est pas absorbé par les châtiments à infliger à ses deux meilleurs élèves', enfin 'Mr Landry descend le Vésuve dans les bras de ses deux meilleurs élèves!'.

Ces jeunes étudiants français en Italie se considéraient comme 'élèves' de Gustave Moreau, qui, plus âgé que ses compagnons, très cultivé et clair dans ses propos, se faisait déjà remarquer par son aptitude pédagogique et son discours lumineux. Quelques mois auparavant, il avait été pour le jeune Edgar Degas, tant à Rome qu'à Florence, un véritable mentor.

Il s'agit, en Italie, de conseils prodigués dans un cercle de camarades artistes, mais on peut se demander si Moreau n'a pas eu aussi une activité de professeur particulier qui lui aurait procuré quelques modestes revenus, même si aucun document financier n'est, semble-t-il, conservé à ce sujet, comme, d'ailleurs, pour la plupart des dépenses techniques, fournitures d'atelier, séances de pose des modèles ou paiement des praticiens. On ne sait dans quelles conditions, alors qu'il était encore élève à l'École des Beaux-Arts, Moreau fit connaissance, dès 1848, du jeune Henri Rupp (1837–1918),[9] fils d'un fabricant de papiers peints, peut-être en apprentissage chez lui dès cette époque. Désignant Moreau comme 'patron', Rupp devait être par la suite un de ses praticiens, au moins vers 1874 et dans les années 1890. Il vivait alors dans un appartement du rez-de-chaussée, 14 rue de La Rochefoucauld. Aide, confident, secrétaire de l'artiste, seul survivant de ses fidèles amis, il fut désigné par lui comme légataire universel et s'acquitta avec une loyale obstination de cette mission. Il fut l'organisateur du musée qu'il réussit à faire accepter par l'État en 1902, quatre ans après la mort du peintre.

C'est sans doute aussi en voulant apprendre à dessiner qu'Alexandrine Dureux (1835–1890) entra en relation avec Moreau qu'elle connut dès le retour d'Italie à l'automne 1859. Des dessins maladroits de la 'chère A.', pieusement conservés et annotés par Gustave Moreau, attestent des efforts studieux de celle qui se contenta par la suite d'être l'âme sœur du peintre resté célibataire.

Il y eut aussi, dans les années de succès, quelques dames du monde et quelques relations qui sollicitèrent des conseils. Si le fils d'Ernest Renan, Ary (1858–1900), un des premiers biographes de l'artiste avec ses articles de 1886 dans la *Gazette des Beaux-Arts*, est influencé par l'art et les sujets de Moreau qu'il étudia en critique d'art, il se déclare seulement élève de Puvis de Chavannes et d'Élie Delaunay. Moreau était ami de longue date de ces deux artistes, Puvis de Chavannes ayant sans doute été rencontré dans l'entourage de Chassériau avant 1856 et Élie Delaunay, pensionnaire à la Villa Médicis, connu en 1858 pendant le séjour romain. Delaunay eut maintes fois l'occasion de servir de médiateur entre Moreau et le monde de l'art, le mettant en relation avec ceux qui allaient devenir ses mécènes les plus importants, Charles Hayem[10] et Antony Roux,[11] ou le proposant pour donner des modèles au costumier de l'Opéra lors de la reprise de la *Sapho* de Gounod en 1883. C'est par lui encore que Moreau fit connaissance de l'écrivain et académicien Ernest Legouvé[12] et de sa famille, dont faisait partie Georges Desvallières. Ce dernier, qui devait demander à Gustave Moreau d'être le parrain de sa fille Sabine, se déclare élève d'Élie Delaunay, de Gustave Moreau et de Jules Valadon et obtient déjà une mention honorable au Salon de 1890.

Il avait donc entamé sa carrière avant que Gustave Moreau ne reçoive du

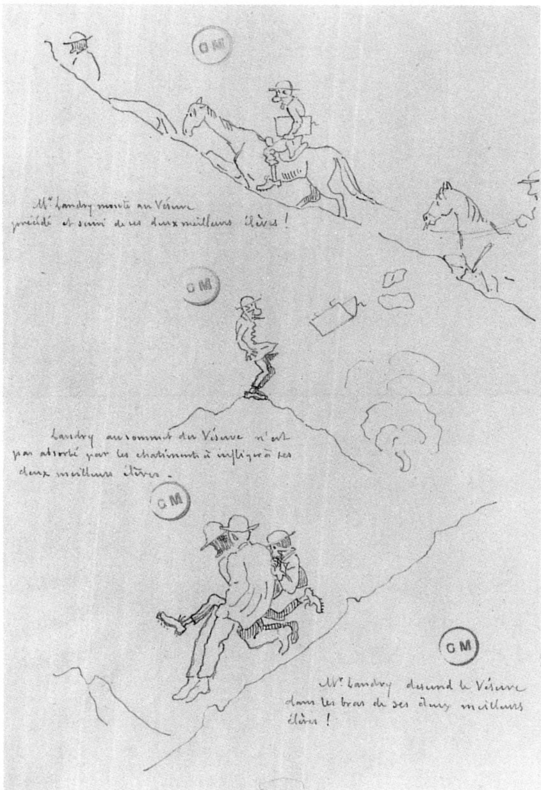

Illustration 3:
LÉON BONNAT,
Gustave Moreau à Vésuve, 1859.
Mine de plomb,
photo: ©RMN, Paris.

sculpteur Paul Dubois, directeur de l'École Nationale et spéciale des Beaux-Arts, une lettre datée du 2 novembre 1891 l'intronisant dans ses nouvelles fonctions: 'Le directeur des Beaux-Arts vous a autorisé, sur ma proposition, à diriger jusqu'à nouvel ordre, l'atelier de M. É. Delaunay. Je vous serai donc obligé si vous vouliez bien vous trouver à l'École mercredi prochain 4 novembre à 9 heures afin que je puisse vous présenter aux élèves.'[13]

Les Archives du Musée Gustave Moreau conservent une liste des 'Élèves inscrits dans l'atelier de Mrs Delaunay et Gve Moreau', datée du 15 octobre 1891 où le nom de Gustave Moreau a été rajouté au crayon bleu. Elle contient soixante-dix-huit noms, notamment ceux de Rouault (inscrit le 3 décembre 1890), de Bussy, de Maxence et de bien d'autres; Moreau la prolonge au fil des arrivées de l'automne 1891 d'une douzaine de mentions plus ou moins précises, par exemple '89, l'élève recommandé par Henner', ou '87, A. Guéniot 25 ans des Arts Décoratifs sur la recommandation de M. Gruyer fils', ce qu'Arthur Guéniot (1866–1951), dans ses mémoires, a confirmé: 'Sur l'avis du cher Gruyer, je me présentai au grand peintre Gustave Moreau, le plus tolérant, disait-on, des trois professeurs de peinture de l'École des Beaux-Arts. Je lui montrai mes dessins et il m'admit de suite à son atelier en attendant d'être reçu au concours d'admission à l'École.'[14]

En effet, outre de nouveaux inscrits, reçus au concours d'entrée,[15] l'atelier accueillait des élèves libres qui préparaient – avec ou sans succès – ce concours, première étape vers les épreuves officielles que couronnait le Prix de Rome. Le plus célèbre est Henri Matisse. Sur la carte de visite que celui-ci remit à Moreau, lorsqu'il vint se présenter, en 1892 sans doute, Moreau a noté 'ancien élève de Bouguereau', Matisse ayant commencé ses études à l'académie Julian et, après son nom, 'de St Quentin/connaît Couturier', ce dernier ayant été un des condisciples de Moreau dans sa jeunesse à l'atelier du vieux peintre néoclassique Picot.[16] Matisse, entré dans l'atelier de Moreau peu après, le 16 mars 1893, fit alors de nombreuses copies au Louvre, tout en se présentant à plusieurs reprises au concours des places, comme l'atteste un dessin daté du 18 février 1895, récemment passé en vente publique.[17] Il n'y fut officiellement accepté que le 29 juin 1895.[18] Il fit aussi des esquisses peintes de compositions historiques, dont deux se trouvent – faussement attribuées à Gustave Moreau, mais très certainement faites par Matisse au temps de 'l'atelier Moreau' d'où la confusion – dans les collection du Musée de la littérature tchèque à Prague.[19] En effet, le souvenir de 'l'atelier Moreau' reste vivace dans l'esprit de ceux qui y sont passés ou de ceux qui ont demandé conseil à l'artiste.

On peut regretter que Georges Rouault, devenu le premier conservateur du Musée Gustave Moreau et particulièrement reconnaissant envers celui qu'il désigne, dans une lettre à André Suarès du 12 février 1914, comme le 'bon, généreux et fraternel Gustave Moreau',[20] ait renoncé à écrire 'un livre important'[21] sur l'enseignement de Gustave Moreau. Il a laissé cependant quelques témoignages précieux et, notamment en 1926, un chapitre célèbre de *Souvenirs intimes*. C'est là qu'il écrit:

Je revois l'homme, son calot sur la tête, vêtu de son tricot 'lainage peuple', comme il disait. Il va de son pas pressé et diligent et je l'entends dire à des élèves guindés ou timides, réticents ou un peu sauvages, tel j'étais: 'Ne me respectez pas tant, aimez-moi un peu'. Il fut pour la plupart d'entre nous un animateur plein de sens et de mesure, capable d'oublier ses préférences devant une œuvre qui était aux antipodes de son inclination foncière ... A l'École, il arrivait le premier et partait le dernier ... Il était plus jeune d'esprit que beaucoup d'entre nous ... L'éminente qualité de Gustave Moreau, c'est qu'il n'était justement pas un professeur au sens habituel du mot mais un émule bienfaisant et comme je l'ai dit, un animateur.[22]

Rouault écrivait encore dans *Soliloques*, en 1944:

A l'atelier Moreau ... on chantait dès le matin, tout en peignant plus mal que bien. Quand le patron arrivait, le silence régnait, car sous son air débonnaire, il se fâchait parfois, prenant au sérieux son doux ministère, allant de l'un à l'autre, débordant le sujet, surtout le samedi, jour de l'Institut, où il corrigeait les esquisses peintes, dans la petite rapinière proche du grand atelier. Il s'en donnait à notre grande joie et plaisance, se mettant en retard pour déjeuner, retenu encore en bas, aux Antiques, par les débutants qui n'avaient pas encore fait choix d'un patron.[23]

Plus précis, Arthur Guéniot raconte:

Le patron était assez impressionnant, il était petit, sa figure vivante et sympathique était encadrée d'une barbe blanche, mais il entrait à l'atelier avec solennité, les jours de correction, le mercredi et le samedi. Le massier l'accueillait à la porte et le débarrassait de son chapeau haut de forme. Il était vêtu d'une jaquete, cravaté d'une lavallière bleue à petits pois blancs. Il ne quittait point ses gants ni sa canne. C'était prudent, sans quoi il eût été tenté, par goût personnel ou sur un désir de l'élève, de prendre pinceau et palette pour donner des indications. Et la séance se fût terminée avant la visite de chaque élève devant son chevalet. Le patron s'asseyait sur le siège même de l'élève et lui faisait tout bas ses remarques, donnait des conseils et des encouragements. Ce passage était rapide car chaque peintre attendait la visite désirée, tandis que le modèle en séance ne pouvait dépasser midi et demie. Gustave Moreau allait déjeuner, di-sait-il, 'd'une côtelette' au Bouillon Duval et l'après-midi se rendait à l'atelier d'élèves qui voulaient lui présenter leur tableau ou au Louvre où il passait en revue des copies. Le mercredi il voyait donc des études pour le dessin et les préparations sur toile, le samedi le travail de la semaine en achèvement. ... Il y avait des semaines où l'on présentait des esquisses d'après un sujet donné. Elles étaient posées en bas d'une cloison avant la revue. C'était merveille d'entendre le jugement du patron. On voyait accourir des élèves de l'atelier voisin, friands des explications précieuses, car leur maître Bonnat, grand portraitiste, ne disait guère les motifs de son choix. ... De leur côté les ateliers de Gérôme et de Bonnat nous appelaient 'les Botticelli' à cause de la passion du patron pour les Primitifs.[24]

Quant au jeune Belge Henri Evenepoël (1872–1899) qui fait la chronique de sa vie quotidienne dans les lettres à son père, il est un témoin de premier ordre, rapportant au fil des semaines – surtout de 1893 à 1896 – de nombreux propos de Moreau. Comme le faisaient beaucoup de jeunes gens, il fit une visite à l'artiste dans sa maison du 14 rue de La Rochefoucauld qu'il raconte dans une précieuse lettre du 2 mars 1893: 'Moreau m'a dit qu'il y a déjà 75 élèves dans son atelier! pour 1 modèle!.'[25] Aussi reste-t-il prudent dans sa réponse, lui demandant de revenir quinze jours plus tard. Alors, en partie grâce à une recommandation de son professeur bruxellois Ernest Blanc-Garin – le Musée Gustave Moreau conserve de nombreuses lettres de ce genre – Evenepoël est accepté, prévenu par Moreau de l'épreuve de bizutage, des brimades traditionnelles qu'il devra subir avec bonne humeur à son arrivée à l'atelier. Il en fera le récit détaillé à son père: 'Lors d'une première séance de correction d'un dessin d'après le modèle, Moreau lui dit: "Tenez, vos jambes, cette partie du bas du corps, sont très bien: vous voyez qu'avec très peu de chose on fait le modelé! il ne faut rien de plus! et je vois déjà que vous avez quitté ce métier par ligne.'"[26] L'enseignement était composé d'une alternance d'études peintes d'après le modèle vivant, d'études d'après l'antique auxquelles Moreau tenait beaucoup, mais qui n'attiraient guère d'élèves[27], d'esquisses enfin de compositions historiques.

Deux mois après son arrivée, Evenepoël se livre à ce dernier exercice sur le thème de Cincinnatus et écrit à son père le 20 mai 1893:

> Moreau m'a très bien corrigé, d'une façon très explicite, me disant le pourquoi et le parce que et me parlant très franchement ... Enfin il me l'a démoli tout à fait, me disant que c'était maintenant que je devais persévérer et ne pas me rebuter. Il m'a dit: 'Vous savez, même vous devriez devenir un Chéret, cela vous sera toujours utile d'aller vous renseigner aux Poussin. Vous y trouverez cette chose qu'on ne peut posséder jeune comme vous êtes, c'est-à-dire le style sans lequel aucune œuvre d'art n'existe réellement'. Et d'enchaîner sur un compliment à Albert Besnard qui possède 'ce fond d'études classiques et d'étude des maîtres. Besnard est un élève de l'École et toujours dans ses choses les plus osées, on voit qu'il sait dessiner un bras, une tête, un torse et qu'elle est dans sa toile'.[28]

L'année suivante, le dimanche 11 mars 1894, Evenepoël va montrer des esquisses de sujets religieux à Moreau chez lui: 'J'ai été ce matin chez Moreau avec mes 2 esquisses. J'y suis resté une heure et demie! matinée des plus intéressantes! je garderai toujours, toujours le souvenir de ce qu'il m'a dit, si simplement quoiqu'avec un enthousiasme qu'il ne retenait pas toujours!.'[29] Ce qu'il expliquait au Louvre – généralement le mercredi après le passage à l'atelier, le samedi après-midi étant réservé aux séances de l'Institut – a fasciné son auditoire, lorsqu'il venait examiner les copies en cours d'après les maîtres. C'est là un des points les plus célèbres, une des particularités de l'enseignement de Moreau.

Indépendamment des dessins à main levée qui se font sans inscription préalable, Philip Walsh[30] a dénombré 596 autorisations de copier demandées par les élèves de Gustave Moreau jusqu'en 1898, et établi une statistique des artistes anciens les mieux représentés: ce sont Rembrandt, Rubens et Titien, tandis que les grands classiques, Poussin, Raphaël ou Vinci, n'apparaissent qu'une douzaine de fois. Deux élèves seulement s'inscrirent pour Claude le Lorrain. Il est vrai que, si Marquet, futur paysagiste, copia le *Débarquement de Cléopâtre*, Rouault rapporte à propos de ce tableau du Lorrain: 'J'avoue à ma honte que je ne partage pas son [celui de Moreau] enthousiasme de façon absolue'.[31] Il ajoute aussi: 'Gustave Moreau nous faisait aimer les beaux Titien, l'épanouissement du *Concert champêtre* du Giorgione pour lequel il avait un faible, mais il était aussi sensible au caractère de certaines fresques primitives...'[32] Enfin, il signale: 'Il me parla souvent de ses deux voyages en Italie.'[33]

Sans doute faut-il noter que Gustave Moreau qui n'avait pas été satisfait de son propre passage à l'École des Beaux-Arts et de ses deux échecs au Prix de Rome, n'avait véritablement trouvé sa manière qu'après son second voyage en Italie, consacré exclusivement à l'étude et à la copie, entre 1857 et 1859, voyage qui lui avait réellement ouvert les yeux sur l'art de la peinture. C'est donc le souvenir de cette expérience personnelle – y compris un certain mépris des concours – qui le guide dans ses conseils à ses élèves. Arthur Guéniot, partant pour Rome, a conservé les notes prises en juillet 1897, lors de sa 'dernière conversation avec le vénéré maître Moreau':

> Passer à Florence, Orvieto, etc. Étudier Luca Signorelli; Crivelli; Giotto; les mosaïstes; Tura. Les copier. Par conséquent avoir leur métier, et pas d'autre prétention que d'y joindre nos sentiments modernes. [...] Faire simple, et s'éloigner du faire lisse et propre.[...] En art désormais, comme l'éducation des masses encore vague se fait peu à peu, il n'y aura plus besoin de finir et de pousser jusqu'au peigné, pas plus qu'en littérature nous aimerons la rhétorique et les périodes bien achevées. – Nos besoins d'expression – tout enrichis par le christianisme – deviennent infinis; en art comme en conversation, héritiers de tant d'art et sachant tant de choses, nous voulons dire beaucoup avec le moins de moyens. Aussi l'art prochain – qui condamne déjà les méthodes de Bouguereau et d'autres – nous demandera seulement des indications, des ébauches, mais aussi l'infinie variété des impressions multiples. On pourra encore finir, mais sans en avoir l'air.[34]

Lui qui refusait l'accès de son atelier à ses élèves – seuls y pénétrèrent vers 1897 Georges Rouault et Émile Delobre qu'il employa pour 'travailler à ses dernières toiles'[35] – , il était attentif à ce que ses élèves ne plagient pas les maîtres et reprochait à Evenepoël d'avoir, dans une esquisse, pastiché le peintre anversois Leys, lui-même pasticheur de Holbein et des gothiques ...[36] Il lui avait déjà déclaré quelques semaines auparavant, à propos de ce même Leys: 'Il ne faut pas faire un pastiche, infiniment inférieur à l'original! Chercher en soi-même les sentiments et les traduire sans préoccupation d'école, là seul est l'art!.'[37]

Il souhaitait aussi que ses élèves soient curieux de tout. Il se rendait lui-même au Salon des Indépendants.[38] Desvallières, dans sa préface à l'exposition de 1926, rappelle: 'Il nous recommandait d'aller visiter toutes les expositions, de surveiller toutes les devantures des marchands de tableaux; quant au Salon officiel d'y surtout examiner les toiles placées "en l'air", 'on y trouve souvent les plus intéressantes.'[39] Ce que confirment les propos de Matisse: 'C'était un homme cultivé, qui incitait ses élèves à considérer toutes les sortes de peintures, tandis que les autres professeurs n'avaient en tête qu'une période, qu'un seul style – celui de l'académisme contemporain – c'est à dire le leur, résidu de toutes les conventions.'[40]

Si les plus prometteurs de ses élèves n'eurent qu'à se féliciter de toute l'attention que leur portait Gustave Moreau, restant en moyenne deux heures à les corriger à l'École le mercredi et le samedi, les recevant chez lui, se rendant à leur atelier, les encourageant, les traitant en amis ('Tous ses élèves sont ses amis et on sent qu'il s'y attache'),[41] il semble qu'il ait eu aussi des moyens de dissuader les plus mauvais ou les moins travailleurs. Il les ignorait. Les propos qu'il tint à un 'amateur' venu lui présenter ses travaux un dimanche matin de novembre 1894 où Evenepoël était chez lui, sont tout à fait caractéristiques: 'Vous ne serez jamais un artiste, tâchez de devenir un homme de goût! Vous avez de l'argent, eh! bien, faites comme M. Sauvageot! collectionnez, et vous aurez bien mérité de l'art! ... que voulez-vous que je vous dise de plus ? vous venez ici pour que je vous dise mon avis, n'est-ce pas ? eh bien! le voilà!.'[42]

Ceux qu'il encourageait et marquait de son influence intellectuelle, de sa haute spiritualité, se distinguèrent par la qualité de leurs œuvres aux expositions de l'École même ou aux Salons. Desvallières se souvient encore en 1926 d'une réaction de Moreau à propos du Caveau du Soleil d'or d'Evenepoël: 'mais si je mets votre toile à l'exposition des travaux d'ateliers, je vais me faire lapider par mes collègues',[43] tandis qu'Evenepoël en fait le récit détaillé à son père dans une lettre du 8 juillet 1896:

> Il lui a apporté des tableaux pour cette exposition d'ateliers, jugée par l'Institut, Gérôme, Bonnat, Bouguereau ... En apercevant mon 'caveau', Moreau s'est écrié: 'très bien, très bien, c'est d'une valeur ...(je passe) ... mais vous ne pouvez montrer cela... vous me feriez tuer!... et cependant je les veux absolument.' Ses hésitations étaient d'un drôle [...] Il a fini par dire: 'Oui, nous l'exposerons, tant pis, nous montrerons autre chose que Léonidas défendant les Thermopyles et qu'Enée portant son père Anchise ...! Ah le casque!!' Comme je sortais de l'École, il m'a rattrapé, et m'a dit: 'Vous savez, vous allez tout à fait me couler. Il y a des gens que cela va exaspérer'.[44]

Un tel épisode sur l'ouverture d'esprit de Gustave Moreau, capable de reconnaître les qualités d'un artiste peignant d'une manière fort éloignée de la sienne – Evenepoël est plus proche de Toulouse-Lautrec et des Nabis que de son maître – est corroboré par l'avis de Roger-Marx dans sa critique sur 'Le Salon de 1895'. Il y remarquait déjà les travaux des élèves de Gustave Moreau dont l'atelier à l'École des Beaux-Arts est 'l'asile de l'originalité militante' et un 'foyer de révolte allumé dans le sanctuaire officiel'.[45]

Si les autres professeurs étaient mécontents, de jeunes peintres tendaient l'oreille et recherchaient les conseils de Moreau. Ce fut le cas de Désiré-Lucas (1869–1949) qui raconta par la suite à la demande de Sabatté, un ancien élève de Moreau, la magistrale leçon qu'il obtint de l'artiste, véritable maître en maïeutique.

Désiré-Lucas était venu voir Moreau dans le petit appartement du 5 rue Pigalle où celui-ci s'était réfugié pendant les travaux d'agrandissement de sa maison du 14 rue de La Rochefoucauld, en vue de créer les grands ateliers destinés au musée. Son envoi au Salon de 1896 avait été refusé et, grâce à l'intervention de Charles Ephrussi, amateur lui-même des œuvres de Moreau, il avait obtenu une consultation, un dimanche matin, chez le maître dont il avait seulement et 'timidement au Louvre écouté les leçons':

Il fut reçu 'paternellement'. Il aligna ses œuvres le long du mur: 'une tête de jeune Ouessantine', exécutée à Brest, l'année de mes quinze ans, sans aucune connaissance, ni direction; des croquis de paysans et de gens en action dont un grand nombre datait de mon enfance. Puis un autre lot d'études faites à l'atelier Bouguereau en 89 et enfin mon tableau refusé au Salon.[...] il me dit: 'Dans tout ce que vous me montrez là, il y a, à côté de choses bien mauvaises, une œuvre de grande qualité et j'aurais pleine confiance en vous si vous pouviez la découvrir tout seul. Voyons, je vais vous laisser ici, une occupation m'appelle. Lorsque je reviendrai, vous aurez selon votre choix placé devant ce mur toutes vos études par ordre de mérite. Jugez-vous vous-même. A tout à l'heure.'

Comment t'expliquerai-je, mon cher ami, ce que j'éprouvai à cette minute. Il me semblait qu'un grand chirurgien venait de me rendre la vue.

Sans le moindre tâtonnement je classai chaque chose à sa place définitive:

La tête de jeune Ouessantine prit la première place; puis mes croquis d'enfance et de jeunesse; ensuite un vide, un grand espace, et très loin, très loin, un peu dans l'ombre, mes études d'atelier.

Mon grand juge apparut. Au premier coup d'œil, il sourit, approuve et me dit: 'Mon petit, vous êtes sauvé. Vous avez vous-même trouvé votre chemin. Vous n'êtes pas fait pour la peinture d'imagination, la nature seule est votre grand

Illustration 4: *L'Atelier de Gustave Moreau à l'École des Beaux-Arts en Décembre 1897* (anonyme, XIXème siècle). Photo: ©RMN, Paris

(Jules Flandrin)

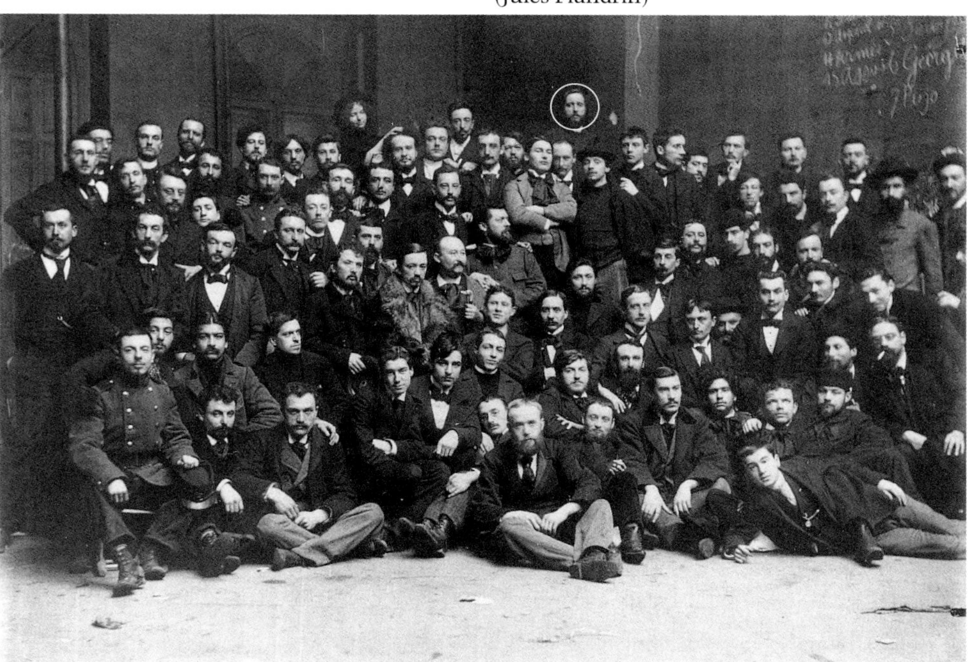

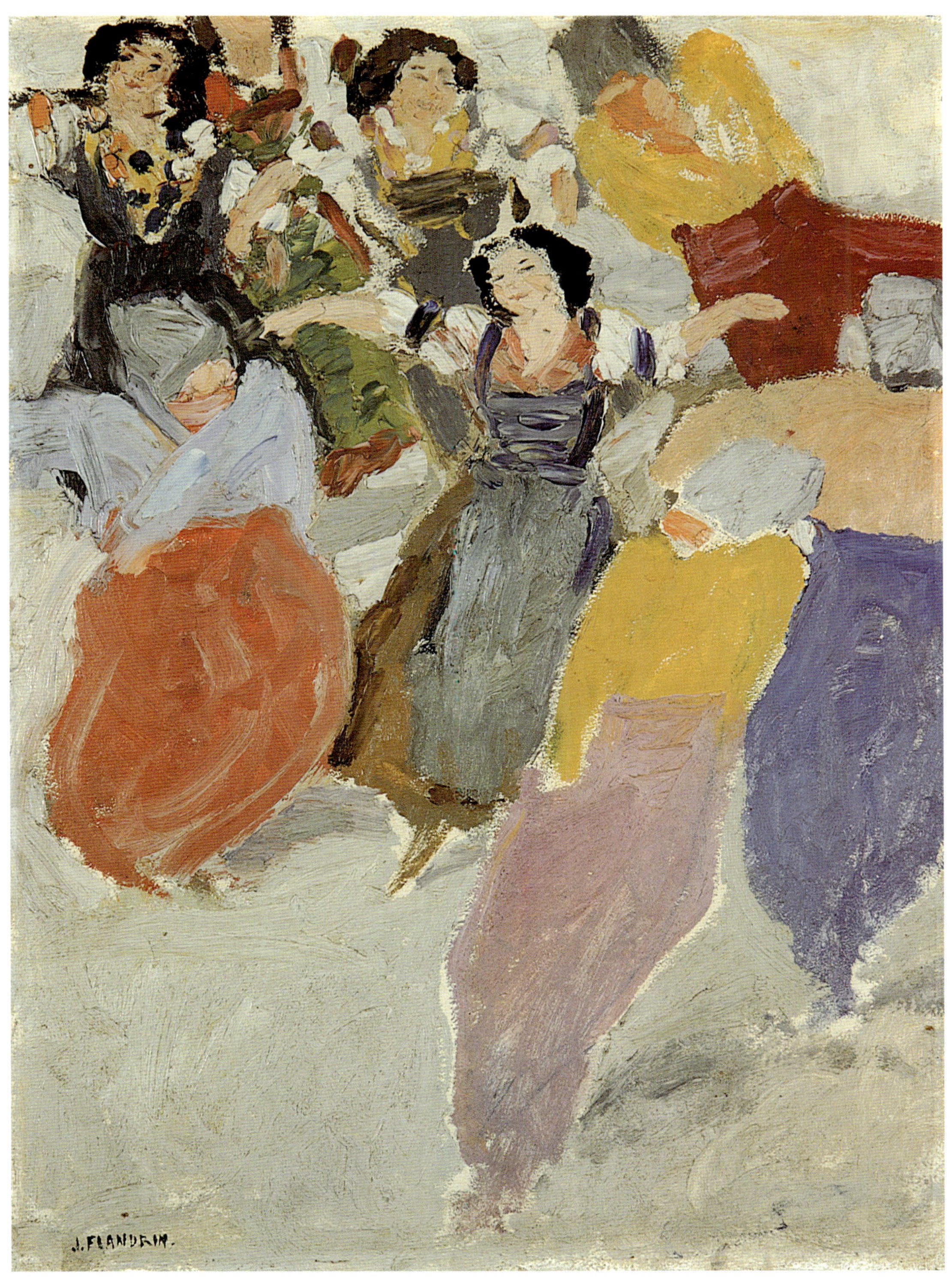

Juliet Simpson 6: JULES FLANDRIN, *The Folk Dance,* 1910. Oil on board, 63 × 48 cms, private collection, Paris.

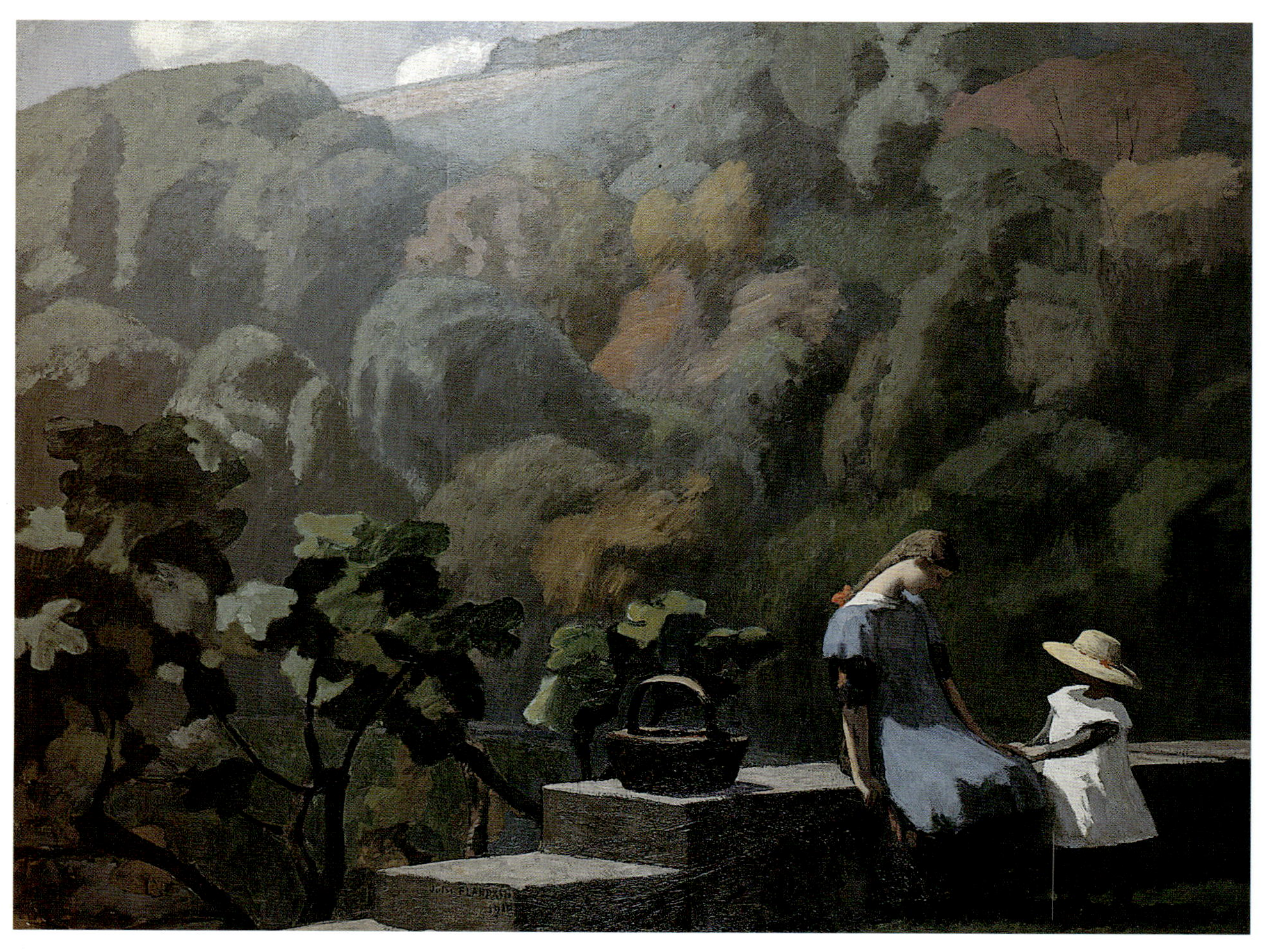

Juliet Simpson 7: JULES FLANDRIN, *The Wooded Gorge*, 1910. Oil on canvas, 230 × 180 cms, private collection, Grenoble.

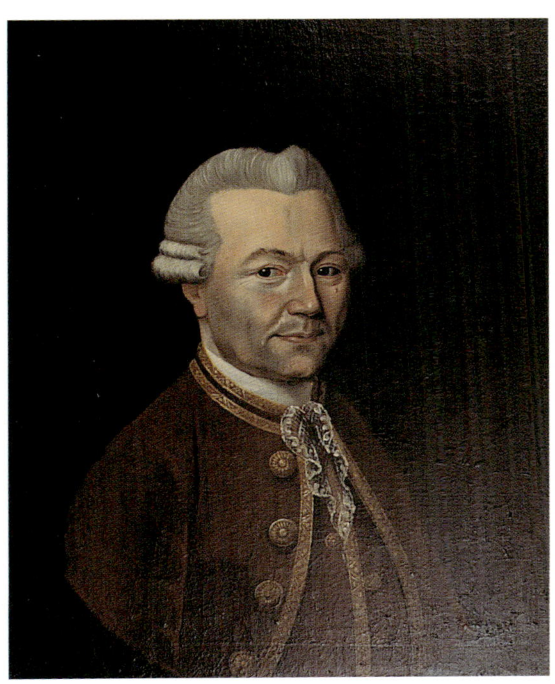

Georges Flandrin 1:
LUNEL, *Antoine Flandrin*, 1780. Oil on canvas,
63 × 50 cms, private collection, Paris.

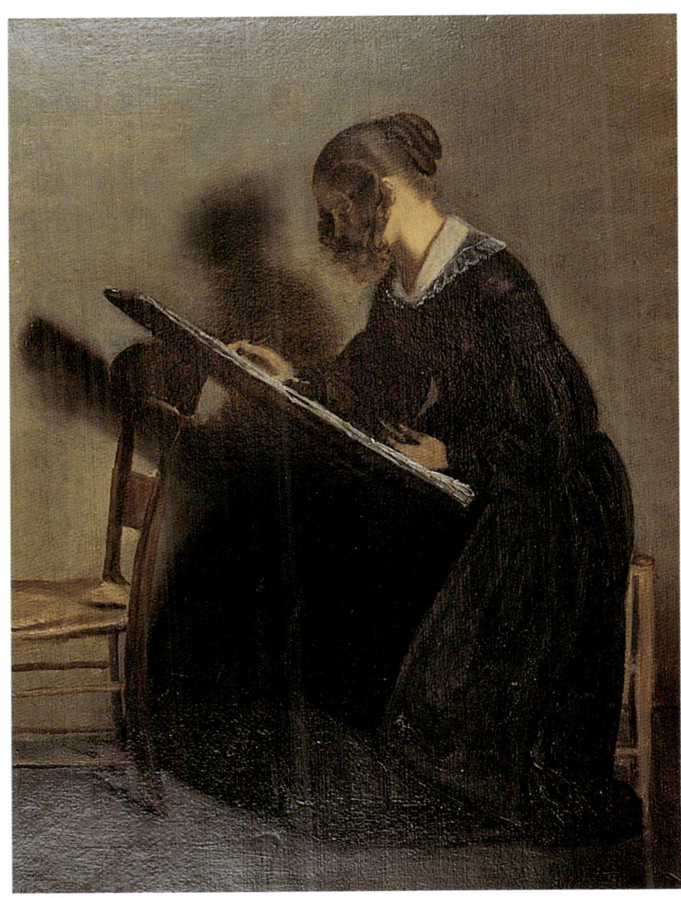

Georges Flandrin 3:
ANETTE GAMEL,
Hélène Gamel Painting, 1840.
Oil on canvas, 43.5 × 31.5 cms,
private collection, Paris.

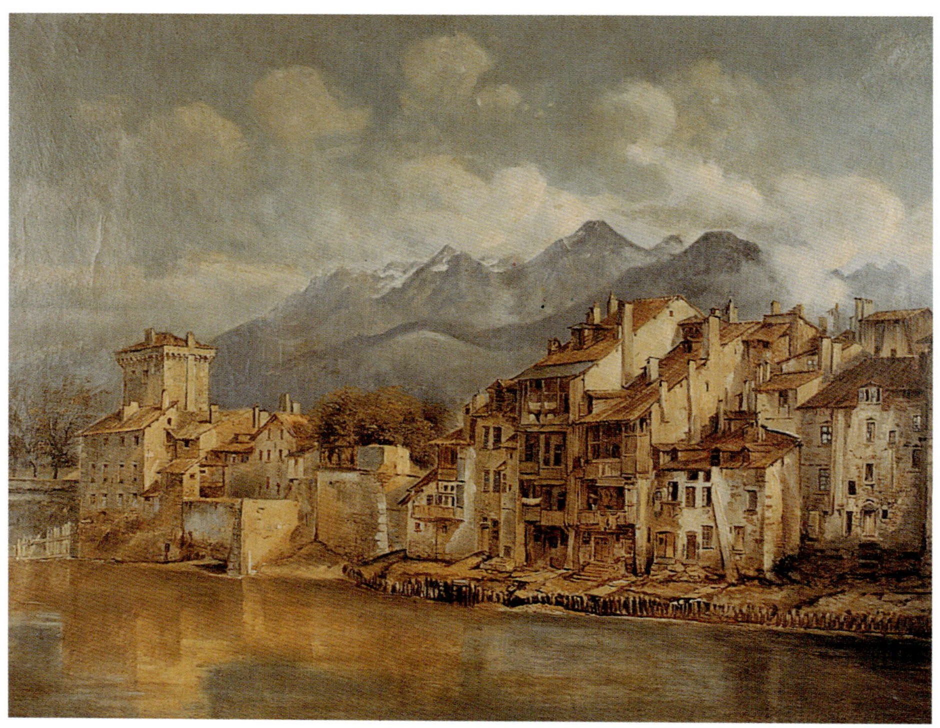

Georges Flandrin 5: HORACE MOLLARD, *Grenoble and the Citadel*, 1830. Oil on canvas, 60 × 72 cms, private collection, Paris.

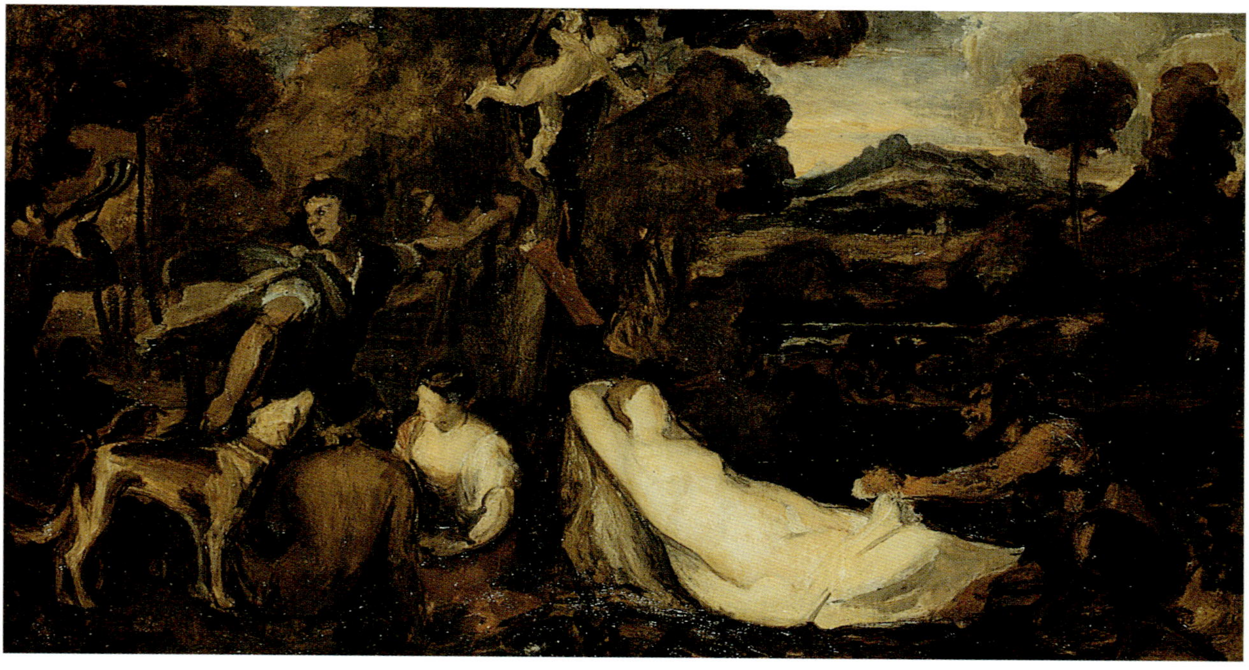

Jon Whiteley 2: JULES FLANDRIN, copy after Titian's *Jupiter and Antiope* (also known as *The Venus del Pardo*), *c.* 1897. Oil on canvas, 66 × 119 cms, private collection, Grenoble.

livre. Quittez Paris, retournez à la campagne et faites ce que vous aimiez quand vous n'étiez qu'un enfant ... Allez, j'ai confiance en vous.'

Hélas! ce fut la première et la dernière fois que je vis Gustave Moreau. L'année suivante, j'arrivais à Paris [...] il venait de mourir.[46] [De fait, il est de ceux qui signèrent lors de son enterrement.]

Ces différents témoignages permettent de restituer ce qui s'est passé entre quelques dizaines de jeunes gens et Gustave Moreau, tant dans les salles du Louvre que dans l'atelier de l'École des Beaux-Arts, situé au premier étage de l'hôtel de Chimay, côté jardin, angle ouest.[47] On en reconnait les fenêtres cintrées et le pilier à droite dans la photographie de groupe offerte en 1897 à Gustave Moreau (ill. 4). Anciens et nouveaux élèves s'y côtoient, à qui, au fil des ans, Moreau avait ouvert des horizons nouveaux. Sans parti-pris, il avait 'développé chez ses élèves une curiosité d'esprit très aiguë et une sensibilité d'œil qui nous a donné l'œuvre d'un Henri Matisse, d'un Marquet, d'un Guérin, d'un Flandrin, d'un Puy, etc ...', comme le rappelle, en 1926, Georges Desvallières.[48]

Il leur avait appris, comme à Evenepoël, 'le style, la matière, l'arabesque et le transformé imaginaire de la couleur'.[49] Les uns et les autres se trouvaient peut-être là lorsqu'il corrigeait le travail d'un des condisciples d'Evenepoël et qu'il attira tout l'atelier autour de lui 'tellement était intéressant ce qu'il disait': '"Notez bien une chose: c'est qu'il faut penser la couleur, en avoir l'imagination. Si vous n'avez pas l'imagination, vous ne ferez jamais de la belle couleur. Il faut copier la nature avec de l'imagination. C'est cela qui fait l'artiste. La couleur doit être pensée, rêvée, imaginée ...".'[50] Hors des chemins de l'académisme, au delà du naturalisme, la voie était ouverte aux futurs fauves.

RÉFÉRENCES

1. Selon les termes de son testament du 10 septembre 1897.

2. Georges Rouault, André Suarès, *Correspondance* (Paris, 1960), p. 7.

3. Un exemplaire, conservé dans les archives de la famille Rouault est reproduit dans le catalogue de l'exposition *Rouault, Première période 1903–1920* (Paris, Musée national d'Art moderne, Centre Georges Pompidou, 1992), p. 180.

4. Georges Desvallières, Préface du catalogue de l Exposition *Gustave Moreau et quelques-uns de ses élèves* (Paris, Galerie Georges Petit, avril 1926), p. 10–11.

5. Une lettre d'Henri Matisse à Paul Eeckout, conservateur du musée des Beaux-Arts de Gand (archives de ce Musée), en date du 19 février 1953, fait état d'un projet qui n'a pas abouti: 'Pour le projet d'exposition Atelier G. Moreau je pense que la collaboration des musées et d'un ensemble d'anciens élèves permetteraient [*sic*] de réunir un choix significatif et intéressant auquel je contribuerais avec plaisir si vous voulez bien me le rappeler au moment opportun.'

6. Exposition *Gustave Moreau* au musée du Louvre, catalogue par Ragnar von Holten, préface par Jean Cassou.

7. Voir le catalogue de l'exposition *Gustave Moreau 1826–1898* (Paris, Grand Palais), 1998.

8. Musée Gustave Moreau, Inv. 16096. Cf. le catalogue de l'exposition *Gustave Moreau e l'Italia* (Rome, Villa Médicis, 1996–7), n° 38 . et p. 35.

9. Voir le catalogue de l'exposition *Gustave Moreau 1826–1898* (Paris, Grand Palais), n° 2 et n° 3.

10. Delaunay avait peint le portrait de Charles Hayem en 1865 (Paris, Musée d'Orsay, R.F. 1137).

11. Sur ce collectionneur, voir l'article de Dominique Lobstein, 'Antony Roux. Portrait d'un collectionneur et mécène', dans *Gustave Moreau, le rêve symbolique, Dossier de l'art*, n° 51 S (octobre 1998), p. 58–64.

12. Delaunay avait peint le portrait d'Ernest Legouvé (1807–1903) en 1874 (Paris, Musée d'Orsay, R.F. 1982–14). Il connaissait aussi le musicien Émile Paladilhe dont il avait fait le portrait à Rome en 1860 (collection particulière) et qui épousa une petite fille de Legouvé, soeur du peintre Georges Desvallières (1861–1950). Jean Paladilhe(1890–1990), conservateur du Musée Gustave-Moreau jusqu'en 1985, était fils du musicien.

13. Archives du Musée Gustave Moreau. Sauf mention contraire, les documents cités dans cet essai en proviennent.

14. Anne Prache, 'Souvenirs d'Arthur Guéniot sur Gustave Moreau', *Gazette des Beaux-Arts* (avril 1966), p. 231. Arthur Guéniot fut reçu officiellement le 23 décembre 1892. Il écrit encore: 'L'atelier formait un bloc très uni autour du patron vénéré Gustave Moreau. Il avait été nommé professeur de peinture à la demande des élèves après qu'il eut fait l'intérim durant la maladie et à la mort du professeur Delaunay' se trompant sans doute pour l'intérim pendant la maladie de Delaunay, rien ne l'attestant par ailleurs.

15. D'après la liste conservée aux Archives nationales, Paris AJ 52 248, 15–19, publiée pour la première fois dans le catalogue *Gustave Moreau et ses élèves* (Marseille, Musée Cantini, 1962), il y eut 7 inscrits à l'automne 1891, 26 en 1892, 17 en 1893, 17 en 1894, 23 en 1895, 13 en 1896, 9 en 1897, 4 en 1898 (dont deux reçus après la mort du peintre). Philip H. Walsh, dans sa thèse de l'Université d'Harvard, *The Atelier of Gustave Moreau at the École des Beaux-Arts* (UMI, 1995, p. 173–4), estime que le nombre d'élèves est sans doute au total de 230 environ et qu'il y en avait une soixantaine présents en même temps. Peut-être y en avait-il un peu plus, comme permet de le penser la photographie d'atelier de 1897, dont l'exemplaire annoté par Evenepoël, conservé aux Musées royaux des Beaux-Arts de Belgique, Bruxelles, donne soixante noms sur soixante-dix-neuf présents, en comptant le modèle féminin.

16. Philibert-Léon Couturier, né en 1823, était entré à l'École des Beaux-Arts en 1844, deux ans avant Gustave Moreau. Il exposait au Salon, dans les années 1880, des sujets de basse-cour. Curieusement, dans l'entretien avec Tériade, paru dans *Art News Annual* (n° 21, 1952) et traduit dans Henri Matisse, *Ecrits et propos sur l'art* (Paris, 1972, p. 113), Matisse s'embrouille un peu et le prénomme Paul-Louis (mêmes initiales). Couturier avait recommandé à Matisse Bouguereau, élève de Picot, entré à l'École des Beaux-Arts en 1846 comme Moreau dont Matisse indique qu' 'il (Couturier) ne cita jamais le nom' (*Ibid.*, p. 113): affaire de goût, peut-être.

17. Son dessin *Homme nu avec épée*, et treize dessins d'autres élèves d'après le même modèle ou d'après l'antique, sont passés en vente à Paris, Drouot Montaigne, le 8 juin 2000, n°8, repr.

18. Pierre Schneider, *Matisse* (Paris, 1984), p. 720.

19. Inv. n° 318 (51/64–89) et 319, (51/64–87) donnés en 1929 et 1931 par Henri Matisse au collectionneur tchèque Rudolf Macek comme 'Atelier Moreau', le premier ayant été prêté et exposé comme Gustave Moreau à la Galerie nationale de Prague il y a une vingtaine d'années. La même donation contient deux peintures, également faussement attribuées à Gustave Moreau, données par Georges Rouault au même collectionneur en 1932 et très certainement faites par Rouault lui-même dans l'atelier Moreau (Inv. 320 (51/64–88) et 321 (51/64–84), les artistes conservant leurs propres exercices d'atelier.

20. Georges Rouault, André Suarès, *Correspondance* (Paris, 1960), p. 96.

21. *Ibid.*, p. 20, lettre à André Suarès du 22 juin 1912. Il est difficile de déterminer quel est le 'jeune homme' qui le lui demandait. Serait-ce Alfred Baillehache (1870–1922) du même âge que Rouault? Ce neveu d'Antony Roux, ami et collectionneur d'œuvres de Gustave Moreau, était

lui-même collectionneur et avait entrepris vers 1906 – au moment où il joue un rôle important dans la préparation de l'exposition *Gustave Moreau* à la Galerie Georges Petit – le catalogue des œuvres de Gustave Moreau sorties de son atelier. Son cahier manuscrit 'remis à jour en 1915' est conservé par la galerie Brame et Lorenceau, à Paris.

22. Georges Rouault, réédité dans *Sur l'art et sur la vie* (Paris, 1971), p. 76–82.

23. *Ibid.*, p. 21.

24. Prache, *art. cit.*, p. 234–5.

25. Henri Evenepoël, *Lettres à mon père* (Bruxelles, 1994), t.1, p. 133.

26. Evenepoël, *op. cit.*, t. 1, p. 144 (lettre du 18 mars 1893).

27. Voir la lettre d'Evenepoël du 28 mars 1898, Evenepoël, *op. cit.*, t. 2, p. 152.

28. Evenepoël, *op. cit.*, t. 1, p. 164.

29. Evenepoël, *op. cit.*, t. 1, p. 293.

30. Walsh, *op. cit.*, p. 192–5.

31. Dans *Souvenirs intimes* (1926), rééd. dans *Sur l'art et sur la vie* (Paris, 1972), p. 79.

32. *Ibid.*, p. 80. A noter que maintenant le *Concert champêtre* est attribué au Titien.

33. *Ibid.*, p. 80. Moreau avait fait un premier voyage en Italie avec sa mère, son oncle, sa tante et sa cousine Emon en 1841 dans le nord de l'Italie. L'abondante correspondance du temps de son second voyage est actuellement sous presse, établie par Luisa Capodieci.

34. Prache, *art. cit.*, p. 235–6.

35. Voir la lettre d'Evenepoël du 22 juin 1898, Evenepoël, *op. cit.*, t. 2, p. 250.

36. Evenepoël *op. cit.*, t. 1, p. 293.

37. Evenepoël, *op. cit.*, t. 1, p. 272 (lettre du 4 février 1894).

38. *Ibid.*, p. 312. Signalé aussi par Desvallières, *op. cit.*, p. 4.

39. Desvallières, *op. cit.*, p. 5.

40. 'Matisse parle à Tériade' (1952), rééd. dans Henri Matisse, *Écrits et propos sur l'art* (Paris, 1972), p. 114.

41. Evenepoël, *op. cit.*, t. 1, p. 330.

42. Evenepoël, *op. cit.*, t. 1, p. 398 (lettre du 12 novembre 1894).

43. Desvallières, *op. cit.*, p. 5. Le tableau d'Everepoël est conservé aux Musées royaux des Beaux-Arts, à Bruxelles (Inv. 7668).

44. Evenepoël, *op. cit.*, t. 2, p. 67.

45. *Gazette des Beaux-Arts*, 1er juillet 1895, p. 18, cité par Cristina Scassellati, 'Correspondance Gustave Moreau/Georges Rouault (1892–1898)', dans le catalogue de l'exposition *Rouault. Première période 1903–1920*, (Paris, Musée national d'Art moderne, Centre Georges Pompidou, 1992), p. 164.

46. Désiré-Lucas, 'Comment j'ai connu Gustave Moreau', *L'Art* (septembre–octobre 1929), p. 140.

47. Selon les recherches récentes d'Emmanuel Schwartz, conservateur à l'École des Beaux-Arts.

48. Desvallières, *op. cit.*, p. 5.

49. Evenepoël, *op. cit.*, t. 1, p. 493 (lettre du 8 novembre 1895).

50. Evenepoël, *op. cit.* (1994), t.1, p. 197 (lettre du 27 juillet 1893).

summary in English by Jon Whiteley

Gustave Moreau and his Studio

Despite having a museum in Paris devoted to his work, Gustave Moreau (1826–1898) was for long better known as the master of Georges Rouault, Georges Desvallières and Henri Matisse than as a painter of importance. Exhibitions in the Galerie Hessèle (1910) and in the Galerie Georges Petit (1926) were the forerunners of a series of exhibitions on the theme of Moreau and his pupils held in Marseille (1962), Japan (1974 and 1984), Marq-en-Baroeul (1990) and Mexico (1996). Following an exhibition in the Louvre in 1961, Moreau's own work has been progessively rediscovered and his importance as an artist in his own right has been acknowledged.

Moreau became a member of the Académie des Beaux-Arts in November 1888. At first, he refused the offer of a teaching post at the École des Beaux-Arts, probably because of the illness of his companion, Alexandrine Dureux, who died in 1890. In 1891 he accepted the post at the École left vacant by the death of Jules-Élie Delaunay and was appointed head of one of the three teaching studios in January 1892. During his stay in Italy from 1857 to 1859, Moreau had gathered a number of informal pupils, including Edgar Degas, who benefited from his advice. These relationships continued after he had returned to Paris. Georges Desvallières already listed Moreau among his teachers before Moreau went to the École. A document, dated 15 October 1891, in the archives of the Musée Gustave Moreau, names 68 students in his class at the École, including Rouault, Bussy and Maxence. In addition to those who had enrolled through the entry competition, there was a number of 'free students' who were preparing for the entry competition, including Henri Matisse, who arrived in 1893 and was finally accepted in 1895. It is regrettable that Georges Rouault, first curator of the Musée Gustave Moreau, did not write his intended book on Moreau's teaching methods; but in his *Souvenirs intimes*, he wrote warmly of his teacher's virtues, chiefly in animating the capacities of his pupils. Further details of Moreau's teaching are found in Arthur Guéniot's memoirs and in the letters of Henri Evenepoël. All insist on the importance Moreau placed on the practice of making copies of Old Masters. Philip Webb has listed 596 applications by Moreau's pupils for permission to copy in the Louvre. Rembrandt, Rubens and Titian were the favourite models. Poussin, Raphaël and Leonardo appear only twelve times while only two pupils applied for permits to copy works by Claude Lorrain. Moreau did not encourage his pupils to imitate the work of other artists but insisted that they should find their own path by copying nature through the faculty of the imagination. He told Evenepoël that without imagination, an artist could not become a fine colourist. The principles of Moreau's teaching opened a path from his studio which led to the formation of the Fauves.

Jules Flandrin and the Old Masters

JON WHITELEY

Artists have always copied the work of their predecessors but never more so than in the nineteenth century.[1] From a modern view point, the quantity of copies produced by nineteenth-century artists seems oddly out of step with the high value which they placed on originality and creativity and the disrespect with which they and their contemporaries, in general, treated handed-down ideas. It is tempting to explain the habit as one of a number of ancient academic practices which were increasingly challenged by innovators; but this is not, on the whole, how nineteenth-century artists saw the place of copies in contemporary art. While the fashion for making copies must, in large part, be due to the widespread acceptance of traditional teaching methods in academic studios, it would be an error to say that academic artists made copies and innovators did not. Delacroix, Degas, Fantin-Latour, Cézanne, Matisse were all dedicated copyists and many others who are normally classed with the innovators made copies on occasion. The expansion of museums across Europe in the course of the nineteenth century provided the opportunity for making copies of famous works of art – none more so than the Louvre – but the motive for doing so lies in a relationship between nineteenth-century art and the art of the past which cuts across the conventional notion of the avant-garde.[2]

Artists learned by making copies. Students at the École des Beaux-Arts spent their first years copying prints, drawings and casts in the belief that they could acquire a grasp of the principles of great art. Variations on this approach were found in all the private teaching studios and were passed down through studio traditions from masters to their pupils. The widespread misconception that the history of art is a history of novelty has led historians to undervalue the importance of the studio tradition for nineteenth-century artists – especially in the case of those artists who have, in retrospect, been recruited into the 'avant-garde' – and the sense of kinship which students felt for artists of the past. Jules Flandrin had little respect for most the professors at the École but made an exception for his own master, Gustave Moreau, whom he admired as an artist and valued as a teacher. Flandrin also readily acknowledged his older antecedents, Ingres and Delacroix, with whom he discerned a link by way of Chassériau and Moreau. In 1900, surveying the paintings on show at the centennial exhibition, Flandrin drew a family tree to prove the point, setting out his links with David, Raphael, Gros, Rubens and the artists of the early Renaissance via Ingres, Delacroix, Chassériau, Moreau and Puvis de Chavannes.[3] The tree is accurate enough but significantly omits

François Picot, Moreau's first master, who was one of the most successful academic teachers of his day. Moreau probably owed a great deal to the lessons of Picot – including a belief in the value of making copies[4] – but Flandrin disliked the academic tradition which Picot and his pupils represented and – apart from Moreau – left them out of the filiation which he marked out between himself and the artists of the fifteenth century. Ingres – an artist held in high regard in the academic tradition – was, however, admitted. Ingres was admired by Flandrin and his contemporaries as an eccentric genius, misunderstood by his immediate followers, and he became a hero figure for a number of avant-garde painters in the *fin de siècle*. Proust's Duchesse de Guermantes, always alert to the latest fashions, was charmed to discover that Ingres, who had always seemed the 'worst of academics', was in reality 'a delicious precursor of art-nouveau'. The exhibition of Ingres's work at the *Salon d'Automne* in 1905, as Roger Benjamin has recently pointed out, marked the high point of this enthusiasm for the artist, particularly among Moreau's pupils who formed an influential group at the Salon.[5] While Delacroix was acknowledged by Flandrin as a link to Rubens and the Venetians via Moreau, Chassériau and Puvis de Chavannes, Ingres was also seen by Flandrin as a link with the Italian painters of the fifteenth century via the same three painters. Moreau, Chassériau and Puvis are not usually seen as mainstream artists but, in this alternative tradition, they appear at a major confluence, inheriting opposing tendencies – line and colour, Classicism and Romanticism, tradition and innovation – and creating a synthesis which developed into the art of the Nabis and the Fauves.

Moreau was an enthusiastic and eclectic copyist. 'Do not be afraid to depend on the Old Masters' he told Evenepoël, 'you will always find what what you are after'.[6] The influence of Moreau on his pupils, several of whom became prominent in the so-called 'Fauve' movement in 1905, ensured that a number of Fauves and their allies – Rouault, Marquet, Flandrin, Manguin, Linaret, Valtat, Piot and Matisse – were also devoted copyists. It was, it seems, Moreau who encouraged Flandrin to undertake his first major painting, a copy of Watteau's *Gilles* (ill. 1), painted in the Louvre in 1896.[7] The copy is both fresh and accurate, conforming to a tradition of facsimile copies which was once an important part of the curriculum at the French School in Rome. The same tradition had, briefly, in 1873, been granted the honour of a state-sponsored Museum in Paris. It has been said that the closing of Charles Blanc's Museum of Copies marked a stage in the transition from tradition to innovation in the years after 1870 but this conclusion needs to be qualified.[8] It is certainly true that with the dispersal of the museum and the ending of the commissions which the Second Empire distributed to artists for copies of state portraits and religious pictures, the professional copyists who had depended on state support faced a bleak future. In compensation, however, the state sustained their hopes by buying copies of famous Old Masters through a Commission which met annually to consider copies offered to the state by artists. This scarcely offered a livelihood but it encouraged artists of Flandrin's generation to compete for the patronage of the government by making copies. Although *Gilles* was not bought by

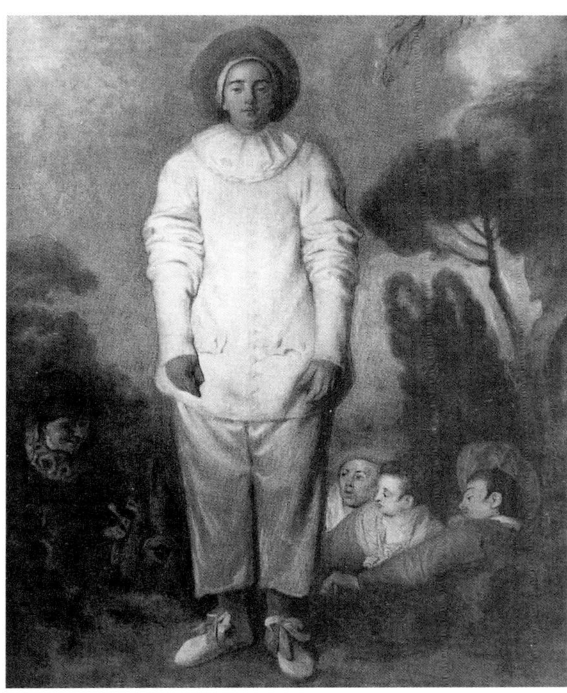

Illustration 1:
JULES FLANDRIN,
copy after
Watteau's *Gilles*, 1897.
Oil on canvas,
184 × 150 cms,
private collection,
Grenoble.

the Commission as Flandrin hoped – it was eventually acquired by his brother Joseph – he continued to paint copies in an attempt to attract a purchase by the state. In 1898, he made several visits to the Louvre for the sake of completing a copy of Titian's *Venus del Pardo* in the hope of selling it to the Commission (col. ill. 2). He also began a study of Veronese's *Wedding Feast at Cana* for his own pleasure: 'My study of the *Wedding Feast at Cana* is not large, a square metre, but what I have undertaken is a considerable thing.'[9] This was the period in Flandrin's life when he executed most of his known copies. Georges Flandrin has suggested a link with the the death of Moreau in 1898 when the studio in the École had lost its charms and Flandrin turned to making copies in the Louvre for consolation.[10] From this period dates a very spirited sketch of Rubens's *Coronation of Maria de' Medici* (cat. 15), an exercise in blue-greys and vibrant reds which may seem exaggerated by comparison with the original, but which corresponds to the way in which he responded to the huge composition. Bonnard was the artist who came to Flandrin's mind when looking at the expanses of red paint in Rubens's work,[11] and he recreated the original with a brio which anticipates the work of the Fauves. Evidently, Flandrin felt the sketches after Rubens and Veronese were among his most successful copies as he exhibited them on at least three occasions. They were admired by early twentieth-century critics as works which were not academic copies but intelligent and spirited interpretations of the originals. 'Jules Flandrin, in copying the *Coronation of Maria de' Medici* and the *Wedding Feast at Cana*, evokes the masters of the past without copying them word for word. He analyses and reconstitutes according to the results of this analysis. Has any pupil of the École des Beaux-Arts seen these copies by Valtat and Flandrin? And, having seen them, has he cast his brushes at the heads of his masters?'[12] In fact, Flandrin's fine sketches would probably not have raised a single academic eyebrow at the time when they were painted. They would not have qualified as finished copies but would have been appreciated as *pochades* or rapid sketches made with the intention of capturing the spirit of the original which, as Albert Boime first pointed out, were commonly encouraged by the most die-hard of academic teachers as an excellent way of educating the eye and learning the art of self-expression.[13]

Negotiations with the state over the sale of the copy after Titian continued slowly. On 5 February, 1900, Flandrin told his mother that he had finished a copy of Poussin's self-portrait in the Louvre which he had begun 'more confidently than last year's Titian and I think it will figure better in the eyes of the Commission than the latter'.[14] On 28 June, Flandrin sent a telegram to his mother with the news that his copy had been bought. His pleasure was dampened by a problem with the payment and the sale was not final until 1903 when the State acquired his copy of Poussin's self-portrait and sent it to the Musée des Andelys.[15] In the same period, the state acquired copies of Raphael's so-called *Portrait of Balthazar Castiglione*[16] and Ingres's *Grande odalisque* (Musée de Montauban).

Following Flandrin's success in selling his copies to the state, he seems to have lost interest in making careful copies in the Louvre but he continued to study the Old Masters as a source of general ideas which he could assimilate into his own painting. In this respect, he developed in tandem with his colleagues from Moreau's studio. 'I studied the masters', recalled Matisse, 'as one studies writers in literature before deciding to take up one or another; above all, I studied without any desire to pick up things but in order to cultivate the mind. I went from a Dutch painter to Chardin, from a Titian to Poussin'.[17] Flandrin, too, went in search of examples from the past which might serve his art. While Watteau, Titian, Rubens, Veronese and Guardi (cat. 37) gave him a sense of the value of colour and Rembrandt taught him about the value of tone and brushwork (cat. 6 and 13), he turned with interest towards Italian art of the fifteenth century as a source of more formal effects, no doubt following Moreau who also copied the Venetians – including the *Venus del Pardo* (ill. 3) – and the artists of the early Renaissance and made of both a complex synthesis of colour and elaborate design. In 1897, Flandrin made a copy of a painting by Uccello (cat. 14). His copies of Fra Angelico's *Coronation of the Virgin* (private coll.), Mantegna's *Parnassus* (private coll.) and a painting attributed to Leonardo (see cat. 5), likewise date from the time he was working in Moreau's studio.

In 1910, the Galerie Bernheim-Jeune acknowledged the importance of copies to the Fauves and their allies by mounting an exhibition of their work after the Old Masters which featured Flandrin's sketches after *The Wedding Feast at Cana* and *The Coronation of Maria de' Medici* as well as copies by Valtat, Matisse, Marquet and others. The exhibition probably evolved in response to the quantity of work of this kind which was available among the innovative artists with whom Bernheim-Jeune

Illustration 3:
GUSTAVE MOREAU,
copy after Titian's
Jupiter and Antiope
(The Venus del Pardo),
1846–9.
Photo: ©Musée Gustave
Moreau, Paris.

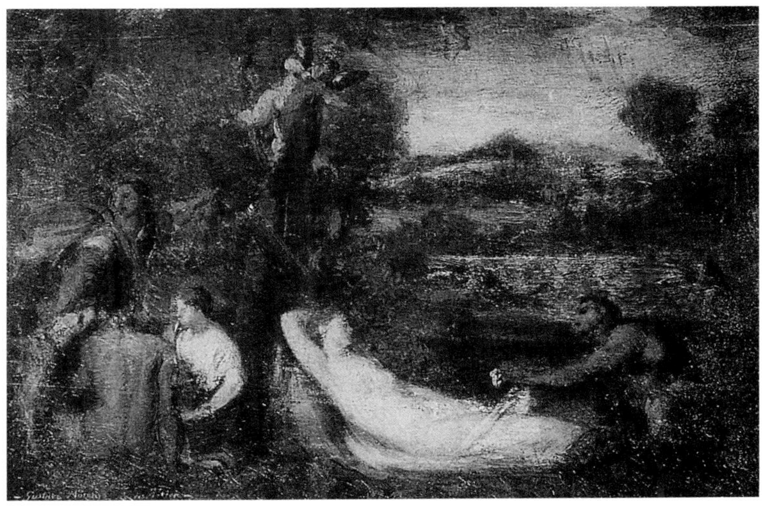

did business. By this date, Flandrin seems to have largely abandoned the practice although the affection for the Old Masters which he acquired while working in the Louvre gave him a lasting interest in their art. He never supposed that being an innovator involved a rejection of past art. In 1899, in a long letter to his father, Flandrin defined innovators as 'those who attempt to think aright and create beauty. They appear to be new in the eyes of those among their contemporaries who have forgotten what beauty is, that is all. But in many respects they resemble the old painters of all past ages who have likewise gone in search of beauty. This is one of the very points which gives them value'.[18] A year later, struck by Auguste Ravier's assimilation of the art of Claude and Poussin, he returned to the theme: 'how well he realises that true progress consists in raising oneself to the level of artists, true artists, of all periods.'[19] He did not, however, believe that good art replicates the art of the past but only that the principles of good art are timeless. In particular, the study of past art teaches the value of studying nature. 'I feel no shame in borrowing wholesale from Angelico and in putting some of my painting into that as at Corenc. I did this in order to convince myself that the Old Masters are nothing but Nature.'[20] In 1902, recalling Moreau's advice, he advised his compatriot, the artist Lucien Mainssieux: 'Do not be afraid to depend on the Old Masters [...] because these Old Masters are Nature herself.'[21] The argument was commonly used in academic circles in the nineteenth century to justify the practice of studying the classic sources in an age when the study of nature was seen by many as the basis of all art. 'You must constantly copy nature and learn how to see it properly', Ingres told his pupils. 'That is why it is necessary to study the works of antiquity and of the Old Masters, not for the sake of imitating them, but, I repeat, for the sake of learning how to see.'[22] Flandrin did not copy the Old Masters for the sake of imitating their compositions but to elicit principles which could be applied to painting contemporary themes. When he went to Italy for the first time in 1909, he was everywhere struck by the similarities between the work of the Old Masters and the details of contemporary life; the fashionable young people he saw there reminded him of Carpaccio and he found echoes of the drawings of Leonardo in the streets of Milan.[23] The link is implicit in the painting of an Italian peasant, entitled *Masaccio*, which he exhibited in 1910. Whenever Flandrin painted scenes of peasant life, the tradition of the pastoral and the pictureque is never far from the surface.

From this time onwards, a certain rigidity and flatness becomes more evident in his art and modern themes are given a veneer of classicism. At a time when Flandrin was becoming increasingly troubled by the direction taken by the avant-garde, he found an appealing alternative in the quattrocentist character which had long been evident in the work of Maurice Denis. His *Homage to Handel* (see cat. 36) painted for the church in Corenc in 1905, is indebted to the example of Denis, and it was Denis's art which came to mind when he visited Siena in 1909.[24] Like Denis, he admired Ingres and, although his liking for Denis had begun to cool by 1908, he still looked back to Ingres as an example of an artist who burnt with the warmth of passion whereas his pupils – among whom he included Denis as a pupil of the pupils – were 'cold as ice'.[25] This tendency culminated in the monumental *Young Horsemen by a Spring* (cat. 62) of 1913, Flandrin's last submission to the Salon of the *Société Nationale des Beaux-Arts*, a composition set ostensibly in his native Corenc but composed with a classical simplicity which was described at the time as 'Poussinesque'. The picture marks a significant point in the return to classical values among a number of French painters in the following years. It was one of Flandrin's most ambitious pictures to date and might have opened the way to a group of works somewhat in the manner of Derain if the war had not intervened.

Flandrin did not subscribe to the Romantic view of art as the untutored outpouring of undiluted inspiration. He placed a high value on inspiration but, like Reynolds, believed that inspiration was worthless unless it was accompanied by an ability to express it through the means of art. He found fault with the later work of Maurice Denis in this respect; too calculated to convey feeling, too academic.[26] This was the problem not only with more ostensibly academic artists such as Detaille, Cormon and Bonnat, but also with Metzinger and Picabia.[27] Linking Cormon and Picabia as fellow academics, as Flandrin knew, was an outrageous but effective thrust, repudiating Cubism without endorsing those who were seen as the enemies of modernism. The new movements – Cubism and Futurism in particular – disturbed Flandrin and he sometimes found difficulty in following the direction taken by old friends and colleagues.[28] By 1912, even Bonnard seemed to have fallen short of the standard of craft which he found in the Old Masters: 'in Bernheim's window, there are works by Bonnard, darned failures in certain respects, the effect is that of some old woman who does the best she can with a trembling hand! My thoughts turn, as if in opposition, to the rape of Europa by Veronese in the Capitoline! Ah, I would like to see that in a window on the Boulevards.'[29]

Flandrin never obviously imitated the Old Masters but they were often in his mind. Like Matisse, he copied their art in order to find a manner of his own. From the art of the past, he found confirmation for his idea that art was the expresson of a response to nature. The idea was hardly new – he would have found it in the art criticism of Baudelaire – but it was flexible enough to allow him to apply it to art of all kinds. The principles which he admired in the work of the Old Masters were applied by him to contemporary art and justified his enthusiasm for Vuillard, Bonnard, Denis, Roussel, Valloton and Sensier, those whom he defined as the 'forerunners of Moreau's pupils',[30] and for his fellow Fauves. He liked Matisse's art, in particular. Even the notorious *Music* and *Dance*, exhibited in 1910, met with his measured approval, although he, himself, never followed Matisse in simplifying his art to this degree: 'I understand his reasoning very well', Flandrin wrote to his brother, enclosing two accurate copies of the paintings in his letter, 'Since the other kind of painting is bad, one must paint the opposite'.[31] His principles did not allow him the same sympathy for what he saw as the more calculating art of the Pointillists, Cubists and Futurists and they were probably responsible for encouraging a traditionalist tendency in his later art. His respect for the past drew him, as it drew Derain in the same period, towards a greater engagement with the values of past art. What Apollinaire said of Derain in 1916 might have been said equally about Flandrin: 'Derain has passionately studied the masters. The copies which he has made of them in the Louvre show his concern to know them. At the same time, by an unequalled daring he has passed over all that contemporary art counts the most daring, to retrieve, with simplicity and freshness, the principles of art and the discipline which springs from it.'[32] Flandrin, too, attempted to retrieve the principles of art with simplicity and freshness and to apply them to the task of creating a modern idiom.

REFERENCES

1. See Marie-Anne Dupuy, 'Les copistes à l'oeuvre', in *Copier Créer* (Paris, 1993), pp. 42–51.
2. The point has been convincingly demonstrated by Jean-Pierre Cuzin and Marie-Anne Dupuy in *Copier Créer*.
3. Georges Flandrin and François Roussier, *Jules Flandrin 1871–1947* (La Tronche, 1992), pp. 57, 69.
4. Pierre-Louis Mathieu, *Gustave Moreau* (Oxford, 1989), pp. 26–8.
5. Roger Benjamin, 'Ingres chez les Fauves', *Art History*, vol. 23, no. 5 (2000), pp. 743–72.
6. 'Ne craignez pas de vous appuyer sur les maîtres, vous vous y retrouverez toujours', cited in Pierre Schneider, *Matisse* (Paris, 1984), p. 57.
7. Flandrin and Roussier, p. 32.
8. Albert Boime, 'Le musée des copies', *Gazette des Beaux-Arts*, vol. 64 (October 1964), p. 247.
9. 'Mon étude des 'Noces de Cana' n'est pas bien grande, un mètre carré, mais c'est la chose qui est grande à faire', cited in Flandrin and Roussier, p. 45. The copy of the *Venus del Pardo* recently appeared at auction in Grenoble (Maître Pierre Blache, Hôtel des Ventes, 12 December 2000, lot 145).
10. *Ibid.*
11. *Ibid.*

12. 'Jules Flandrin, d'après le couronnement de Marie de Médicis de Rubens et d'après les *noces de Cana* de Veronèse, évoque les maîtres sans les copier textuellement. Il analyse et reconstitue selon les données de cette analyse. Quel élève de l'école des Beaux-Arts a-t-il vu ces copies de Valtat et de Flandrin? A-t-il, les ayant vues, jeté ses pinceaux à la tête de ses maîtres ...?', Léon Werth, cited *ibid.*, p. 40.

13. Albert Boime, *The Academy and French Painting in the Nineteenth Century* (London, 1971), p. 128.

14. 'Je mets la dernière main à une copie du portrait de Poussin par lui-même au Louvre. Je l'ai entreprise cet hiver, avec je crois plus de sûreté que le Titien de l'année passée et je crois qu'il fera bien meilleure figure devant la commission que celui-ci', cited in Flandrin and Roussier, p. 53.

15. Archives nationales F 21/4500B. I am grateful to Dr Juliet Simpson for tracing all references to Flandrin's copies in the archives of state acquisitions.

16. *Ibid.*, F 21/4909B, dossier 10, pièce 20 [cahiers des musées]; the copy was sent to the Musée de Mont-de-Marsan in the Landes. This painting, along with the copy of Ingres's *Grande odalisque* (*ibid.*, F 21/4909B, dossier 10, pièce 22) acquired at the same time, is listed as the work of 'M. Flandrin'; there is a vestigial possibility that these were copies by either Hippolyte or Paul Flandrin, acquired from the estate of Paul who died in 1902. As Mme Lacambre has kindly pointed out, the copy of Ingres's *Grande odalisque* is attributed to Hippolyte Flandrin in the catalogue, *Ingres et son temps* (Paris, 1965), no. 123, but the date 1903, given in the catalogue, suggests an attribution to Jules.

17. 'Vous voyez, j'étudiais, selon mes attirances, les maîtres comme dans les lettres on étudie les auteurs, avant de décider pour l'un ou pour l'autre; surtout sans le désir de piger des trucs, mais par culture d'esprit. J'allais d'un Hollandais à Chardin, d'un Titien à Poussin', cited in *Copier Créer*, p. 348.

18. 'ce sont ceux tout simplement ceux qui s'efforcent de penser bien et de faire beau. Ils ont l'air nouveau pour ceux de leur génération qui ont oublié ce qui était beau, voilà tout. Mais ils ressemblent sous bien des rapports aux vieux de tous les siècles passés qui ont aussi cherché le beau', cited in Flandrin and Roussier, p. 47.

19. 'Comme il sait bien ce que c'est que Poussin et Claude Lorrain. Comme il voit bien que le vrai progrès consiste à s'élever au niveau des artistes, de vrais, de tous les temps', cited *ibid.*, p. 55.

20. 'Je n'ai pas rougi de prendre de toute pièce, de l'Angelico, et d'y mettre de ma peinture comme à Corenc. Je l'ai fait pour bien me persuader que les Maîtres c'est la nature même', cited *ibid.*, p. 57.

21. 'Ne craignez pas de vous appuyer sur les maîtres [...] car, les Maîtres, c'est la Nature', cited *ibid.*, p. 69.

22. 'Il faut copier la nature toujours et apprendre à la bien voir. C'est pour cela qu'il est nécessaire d'étudier les maîtres, non pour les imiter, mais, encore une fois, pour apprendre à voir', cited in Henri Delaborde, *Ingres* (1870), p. 139.

23. Flandrin and Roussier, p. 105.

24. *Ibid.*, p. 106.

25. 'froids comme glace', cited *ibid.*, p. 95.

26. *Ibid.*, p. 168.

27. *Ibid.*

28. *Ibid.*

29. 'En vitrine chez Bernheim, il y a des Bonnard bigrement ratés aussi, par certains côtés, la sensation d'une bonne vieille dame qui a fait d'une main tremblante, tout ce qu'elle a pu! Je revois en pensée comme opposition, l'enlèvement d'Europe de Veronèse au Capitole! Ah j'aimerais voir ça dans une vitrine, sur les Boulevards ...', cited *ibid.*, pp. 131–3.

30. 'ce groupe d'amis qui qui a précédé les élèves de Gustave Moreau', cited *ibid.*, p. 241.

31. 'Je comprend très bien son raisonnement. Puisque l'autre peinture est mauvaise, il faut prendre l'opposé', cited *ibid.*, p. 120.

32. Cited in Jane Lee, *Derain* (Oxford, 1990), p. 49.

THE CATALOGUE

Juliet Simpson

1

Flandrin and Moreau
Copy and Creation

Abbreviations and referencing systems are given in the Editor's Note.
Catalogue entries illustrated in colour are denoted by an asterisk* after the title.
Cat. 41, 47, 59 and 71 are not included in the exhibition.

1   *Path through the Trees**
1886
Chemin sous les arbres

OIL ON PANEL, 23.5 × 14.5 CMS.
INSCRIBED WITH MONOGRAM 'J.F' ON RECTO LOWER LEFT
PROV.: THE ARTIST; BY DESCENT TO THE PRESENT OWNER

Flandrin's earliest works were paintings and drawings of the scenery of his native Dauphiné, especially the surrounding landscape of the Flandrin family home at Corenc, near Grenoble.

This small landscape, one of the first of a series painted on panel and board (see cat. 2 and 4), shows the marked influence of the Barbizon school, especially Corot, on Flandrin's work at this stage. The device of the pathway leading from the dappled foreground to a brilliant sunlit distance is characteristic of the Barbizon school, but also indicates Flandrin's emerging interest in creating balanced compositions with a strong emphasis on structure and pattern.

Private Collection, Grenoble

2   *The Massif of the Chartreuse, the Pinéa seen from Saint-Egrève*
(UNDATED) *c.*1889
Contreforts de la Chartreuse, la Pinéa, vus de Saint-Egrève

OIL ON BOARD, 16.5 × 22.5 CMS.
PROV.: THE ARTIST; BY DESCENT TO THE PRESENT OWNER

The two summits of the Pinéa and Saint-Egrève, north west of Corenc, form part of the vast Massif of the Chartreuse which extends towards Grenoble, the valley of the Isère, and to the Montagne de Lans in the south. This view from Corenc, a favourite of Flandrin's in his youth, was painted from the plain of the Isère looking westwards from Corenc and includes the southerly summits of the Chartreuse, with the Pinéa visible between the

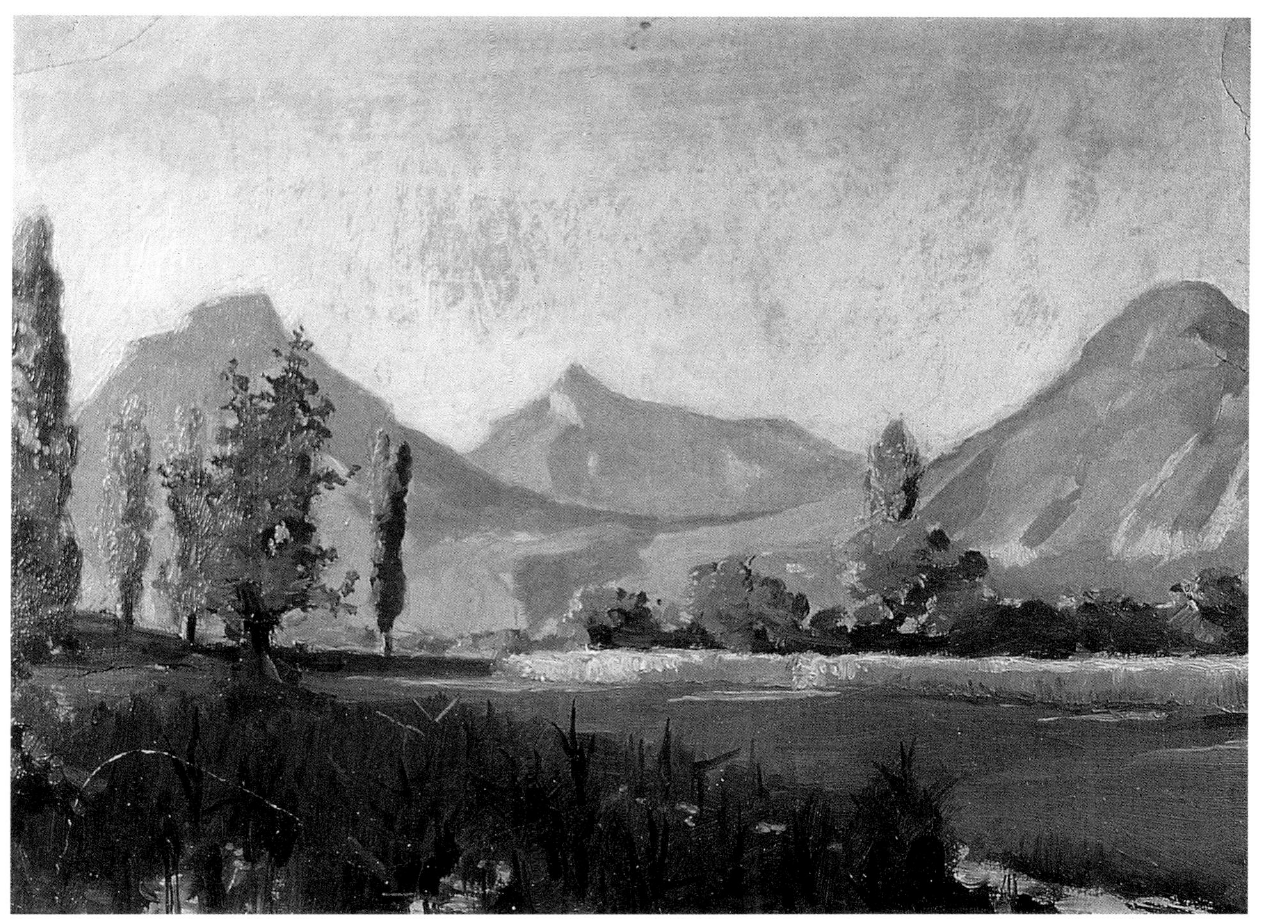

2 *The Massif of the Chartreuse, the Pinéa seen from Saint-Egrève* (undated), *c.*1889

two other peaks. There is a clear debt, here, to eighteenth- and nineteenth-century Dauphinois traditions of topographical landscape painting,[1] although the stark simplicity of Flandrin's view also suggests a concern to develop a more individual and expressive treatment of his subject-matter.

Private Collection, Paris

[1] Notably to the Grenoblois group of landscapists, including Jacques-André Treillard (1712–94), Jean Achard (1807–84) and Diodore Rahoult (1891–74), which Flandrin admired in his youth: *Flandrin Archives*, Paris and Grenoble.

3   *Avenue of Blackberry Bushes, Garden at Corenc**
1890
Allée des mûriers, jardin de Corenc

OIL ON CANVAS, 22 × 26 CMS.
INSCRIBED WITH MONOGRAM 'JF' ON RECTO LOWER LEFT
PROV.: THE ARTIST; BY DESCENT TO THE PRESENT OWNER
EXH.: GRENOBLE, GALERIE ROUX, 1890

Painted at nineteen years of age during Flandrin's apprenticeship with the Grenoble printing firm Allier, this was the first of Flandrin's works to be publicly exhibited. The subject of the family house and garden at Corenc accords with Flandrin's interest in depicting the local colour and ambience of his familial environment. The house at Corenc, a frequently occurring motif in Flandrin's work, would remain emblematic of childhood ideals, family security, and of an untroubled, wholesome vision of nature throughout his career. But the quasi-impressionist treatment of forms and bold brushwork indicate a more modern approach to landscape than hitherto, anticipating the brilliant colourism that would characterize Flandrin's art from 1898 onwards.

Private Collection, Paris

4   *Sunset*
1892
Coucher de soleil
OIL ON PAPER MOUNTED ON PANEL, 17.5 × 26.5 CMS.
INSCRIBED WITH MONOGRAM 'JF' AND DATED '92' ON RECTO LOWER LEFT
PROV.: THE ARTIST; BY DESCENT TO THE PRESENT OWNER

This remarkably free oil sketch, painted prior to Flandrin's departure for Paris in 1893, appears to have been part of a series of landscape *pochades* (rough sketches) produced in conjunction with his more finished, topographical views of his local scenery. The dramatically simplified forms and vigorously worked surface show Flandrin's capacity to work in a variety of

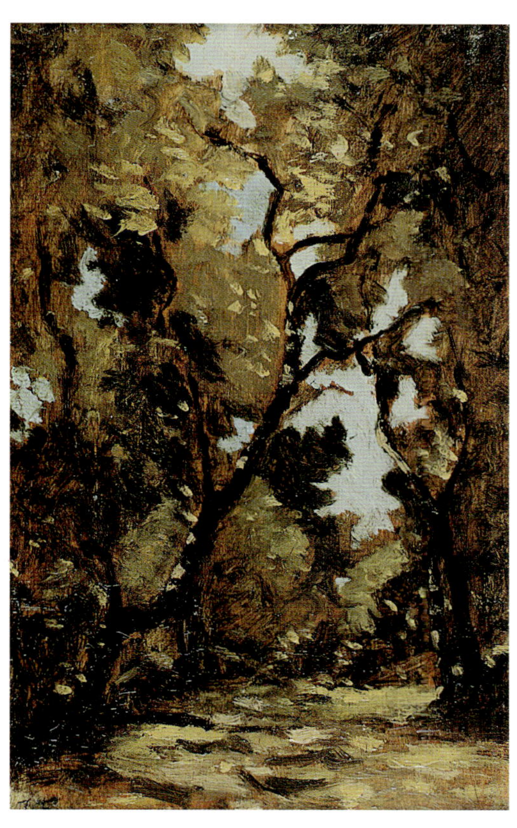

1 *Path through the Trees*, 1886

3 *Avenue of Blackberry Bushes, Garden at Corenc,*
1890

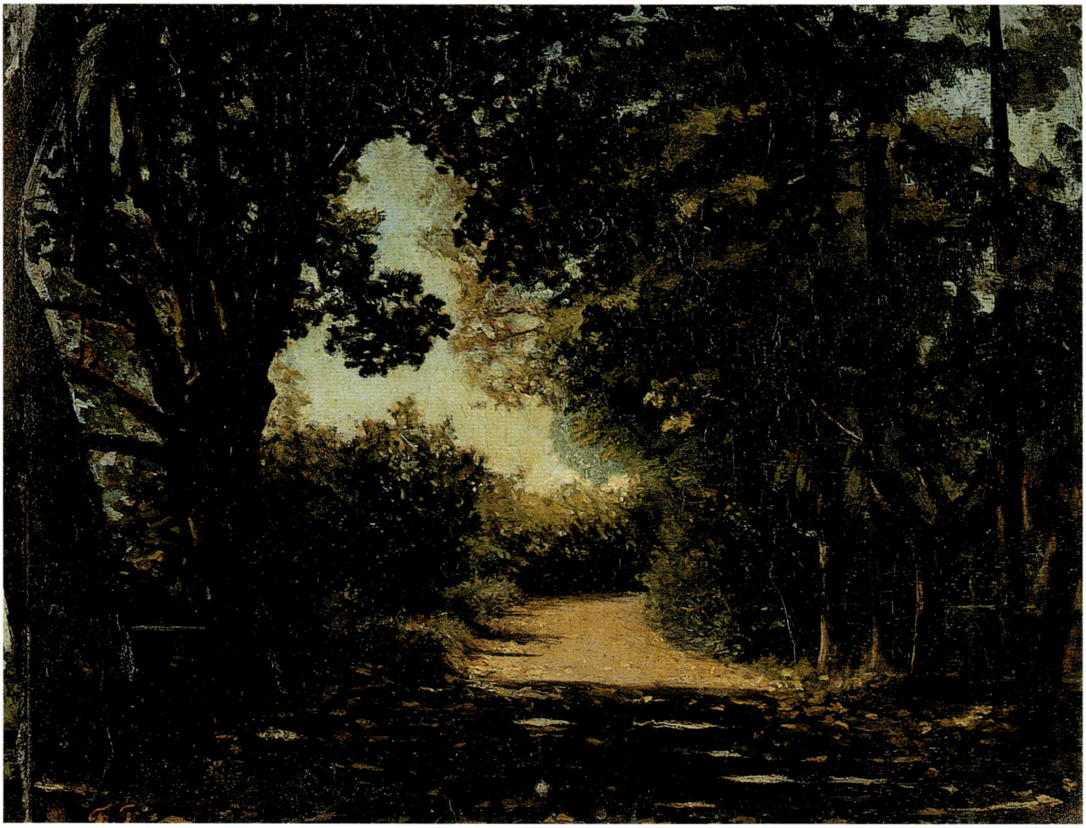

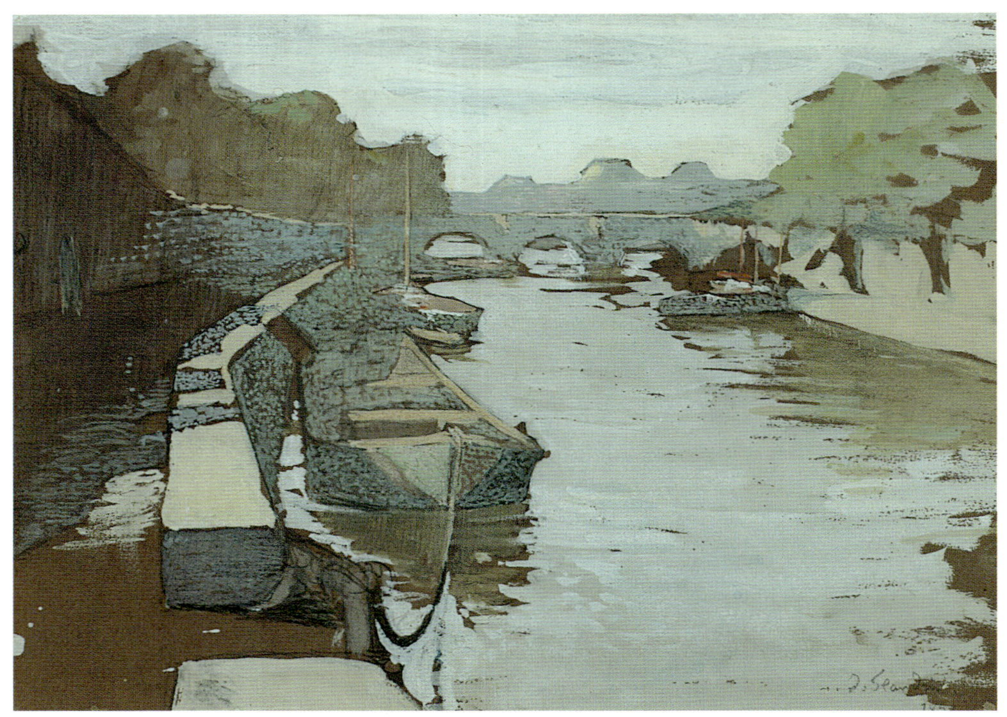

7 *Barge at the Quayside with the Pont-Neuf in the Background*, 1894

8 *Shady Street, Paris* (undated) *c*.1895

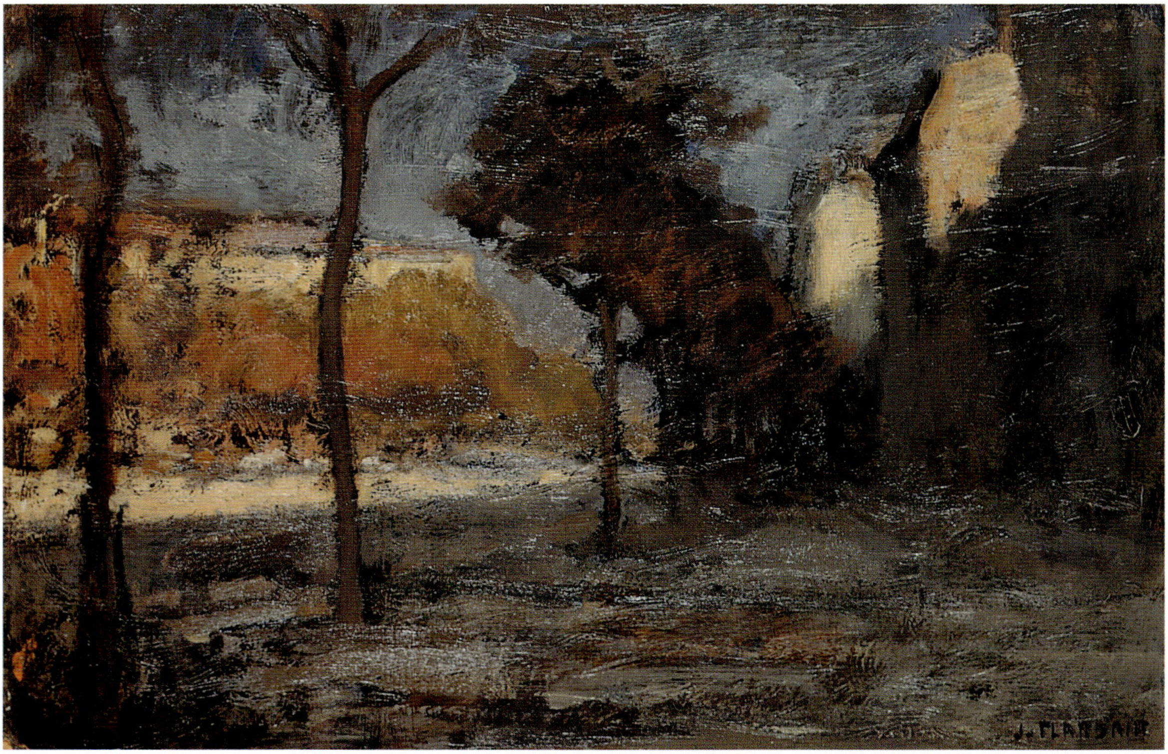

10 *Portrait of Adèle Lizambert*, 1895

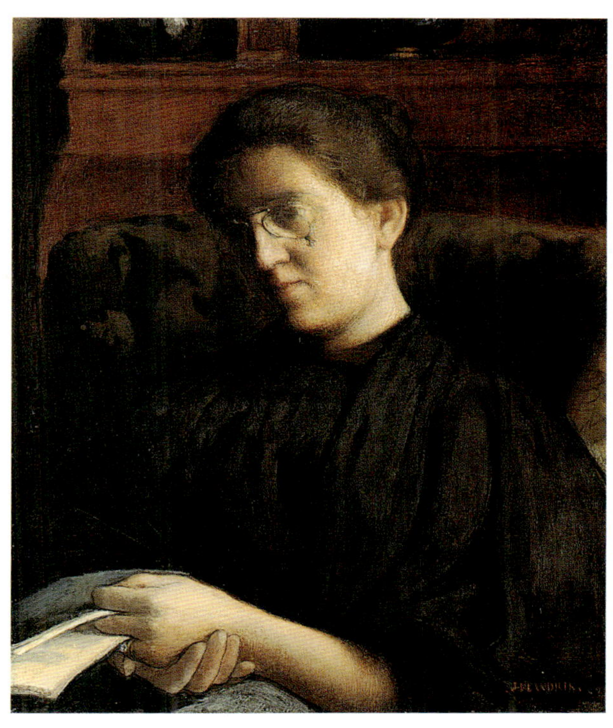

15 *Copy after Rubens, 'The Coronation of Maria de' Medici'* (undated) *c.* 1897

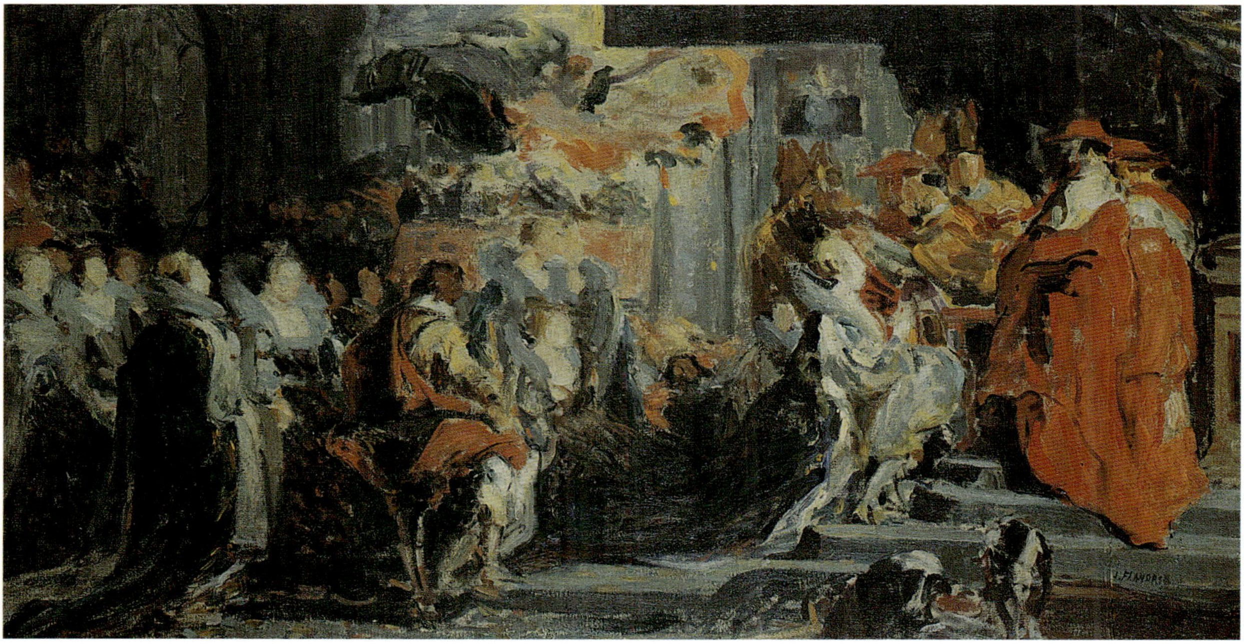

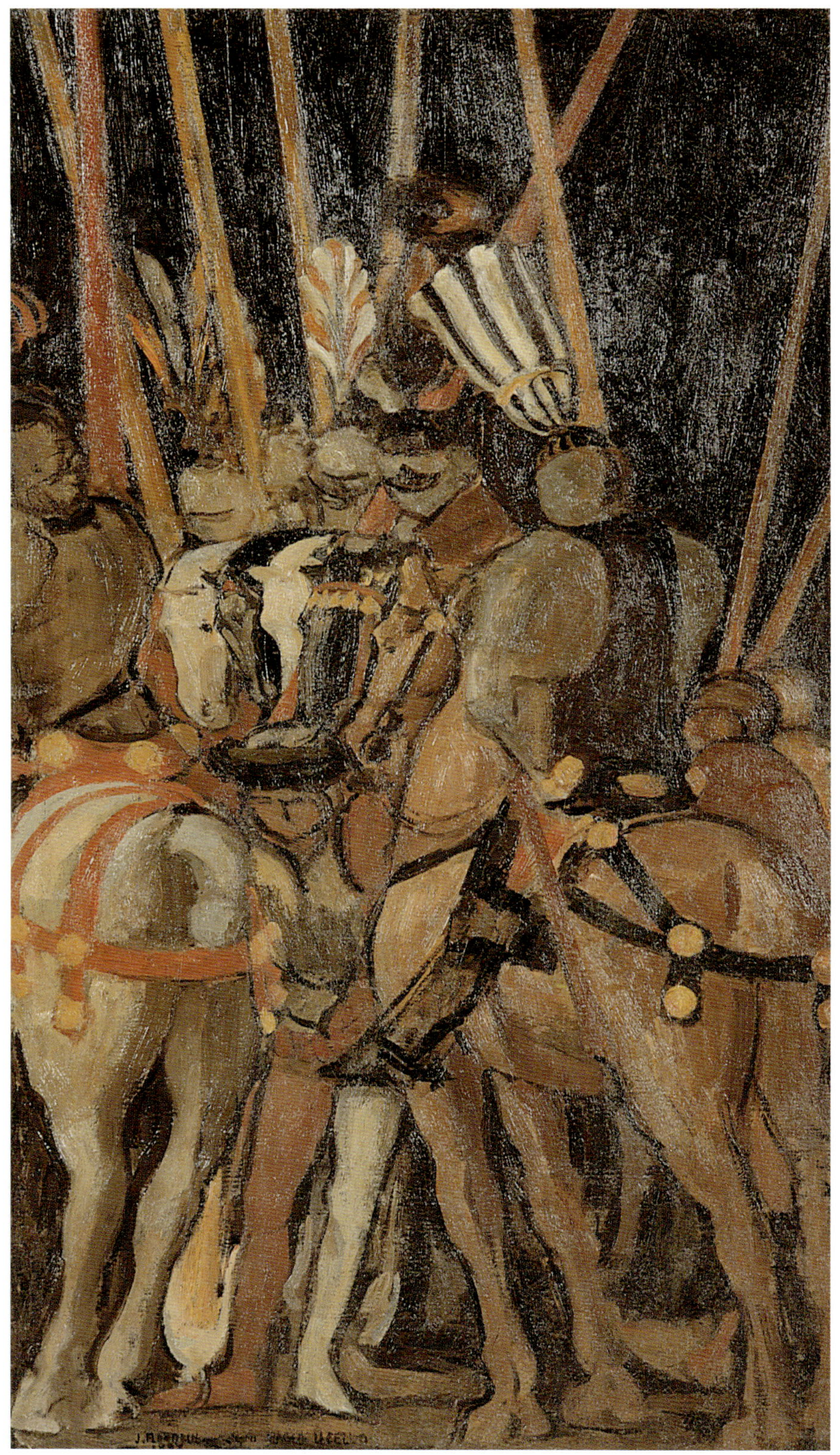

14 *Copy after Paolo Uccello, 1897*

different traditions and styles, even at this early stage. There is also a striking similarity to Gustave Moreau's numerous and atmospheric studies of
twilight landscapes[1] echoed by Flandrin in his later *Alps at Twilight, Corenc*
(1898: cat. 23), suggesting the daring qualities which were to mark
Flandrin out as one of Moreau's most talented pupils.

Private Collection, Grenoble

[1] See, for example, *Peintures, cartons, aquarelles etc. exposés dans les galeries du Musée
Gustave Moreau* (Paris, 1990), cat. nos 111 and 120 (pp.54–5).

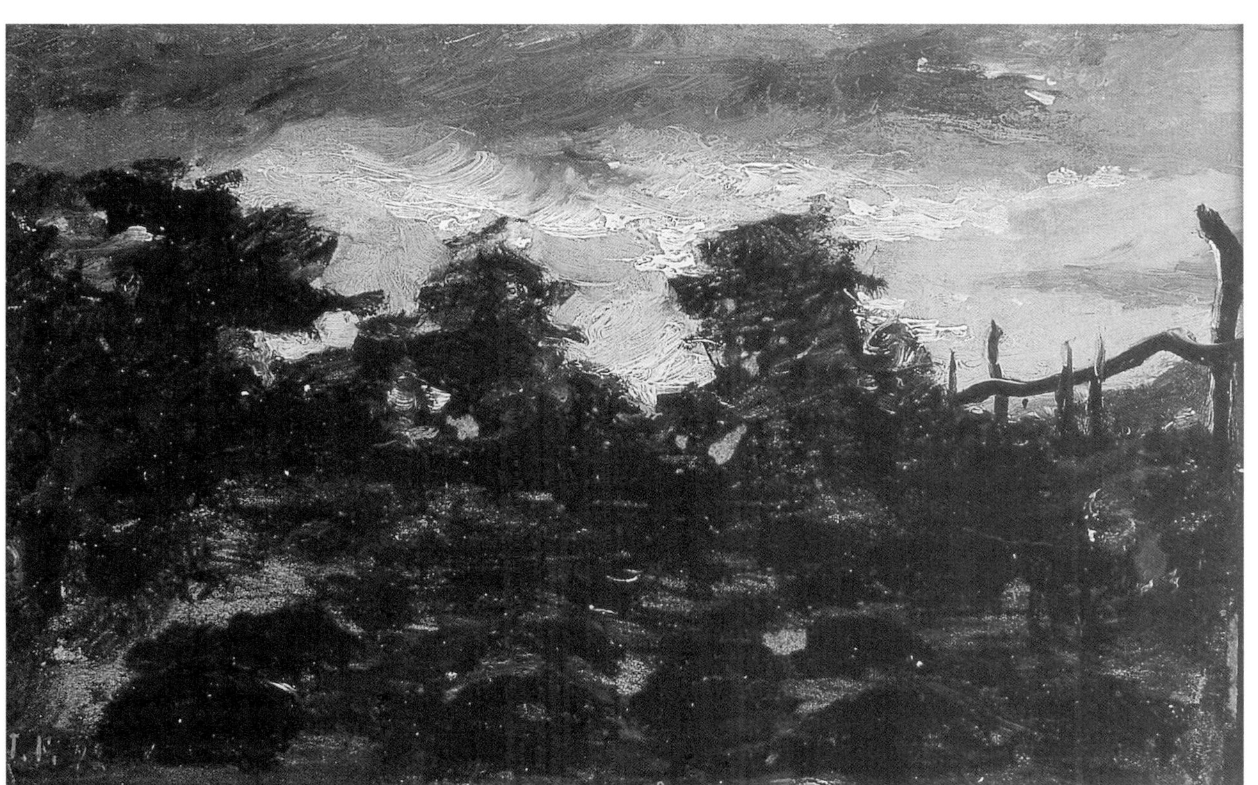

4 *Sunset*, 1892

5   *Virgin and Child after Leonardo da Vinci*
1894–6
Vierge à l'enfant d'après Vinci

INDIAN INK, 17 × 15 CMS.
INSCRIBED 'JULES FLANDRIN' ON RECTO LOWER LEFT, AND 'VINCI'
LOWER RIGHT
PROV.: THE ARTIST; BY DESCENT TO THE PRESENT OWNER

Amongst Flandrin's first works following his arrival in Paris in October 1893 are a series of copies after masterpieces he encountered in the Louvre (see cat. 6, 13, 14 and 15).[1] Copying was an essential part of a young artist's education at this period, forming the core of the teaching curriculum at the Paris École des Beaux-Arts. But under Moreau's guidance from 1895 to 1898, Flandrin and his contemporaries, notably Georges Rouault, Henri Matisse and Albert Marquet, were encouraged to see copying not so much in terms of slavish imitation, but rather as a process of interpretation – as a means to apply the lessons of the 'masters' in the context of the present. Moreau's favoured artists included, as well as the Masters of the High Renaissance, Rembrandt, Rubens and Titian: an eclecticism which contrasted with the dominant vogue for the great representatives of the classical tradition, Raphael and Poussin, promoted by the École des Beaux-Arts.[1] Flandrin's copy is based on a painting by Cesare da Sesto (Hermitage), then attributed to Leonardo. Flandrin was doubtless inspired by Moreau's enthusiasm for Leonardo, although, perhaps surprisingly, his works were not copiously copied by Moreau's students.[2] More characteristic of Moreau's influence at this time, are Flandrin's copies after Rembrandt (see cat. 6 and 13), Titian, Rubens (cat. 15) and Veronese, as well as of the so-called Florentine 'Primitives', notably Fra Angelico, Mantegna and Uccello (cat. 14), and works by eighteenth-century French masters (Flandrin made a large copy after Watteau's *Gilles* in 1897, which was highly praised by Moreau[3]).

Private Collection, Paris

[1]See Larry J. Feinberg, 'Gustave Moreau and the Italian Renaissance', in Lacambre *et al.*, *Gustave Moreau: Between Epic and Dream* (Paris, Princeton, 1998), pp. 5–13.
[2]According to Philip Walsh, only a dozen requests to copy Leonardo were registered by Moreau's students: *The Atelier of Gustave Moreau at the École des Beaux-Arts*, unpublished Ph.D. thesis (Harvard, 1995), p. 193 (I am very grateful to Mme Lacambre for drawing this study to my attention).
[3]In Flandrin and Roussier, p. 31–2.

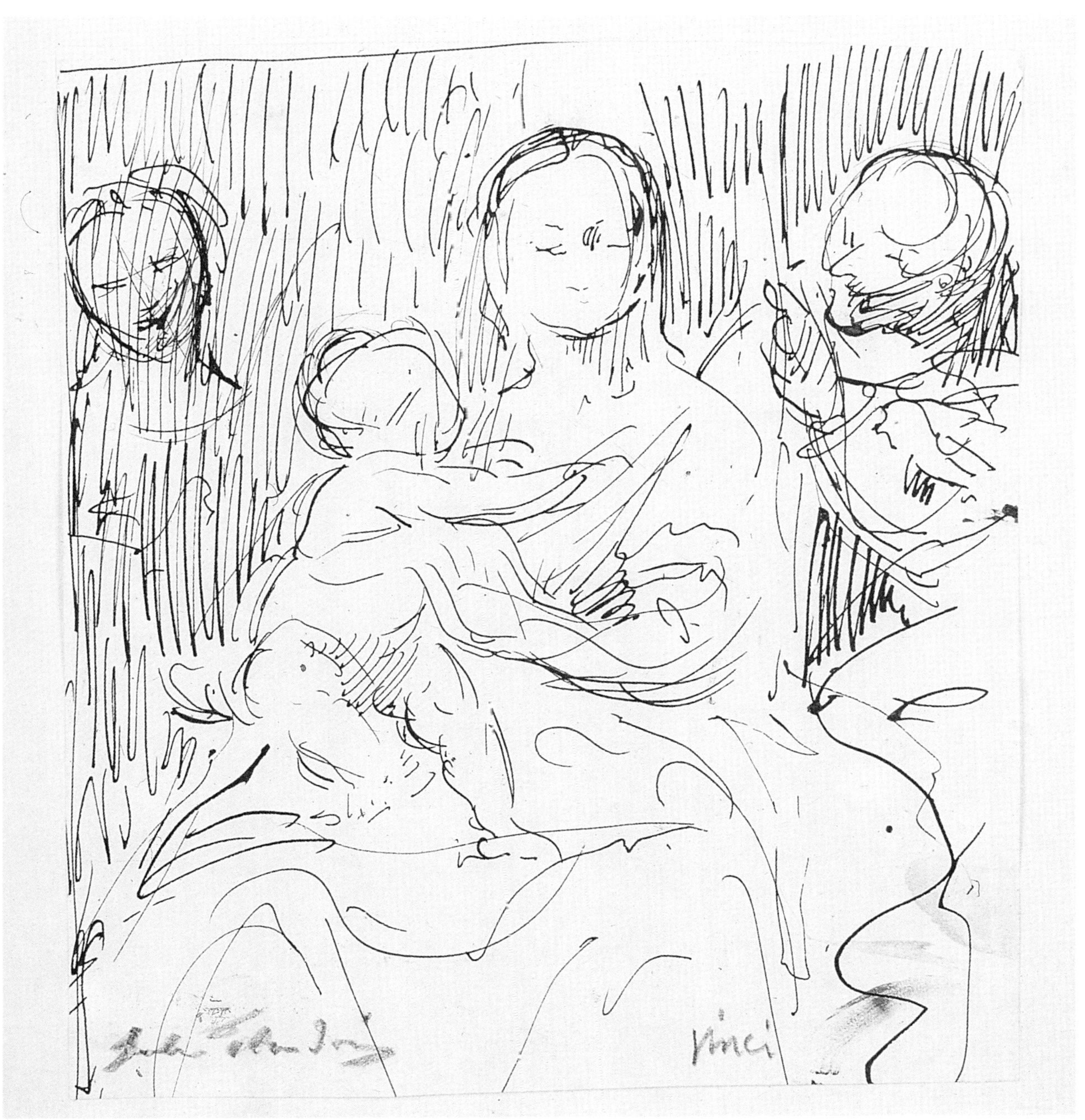

5 *Virgin and Child after Leonardo da Vinci*, 1894–6

6   *'Group' after Rembrandt*
1894–6
'Groupe' d'après Rembrandt

INDIAN INK, 12 × 16 CMS.
INSCRIBED WITH MONOGRAM 'J.F. D'APRÈS REMBRANDT' ON RECTO
LOWER RIGHT
PROV.: THE ARTIST; BY DESCENT TO THE PRESENT OWNER

This sketch is based on Rembrandt's *Family Group* (Herzog Anton Ulrich-Museum, Brunswick). The summary outlines of the figures against a loosely-drawn *chiaroscuro* background show Flandrin's absorption of Moreau's teaching methods and advice which involved the production of numerous 'free-style' sketches (*pochades*) in front of the original to capture the essentials of subject and style.

Private Collection, Paris

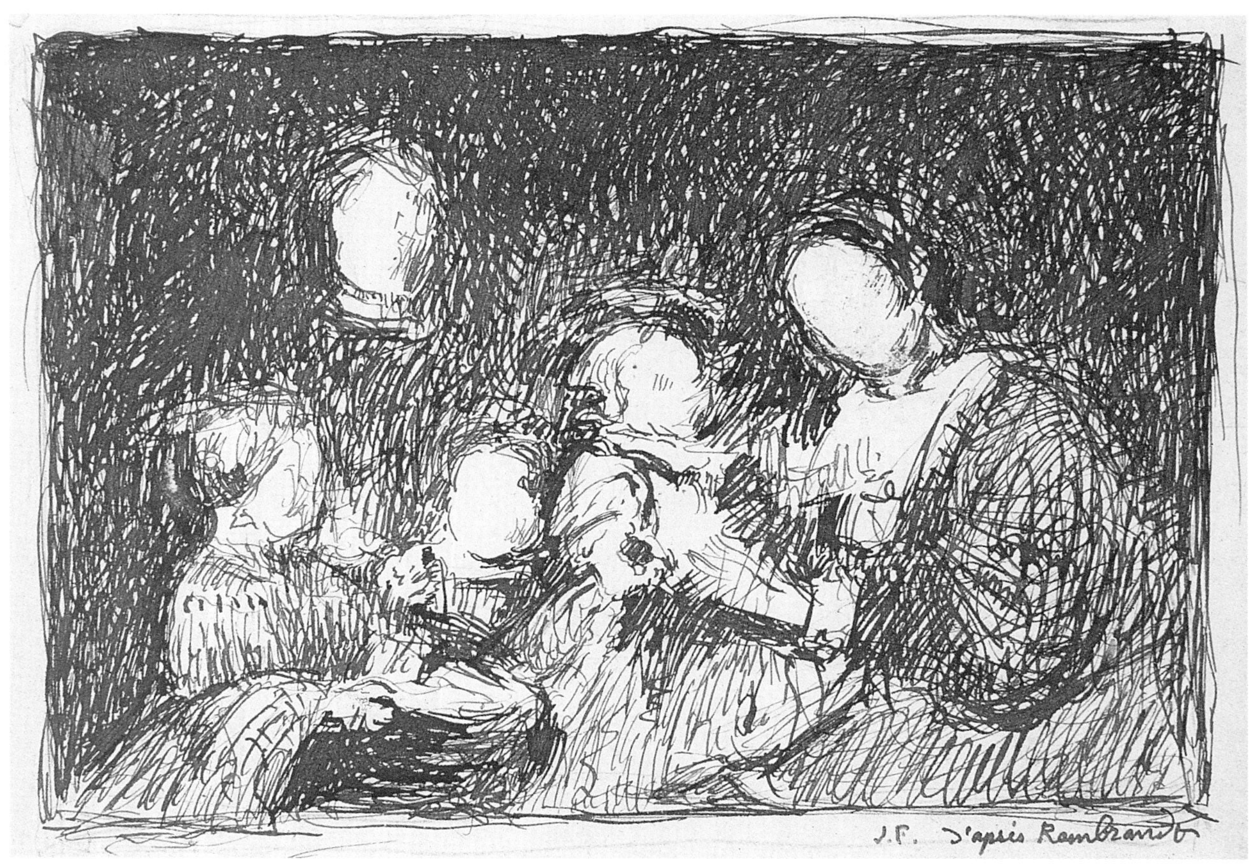

6 *'Group' after Rembrandt*, 1894–6

7 *Barge at the Quayside with the Pont-Neuf in the Background**

1894
Péniche à Quai avec le Pont-Neuf au fond

GOUACHE, 22.5 × 30 CMS.
INSCRIBED 'J. FLANDRIN' AND DATED '94' ON RECTO LOWER RIGHT
PROV.: THE ARTIST; BY DESCENT TO THE PRESENT OWNER

Dating from Flandrin's first year in Paris, this small river-side scene provides an indication of sources and ideas that were to preoccupy Flandrin after 1894. Views of the Seine, its bridges, and quayside hinterlands were popular subjects for the Impressionists. During the 1870s, Alfred Sisley had painted the barges and canal-side loading quays of the Canal Saint-Martin,[1] a theme taken up by Monet in his gritty *Unloading Coal* of 1875 (Private Collection, Paris). Flandrin's debts to his immediate predecessors are apparent in the manner in which the industrial motif of the barge is juxtaposed against the picturesque outlines of the distant Pont Neuf. This idea was to be developed later, in his much more overtly Impressionistic *Quayside Boat on the Seine* (1896),[2] and in *The Seine at Sunrise* (1902: cat. 33) where the wide expanse of water and sky enables Flandrin to explore the nature of light, atmosphere, and most significantly, relationships between light and colour effects.

Private Collection, Paris

[1]See MaryAnne Stevens, *et al.*, *Alfred Sisley* (New Haven and London, 1992), cat. 9 (p.100).
[2]In Flandrin and Roussier, p.30.

8   *Shady Street, Paris**
(UNDATED) *c.*1895
Rue ombragée, Paris

OIL ON CANVAS, 31 × 46 CMS.
INSCRIBED 'J.FLANDRIN' ON RECTO LOWER RIGHT
PROV.: THE ARTIST; BY DESCENT TO THE PRESENT OWNER
LIT.: FLANDRIN AND ROUSSIER, P.30.

One of a series of views of Paris streets and buildings dating from Flandrin's early years in Paris, this jewel-like painting shows Flandrin beginning to use colour in a way which would be the hallmark of his later work. The limited range of bright tonalities and broadly applied strokes of paint are markedly Impressionist in character. Flandrin, like any ambitious young artist of the period, was beginning to acquaint himself with the Paris collections and prominent dealer-galleries where avant-garde art was being exhibited. However, this is combined with an intimacy, a simplicity, as well as a decorative approach to colour which suggests contact with newer sources of inspiration: with Nabi art, in particular, Bonnard's and Vuillard's – influences which were to become dominant in Flandrin's work around 1897.

Private Collection, Grenoble

9   *Marval Reading*
*c.*1895
Marval lisant

INDIAN INK, WASH AND PEN, 10 × 11.5 CMS.
INSCRIBED WITH MONOGRAM 'J.F.' ON RECTO LOWER LEFT
PROV.: THE ARTIST; BY DESCENT TO THE PRESENT OWNER
LIT.: FLANDRIN AND ROUSSIER, P.43; SPURLING, P.227.

This delicate wash and pen drawing is the first known portrait of Flandrin's mistress, the Grenoblois couturier, Marie Vallet (1866–1932) whom he met and fell in love with in 1895. Vallet, a lover of Flandrin's friend and contemporary, the Grenoblois painter François-Joseph Girot (1873–1916), was to have an enormous influence on Flandrin's life and art

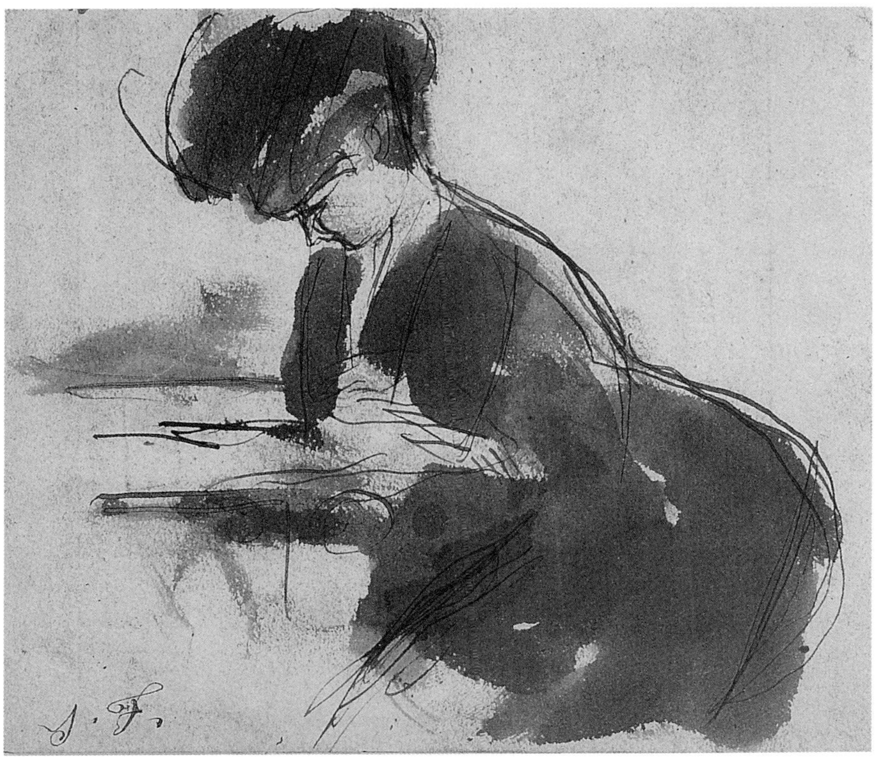

9 *Marval Reading, c.*1895

until he left Paris permanently in 1931. Joining Flandrin in 1895 in his rented apartment at 9 rue Campagne Première in the 14th arrondissement near the Luxembourg Gardens, Vallet became Flandrin's constant companion, in art as well as in love. Taking up painting around 1900, she began styling herself as the artist 'Jacqueline Marval': the name she adopted for the rest of her life. Her bold and daring paintings, which matched her striking appearance and flamboyant personality, drew admiration from Flandrin's male contemporaries, from Matisse and Marquet who became close friends in the late 1890s,[1] and from numerous eminent critics including Claude Roger-Marx and Charles Morice. Flandrin's portrait, with its cursory form, fluid, open contours and smudgy ink washes may be seen as a visual counterpart to Marval's energetic and impetuous presence, shown here, barely poised over a table as if ready to spring up at a moment's notice.

Private Collection, Grenoble

[1]See Spurling, pp.225–8.

10   *Portrait of Adèle Lizambert**
1895
Portrait d'Adèle Lizambert

Oil on canvas, 61 × 50 cms.
Inscribed 'J. FLANDRIN' on recto lower right
Prov.: The artist; by descent to the present owner
Lit.: Flandrin and Roussier, p.32.

This early portrait of Flandrin's sister shows Flandrin working in an 'Old Master' style, characteristic of his other family portraits at this period. The dark interior, half-lit figure, and earthy tonalities are clearly indebted to Dutch seventeenth-century painting, as well as to that of the eighteenth-century French school, in particular, Chardin. Similar tendencies are evident in Matisse's contemporary work, as in his Chardinesque *Woman Reading* (1895: Musée national d'Art moderne, Paris) which attest the marked influence of Moreau's tastes and ideas on the evolution of his pupils' art. Flandrin may also have been working in a consciously traditional style in order to gain entry to the Salon of the *Société Nationale des Beaux-Arts*. Following his initial success in 1897 with a series of crepuscular portraits of family and friends, he was soon to abandon careful modelling and dark tonalities in favour of Symbolist and Nabi-inspired colour and a freer more decorative treatment of form (see cat. 16, 17, 19, 25 and 26).

Private Collection, Grenoble

11   *'Snow Reverie'*
1896
'Songe de neige'

Lithograph, 36 × 51.5 cms.
Inscribed 'J.FLANDRIN' and dated '96' on recto middle left
Prov.: The artist; by descent to the present owner

Flandrin's apprenticeship with the Grenoble printing-firm Allier between 1889 and 1893 had provided him with a strong grounding in decorative art techniques. He spent his first year in Paris registered at the École des Arts

Décoratifs while preparing for his entry to the École des Beaux-Arts, which continued to fuel an interest that animated his entire artistic career. The illustration for Henri Francou's poem, *Songe de neige*, is likely to have been produced during a vacation spent at Corenc and shows Flandrin's considerable feeling for design; for bold compositional arrangements and pattern-making. It also indicates, that, as with his drawings of the period, lithography and print-making increasingly provided vehicles for exploring experimental ideas and compositional techniques which were only just beginning to be manifest in his paintings.

Private Collection, Paris

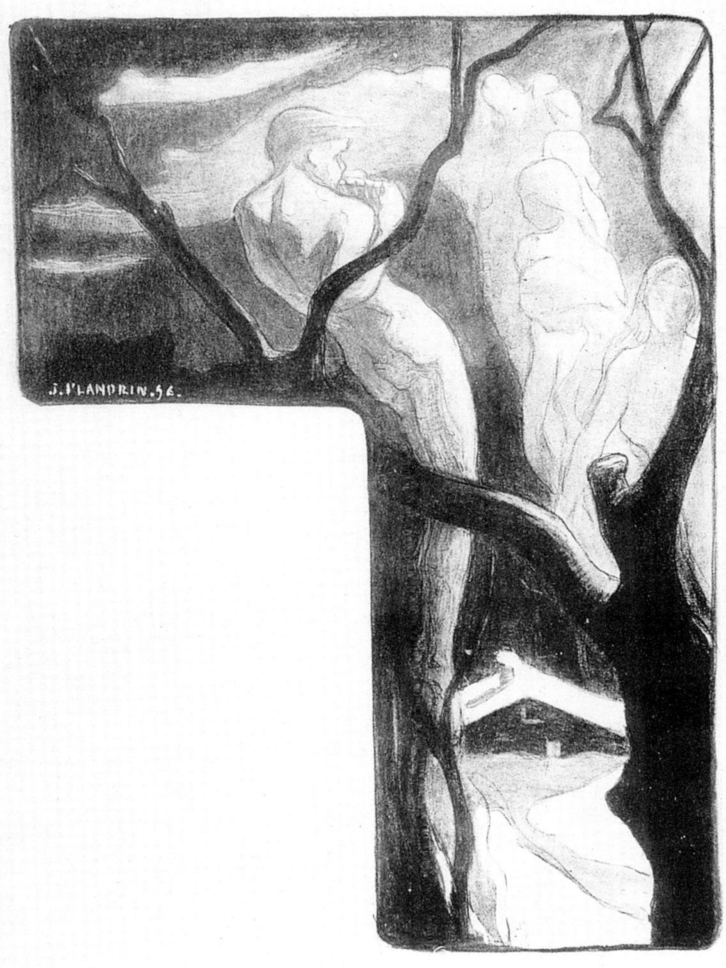

11 *'Snow Reverie'*, 1896

12   *Marquet and Camoin Sketching in the Louvre*
1897
Marquet et Camoin dessinant au Louvre

COLOURED PENCIL, 20.5 × 14 CMS.
INSCRIBED 'JULES FLANDRIN MARQUET AND CAMOIN DESSINANT AU
LOUVRE.' ON RECTO LOWER LEFT, AND DATED '1897' LOWER RIGHT
PROV.: THE ARTIST; BY DESCENT TO THE PRESENT OWNER
LIT.: FLANDRIN AND ROUSSIER, P.35.

See cat. 5.

Private Collection, Grenoble

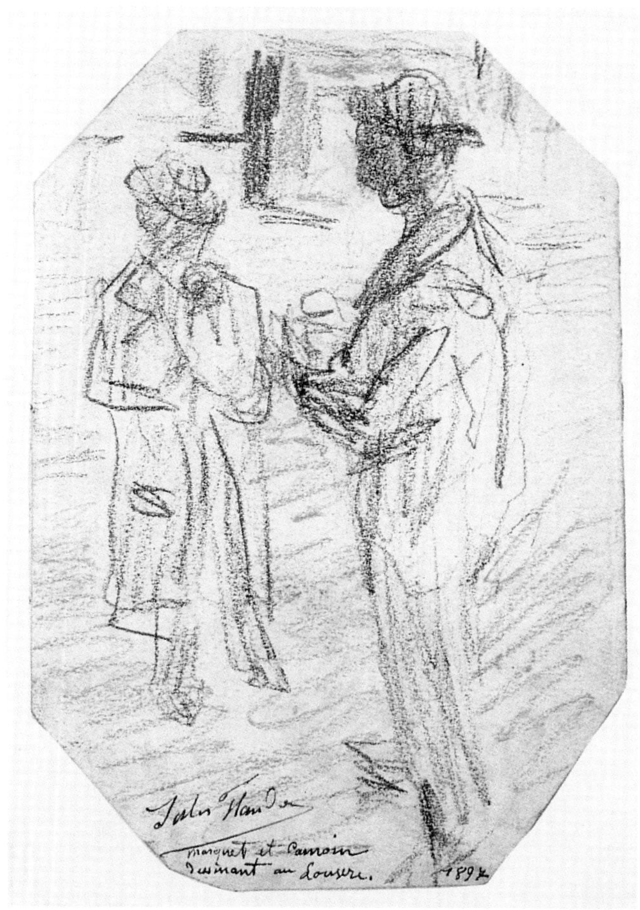

12 *Marquet and Camoin Sketching in the Louvre, 1897*

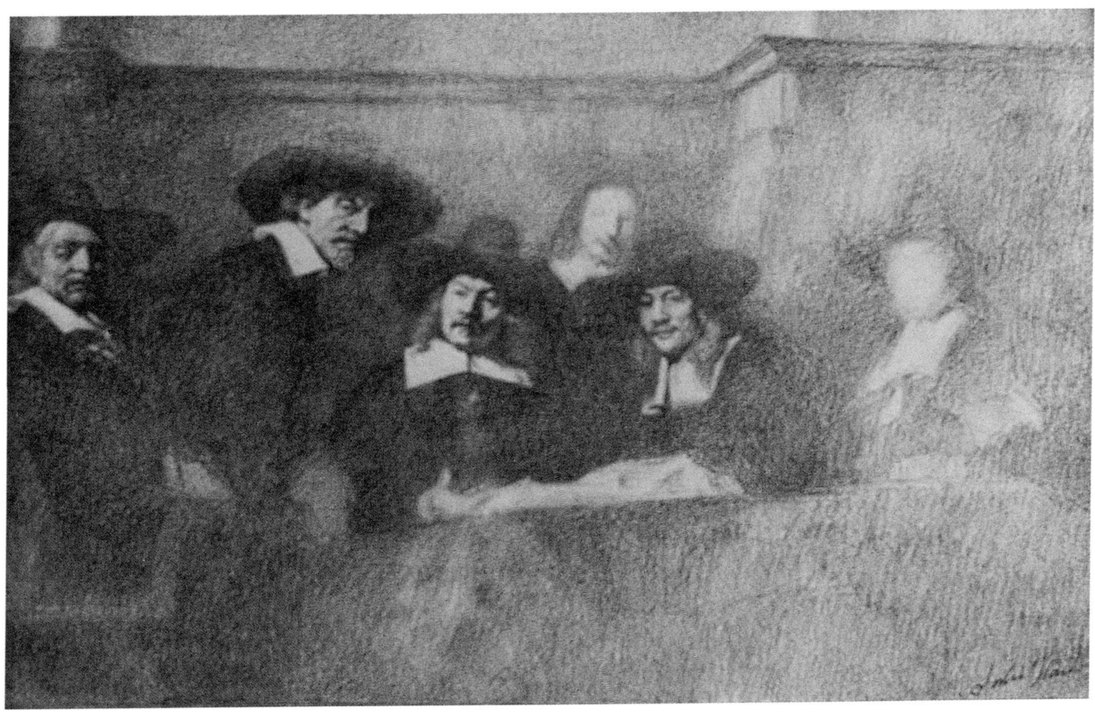

13 *Study after Rembrandt's 'The Anatomy Lesson' (undated), c.*1896–8

13 *Study after Rembrandt's 'The Anatomy Lesson'*
(UNDATED) *c.* 1896–8
Étude d'après 'la leçon d'anatomie' de Rembrandt

PENCIL, 19 × 29 CMS.
INSCRIBED 'JULES FLANDRIN' ON RECTO LOWER RIGHT
PROV.: THE ARTIST; BY DESCENT TO THE PRESENT OWNER

See cat. 5 and 6.

Private Collection, Paris

14   *Copy after Paolo Uccello**
1897
Copie d'après Paolo Uccello

Oil on canvas, 118 × 66 cms.
Prov.: The artist;… Marcel Sahut Collection, from whom
bought by the present owner, *c.*1972
Exh.: Grenoble, *Salon de Grenoble*, 1931

Flandrin's copying activities reached a peak in 1897 with his production of large-scale copies after Watteau, Rubens (cat. 15), Titian, Veronese and Uccello. At this time, Flandrin was spending several afternoons a week in the Louvre, engaged in concentrated study of the Masters, and usually in the company of several of Moreau's students, including Matisse, Marquet, Camoin (see cat. 12), Charles Guérin, Georges Desvallières and the Belgian, Henri Evenepoël. Indeed, as the critic Roger-Marx noted in 1895, Moreau's students stood out from their contemporaries for what he describes as their skilful and imaginative interpretations of the art of the past; by their 'profoundly intelligent sense of the original and their lively translation of it'.[1] Along with his copy after Watteau's *Gilles*, the copy after part of Uccello's *The Battle of San Romano* is a more faithful imitation of its source than Flandrin's other work of the period. As with his *Gilles*, this may have reflected Flandrin's desire to achieve State recognition[2] with an 'acceptable' apprentice-piece in a period when 'free' and imaginative interpretations of the Masters were still being discouraged by the École des Beaux-Arts and by the upholders of Academicism[3] (a situation which was largely reversed by the time of the celebrated *D'après les Maîtres* exhibition at the Galerie Bernheim-Jeune in 1910). Flandrin may also have been drawn to the strong sense of design and pattern in Uccello's painting – a taste consistent with Moreau's teachings, as well as with the Nabis' interest in the art of the Florentine 'Primitives'.

Private Collection, Grenoble

[1]Quoted in Flandrin and Roussier, p. 32.
[2]See *ibid.*, pp. 40–1.
[3]As noted by Walsh who points out that imaginative copies were much less likely to sell for this reason: *op.cit.*, pp. 196-7.

15   *Copy after Rubens, 'The Coronation of Maria de' Medici'**

(UNDATED) *c.* 1897

Copie d'après Rubens, 'le couronnement de Marie de' Médicis'

OIL ON CANVAS, 69 × 131 CMS.
PROV.: THE ARTIST, FROM WHOM BOUGHT BY DRUET, 1906;... TO PRESENT OWNER
EXH.: PARIS, GALERIE DRUET, 1906, PARIS, GALERIE BERNHEIM-JEUNE, 1910
LIT.: WERTH, *La Phalange*, MAY 1910; ZAVIE, *Le Feu*, NO.62 (JUNE 1910), P.269; FLANDRIN AND ROUSSIER, P.31; CF. *Copier Créer*, CAT. NO.150F.

This painting was included in Flandrin's first solo show at Eugène Druet's gallery in 1906, and in the celebrated *D'après les Maîtres* exhibition organized by the Galerie Bernheim-Jeune in 1910. It demonstrates a much more daring conception of copying than the works after Watteau and Uccello (cat. 14), in its free rendition of its source. Following Moreau's advice to seek inspiration from the masters rather than to slavishly imitate them, we see Flandrin, here, attempting to highlight the essential qualities of the original. Like his contemporary copy after Veronese's *Wedding Feast at Cana*,[1] the Rubens copy deliberately simplifies its source in order to draw attention to the hallmarks of Rubens's style: to the painting's sense of drama and movement, conveyed in Flandrin's vigorously abbreviated forms, and bold colour harmonies of red and blue which are proto-Fauve in character.[2]

Private Collection, Grenoble

[1]In *Copier Créer*, cat. no.150f.
[2]For comparisons with other avant-garde copies of the period, notably by Cézanne, Matisse, Derain and Picasso, see Roger Benjamin, 'Recovering Authors: the Modern Copy, Copy Exhibitions and Matisse', *Art History*, 12, no.2 (1989), pp. 176-201.

16   *My Portrait (Self-Portrait in the Studio)**
1897
Mon portrait (autoportrait à l'atelier)

OIL ON BOARD, 65 × 50 CMS.
INSCRIBED 'J.FLANDRIN' ON RECTO LOWER LEFT
PROV.: THE ARTIST; BY DESCENT TO THE PRESENT OWNER
EXH.: GRENOBLE, *Salon de Grenoble*, 1931
LIT.: FLANDRIN AND ROUSSIER, P.47; SPURLING, P.226.

An early achievement of Flandrin's new assurance with colour was a portrait of himself quite different in character from the rather intense series of self-images (drawings) dating from his apprenticeship with the Allier firm. It shows Flandrin in his studio at rue Campagne Première surrounded by paintings, presumably his own. The easy stance, slightly crossed legs, and appraising gaze turned towards a painting on the easel in front of him, convey an impression of confidence and cultivated insouciance, emphasized by his smartly turned-out, unworkmanlike appearance – a marked contrast with the later 'hands-on' 1924 self-portrait of Flandrin the artist (cat. 70), his open shirt and unbuttoned cuffs denoting the activity of creation. In the earlier work, the simplified forms, and bold tones suggest new directions in Flandrin's art, including his portraiture, in this period: towards the composition conceived as an expressive arrangement of shape and colour, corresponding with the latest tendencies in avant-garde art, notably those promoted by the Symbolist movement.

Private Collection, Grenoble

17 *Portrait of François Flandrin in Blue**
1897
Portrait bleu de François Flandrin

OIL ON CANVAS, 81 × 46 CMS.
INSCRIBED 'J.FLANDRIN' ON RECTO LOWER RIGHT
PROV.: THE ARTIST;... TO THE PRESENT OWNER
LIT.: FLANDRIN AND ROUSSIER, PP. 38, 43.

This portrait of Flandrin's younger brother is one of group of works produced between 1897 and 1899 (cat. 18, 19, 20, 22 and 24) which demonstrate a clear debt to Symbolist art, in particular to the art of the Nabis. François Flandrin, known also as 'Henri Franck', was an accomplished musician, and also keen to follow in Jules's footsteps and pursue a career as a professional artist – an ambition which earned him a degree of success in Parisian circles at the turn of the century. The portrait portrays François as a *fin-de-siècle* aesthete, with his languid pose, long locks and heavy-lidded stare from behind his *pince-nez*, exploiting characteristic themes and devices associated directly with Symbolism. The introspective, dream-like, almost melancholy quality of the image is emphasized by the unreal, stylized landscape against which the figure is placed, and by the use of blue, mauve and ochre tonalities, suggestive of sunset and twilight; of the borderline between reality and dream. Taking his inspiration from Gauguin, Émile Bernard and their younger Nabi disciples, Flandrin's portrait attempts to evoke the mood of his subject, as well as to suggest his inner life, through its expressive treatment of form and 'correspondences' between shape, pattern and colour. Close parallels may be noted with Maurice Denis's work of the early-to-mid 1890s, such as *The Sacred Wood* (1893: Musée national d'Art moderne, Paris), where the other-wordly subject-matter is expressed in the language of simplifying stylizations, flattened-out space, and fluid arabesques.

Private Collection, Paris

18   *Study of a Woman at her Toilet*
1897
Étude de femme, toilette

LITHOGRAPH, 36 × 51.5 CMS.
PROV.: THE ARTIST; BY DESCENT TO THE PRESENT OWNER
EXH.: PARIS, *Société Nationale des Beaux-Arts*, 1898
LIT.: BERNARD, *Le Reveil du Dauphiné*, JUNE 1898; DE FLANDRESY, *La Gravure, les graveurs Dauphinois* (GRENOBLE, 1901), P.237; FLANDRIN AND ROUSSIER, PP.36-7.

Together with its pendant *Study of a Woman, Knitting* (*Étude de femme, le tricot*, 1898[1]), this rear-view study of Marval was one of Flandrin's first works to receive critical acclaim following its exhibition at the 1898 *Société Nationale*. A reworking of a slightly earlier version (c.1897) depicting Marval at her toilet, intended for a tapestry project, the lithograph demonstrates Flandrin's debts to the traditions of sixteenth-century Venetian and seventeenth-century Dutch art, as well as to more recent ideas deriving from Symbolism. It also reveals Flandrin's considerable abilities as a printmaker, and his interest in experimenting with a variety of artistic media which was to be a consistent feature of his later work. In keeping with other portraits of the period, notably, the *Portrait of François Flandrin Reading* (cat. 24), Flandrin exploits Rembrandtesque *chiaroscuro* effects, and the particular characteristics of the lithographic medium to create a combination of intimacy and Symbolist inwardness. Marval's neck and back emerge sculpturally from the densely-hatched *sfumato* ground which, at the same time, conceals her face from view, suggesting a sense of mystery and introspection. The strongly-marked, fluid contours, more overt in cat. 24, attest the influence of Nabi art, as well as Toulouse-Lautrec's and Jules Chéret's posters, with their bold patterns and decorative forms, which Flandrin had begun to collect avidly around 1896.

Private Collection, Paris

[1]Titled *Étude à la lampe (dessin)* (no.1482) in the 1898 *Société Nationale* catalogue; in Flandrin and Roussier, p.36.

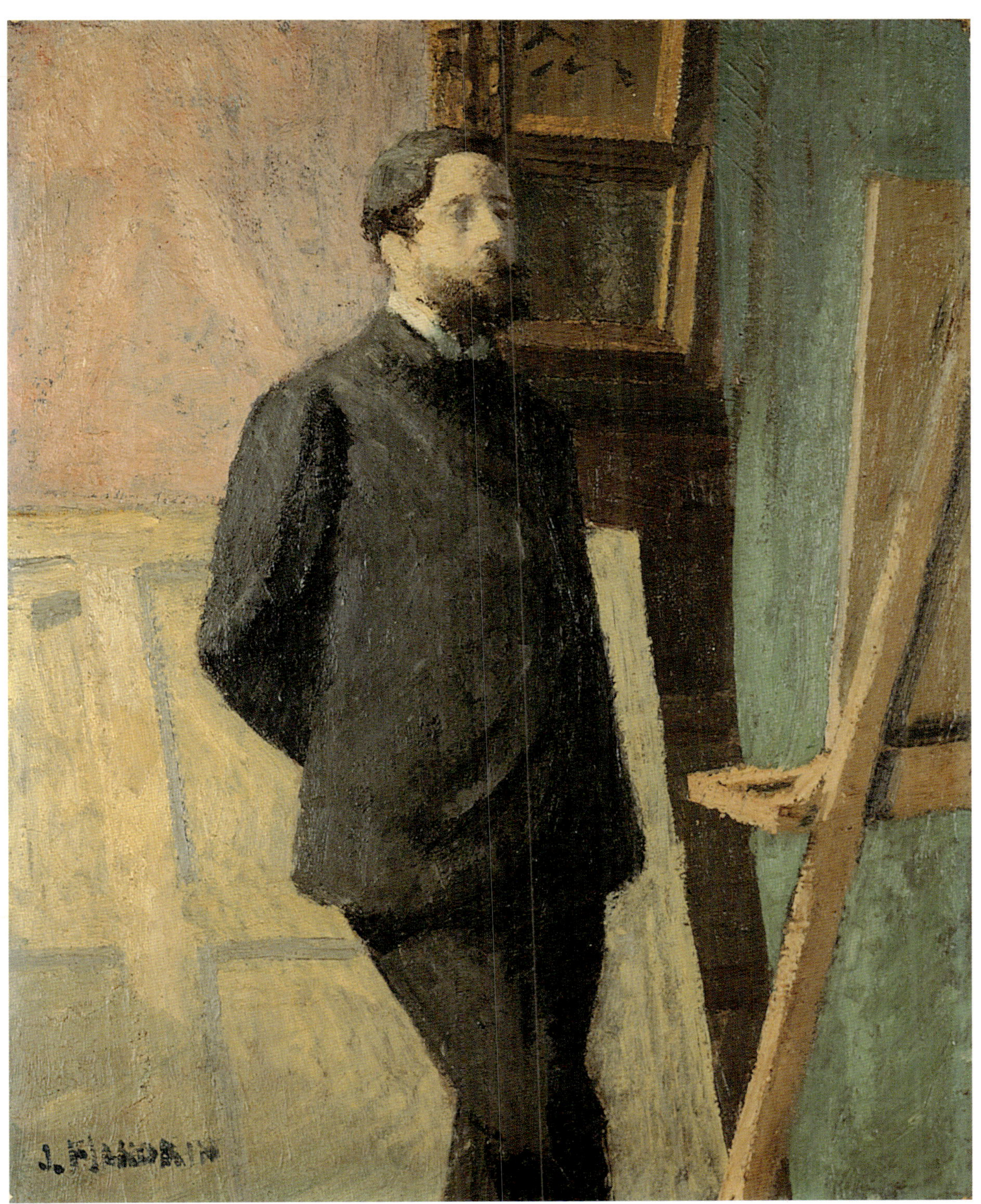

16 *My Portrait* (*Self-Portrait in the Studio*), 1897

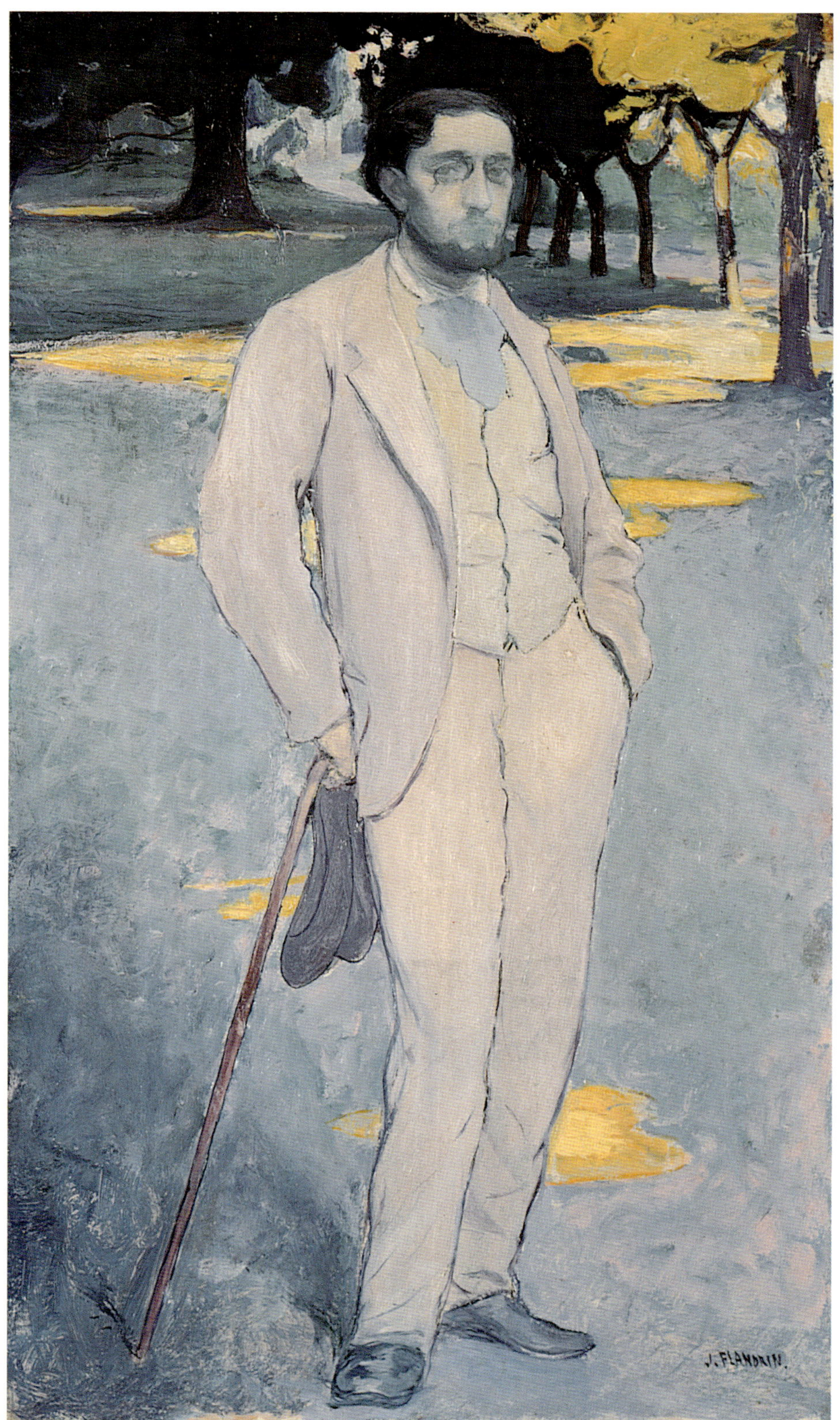

17 Portrait of François Flandrin in Blue, 1897

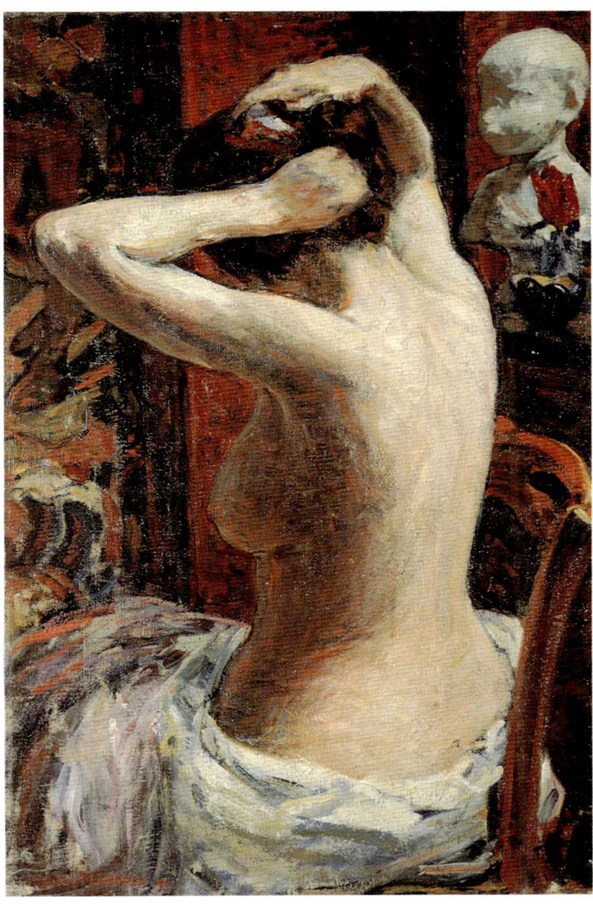

19 *The Toilet (Marval)*, 1897

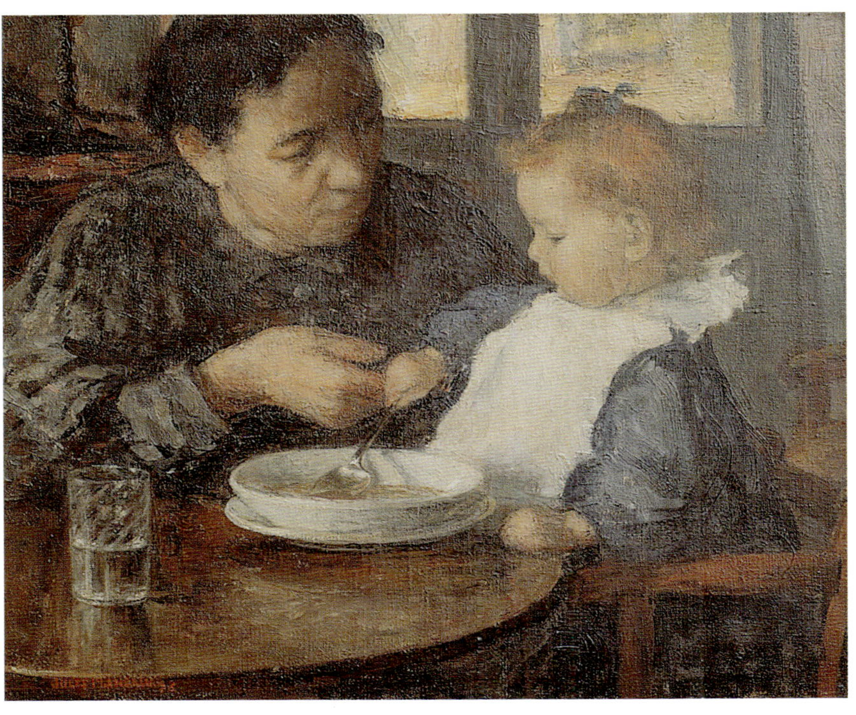

21 *Grandmother Giving Soup to her Grand-daughter*, 1898

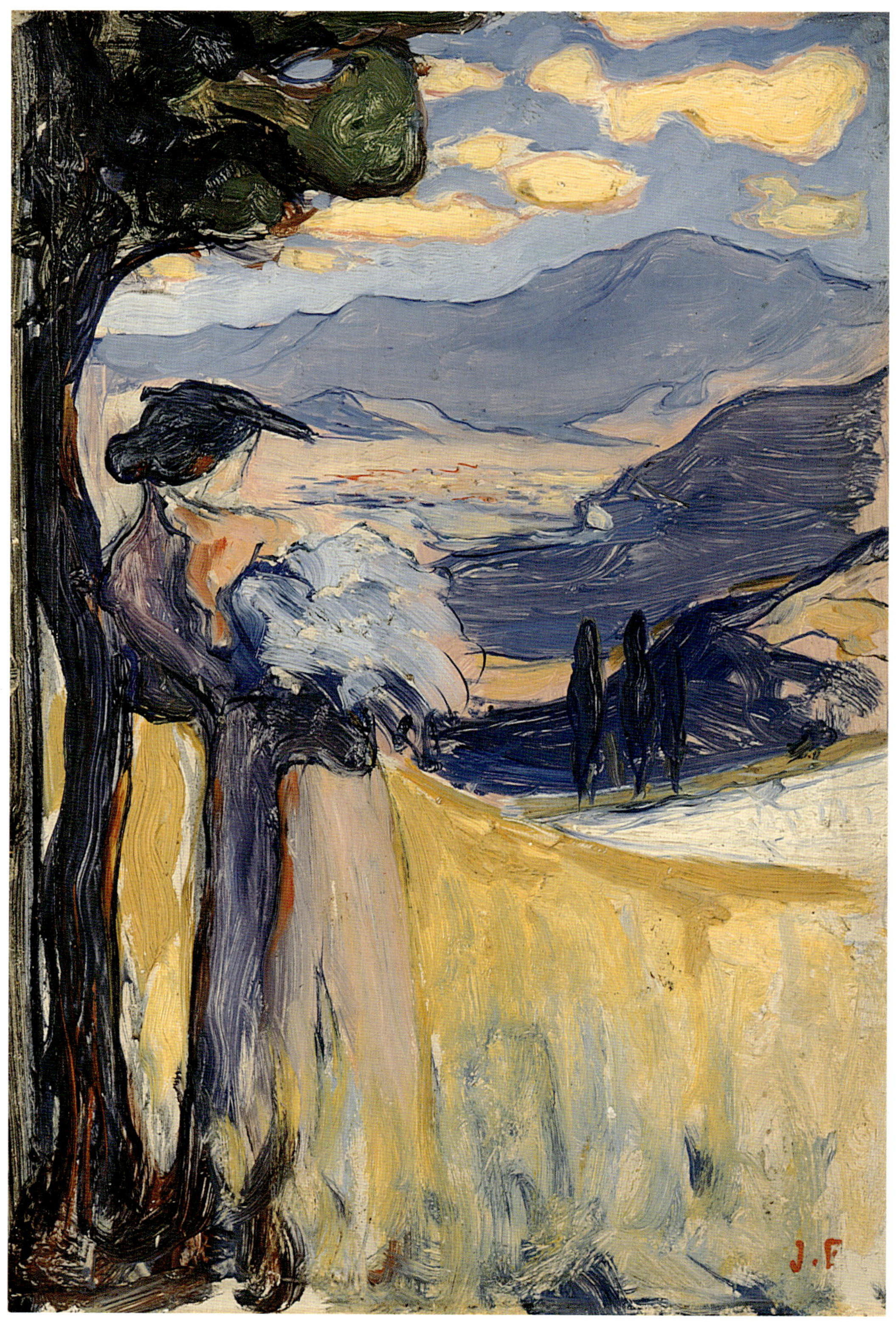

20 *Woman with a Bouquet in front of 'Le Moucherotte' (Marval)* (undated) *c.*1897

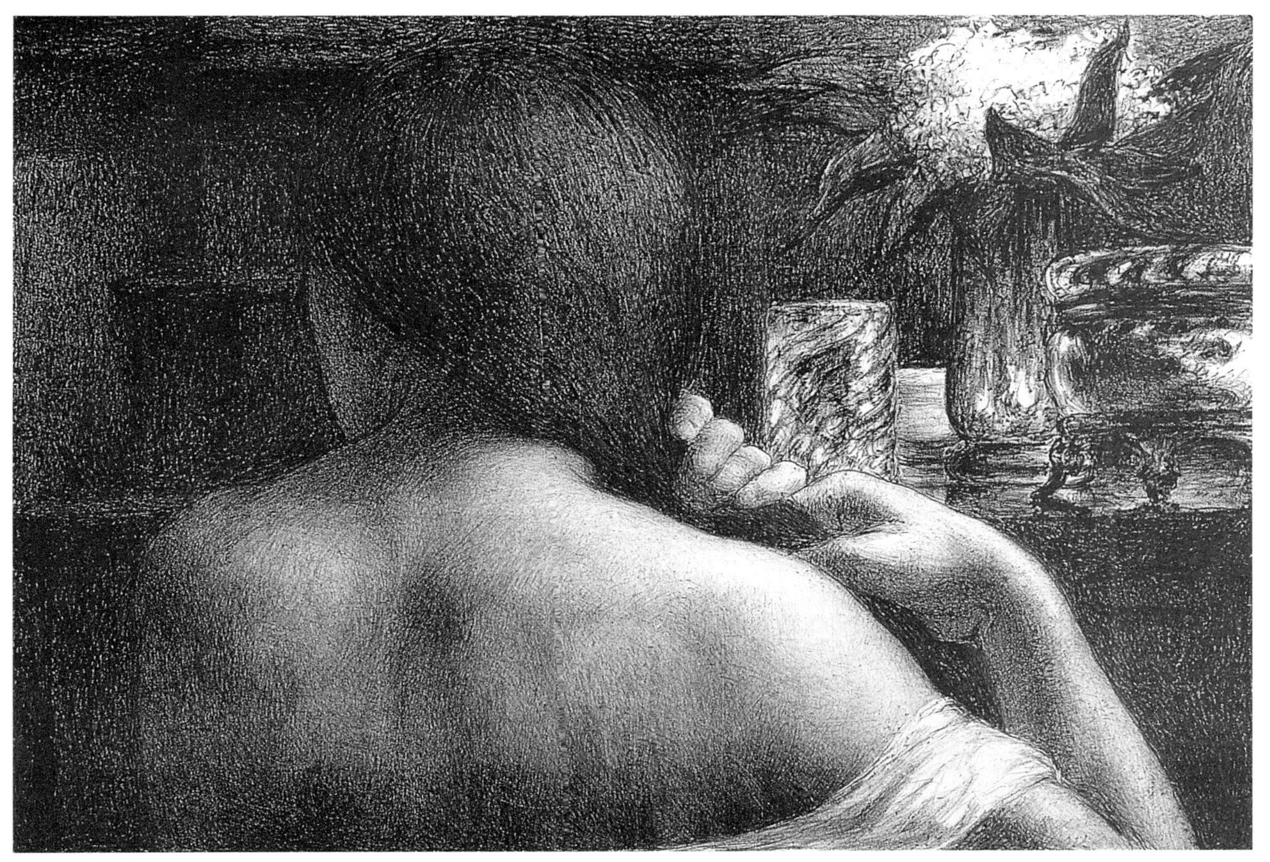

18 *Study of a Woman at her Toilet*, 1897

19   *The Toilet (Marval)**
1897
La Toilette (Marval)

OIL ON CANVAS, 92 × 60 CMS.
INSCRIBED 'JULES FLANDRIN' AND DATED '97' ON RECTO LOWER
LEFT
PROV.: THE ARTIST; BY DESCENT TO THE PRESENT OWNER
EXH.: PARIS, *Société Nationale des Beaux-Arts*, 1899
LIT.: BERNARD, *Le Reveil du Dauphiné*, JUNE 1899; FLANDRIN AND
ROUSSIER, P. 24.

The model for this nude, one of only two painted by Flandrin, was once again Marval, painted repeatedly by Flandrin throughout his Paris career (see cat. 20, 27, 32 and 53), and the main source of inspiration for his female subjects in general. Although the work appears in the catalogue for Flandrin's 1906 Druet exhibition,[1] it was never shown, replaced instead with his *Virgin and Child* (1903)[2], the Virgin's features bearing a close resemblance to those of Marval's. Flandrin's friend and compatriot Félix Jourdan, whom he met in 1904, suggested a reluctance on Flandrin's part to see the work exhibited owing to his self-imposed taboo on nude subject-matter. The painting is certainly unique of its kind in Flandrin's *oeuvre*; the other nude, also modelled on Marval, visible in a photograph (*c.*1895) of the interior of Flandrin's studio in rue Campagne Première, has now been lost. The surviving work evokes the powerful and magnetic presence of Marval in Flandrin's life, combining his interest in sixteenth-century Venetian art, Rubens and Ingres – in Marval's powerfully sculptural body, the rich colours and sensuous handling of paint – with the decorative intimacy of contemporary Nabi painting, notably Bonnard's.

Private Collection, Grenoble

[1]The title, *La Toilette* is deleted and replaced by *La Vierge et l'enfant*, written by hand: *Flandrin Archives*, Paris.
[2]Reproduced in Flandrin and Roussier, p. 75.

20   *Woman with a Bouquet in front of 'Le Moucherotte'*
      *(Marval)**
(UNDATED) *c.*1897
Femme au bouquet devant le Moucherotte

OIL ON BOARD, 33 × 22 CMS.
INSCRIBED WITH MONOGRAM 'J.F' ON RECTO LOWER RIGHT
PROV.: THE ARTIST; BY DESCENT TO THE PRESENT OWNER
LIT.: FLANDRIN AND ROUSSIER, P.53.

This fanciful image of Marval posed against the landscape around Corenc
is Flandrin's most consciously Nabi work of the period, with its decorative
deformations of shape and colour patterns. The vigorously worked foreground surface, however, represents the first appearance of the intense
colourism and free handling of paint which matured in *The Little School
Boy* (cat. 34).

Private Collection, Grenoble

21   *Grandmother Giving Soup to her Grand-daughter**
      1898
      Grand-mère donnant à manger à sa petite fille

OIL ON CANVAS, 46 × 55 CMS.
PROV.: THE ARTIST; BY DESCENT TO THE PRESENT OWNER
EXH.: PARIS, *Société Nationale des Beaux-Arts*, 1899[1]; GRENOBLE,
SOCIÉTÉ DES AMIS DES ARTS, 1899; GRENOBLE, MUSÉE DE
GRENOBLE, 1972
LIT.: BERNARD, *Le Reveil du Dauphiné*, JUNE 1899; BOYER D'AGEN, *Le
Figaro illustré*, JULY 1899

From 1896 onwards, Flandrin consistently appears to have treated his
portraits, particularly of close family and friends (many of which, like *The
Little School Boy*, were never shown during his lifetime) as vehicles for
experimenting with new ideas and techniques. The models for this
intimate domestic scene[1] were Flandrin's mother and his niece, Dédé – a
relatively rare example in his *oeuvre* of a mother and child group. The
figures have a greater sense of solidity and volume than some of the

portraits of this period, which, together with the impressionist *facture*, suggest a tentative Cézannian tendency, which was to become more marked in Flandrin's work around 1907–8.

Private Collection, Grenoble

¹Titled *Le Déjeuner* (no. 572, also illustrated) in the 1899 *Société Nationale* catalogue.

22 *The Climb up to Bert's**
(UNDATED) *c.*1898–1900
La Montée chez Bert

OIL ON BOARD, 27 × 21.5 CMS.
INSCRIBED WITH MONOGRAM 'J.F.' ON RECTO LOWER LEFT
PROV.: THE ARTIST; BY DESCENT TO THE PRESENT OWNER

Bert, a family friend, was the owner of the house at Corenc that was later the home of the Grenoblois artist, Henriette Deloras, Flandrin's future wife. Given eventually to his elder brother, Joseph Flandrin, this painting was never exhibited during Flandrin's lifetime. The hastily sketched forms, bright tonalities and improvised brushwork share many similarities with Flandrin's early landscape *pochades*. But this also shows an experimentalism which is marked by his contact with newer concerns, notably with Impressionism and Symbolism (see cat. 23, 25 and 26).

Private Collection, Grenoble

23   *The Alps at Twilight, Corenc**
1898
Les Alpes au crépuscule, Corenc

OIL ON CANVAS, 27 × 46 CMS.
INSCRIBED 'J. FLANDRIN' AND DATED '98' ON RECTO LOWER LEFT
PROV.: THE ARTIST; BY DESCENT TO THE PRESENT OWNER
EXH.: GRENOBLE, SOCIÉTÉ DES AMIS DES ARTS, 1899
LIT.: BERNARD, *Reveil du Dauphiné*, JUNE 1899; FLANDRIN AND
ROUSSIER, PP. 19, 43.

During his period spent in Moreau's *atelier* between 1895 and 1898, Flandrin was concentrating mainly on copies and portraits, engaged in a process of synthesizing lessons drawn from different traditions in the history of art with influences deriving from the contemporary avant-garde: from Impressionism, Symbolism and 'Intimism'. This small painting denotes an important stage in the development of his work, indicating a renewed interest in landscape subjects, as well as his discovery of light and colour, inspired by Matisse's example, the 'Ravier of sunshine', as Flandrin called him.[1] The crepuscular theme and compositional devices, such as the dark, indistinct forms in the foreground silhouetted against a luminous sky, still show a clear debt to Moreau. But the juxtaposition of daubs of bright, unmixed pigment, first demonstrated in *The Toilet* (cat. 19), to create sunset effects, derives directly from Matisse's brilliantly colourful Corsican landscapes of 1898, one of which (his *Vue de Corse*), Matisse gave to Flandrin and Marval on his return to Paris, probably during the late summer or early autumn of the same year.[2]

Private Collection, Paris

[1]A comparison with the pre-Impressionist artist, François-Auguste Ravier
(1814–1895), admired by Flandrin; cited in Flandrin and Roussier, p. 43.
[2]According to Georges Flandrin (Flandrin and Roussier, p. 61, n. 62); the work was eventually auctioned following Marval's death in 1932: *Vente des tableaux de la collection Jacqueline Marval*, Hôtel Drouot, Paris, 21 December 1932.

24 *Portrait of François Flandrin Reading*
1898
Portrait de François Flandrin lisant

Pencil, 44 × 31.5 cms.
Prov.: The artist; by descent to the present owner
Exh.: Grenoble, Société des amis des arts, 1899
Lit.: Flandrin and Roussier, p.39.

See cat. 18.

Private Collection, Paris

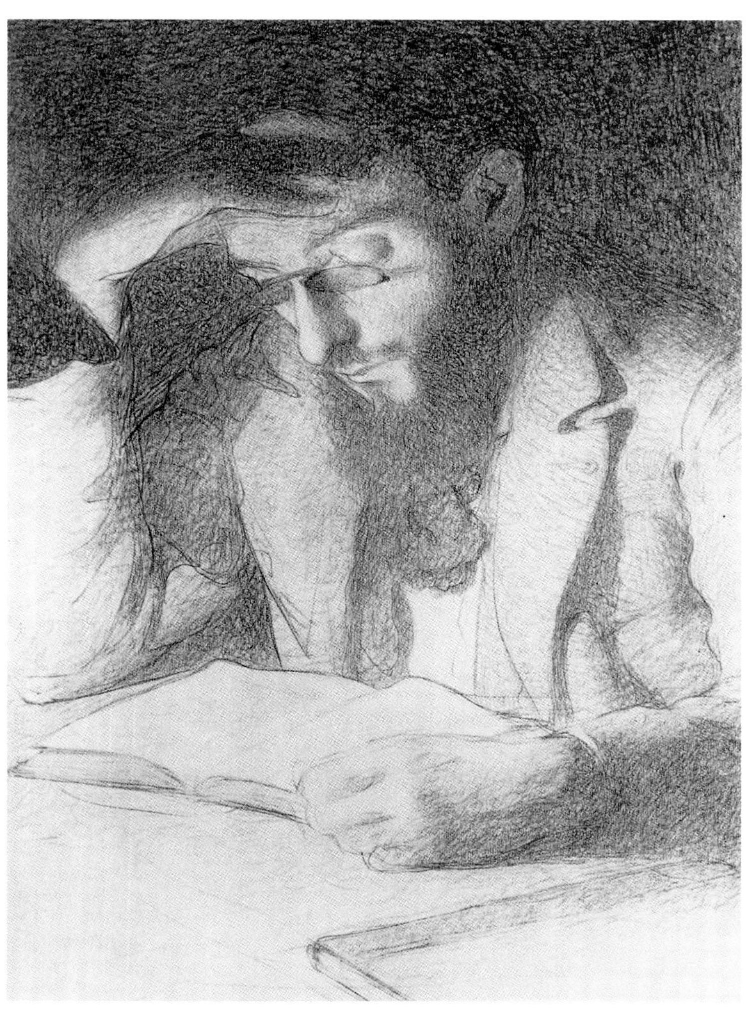

24 *Portrait of François Flandrin Reading*, 1898

2

The Eclectic Eye

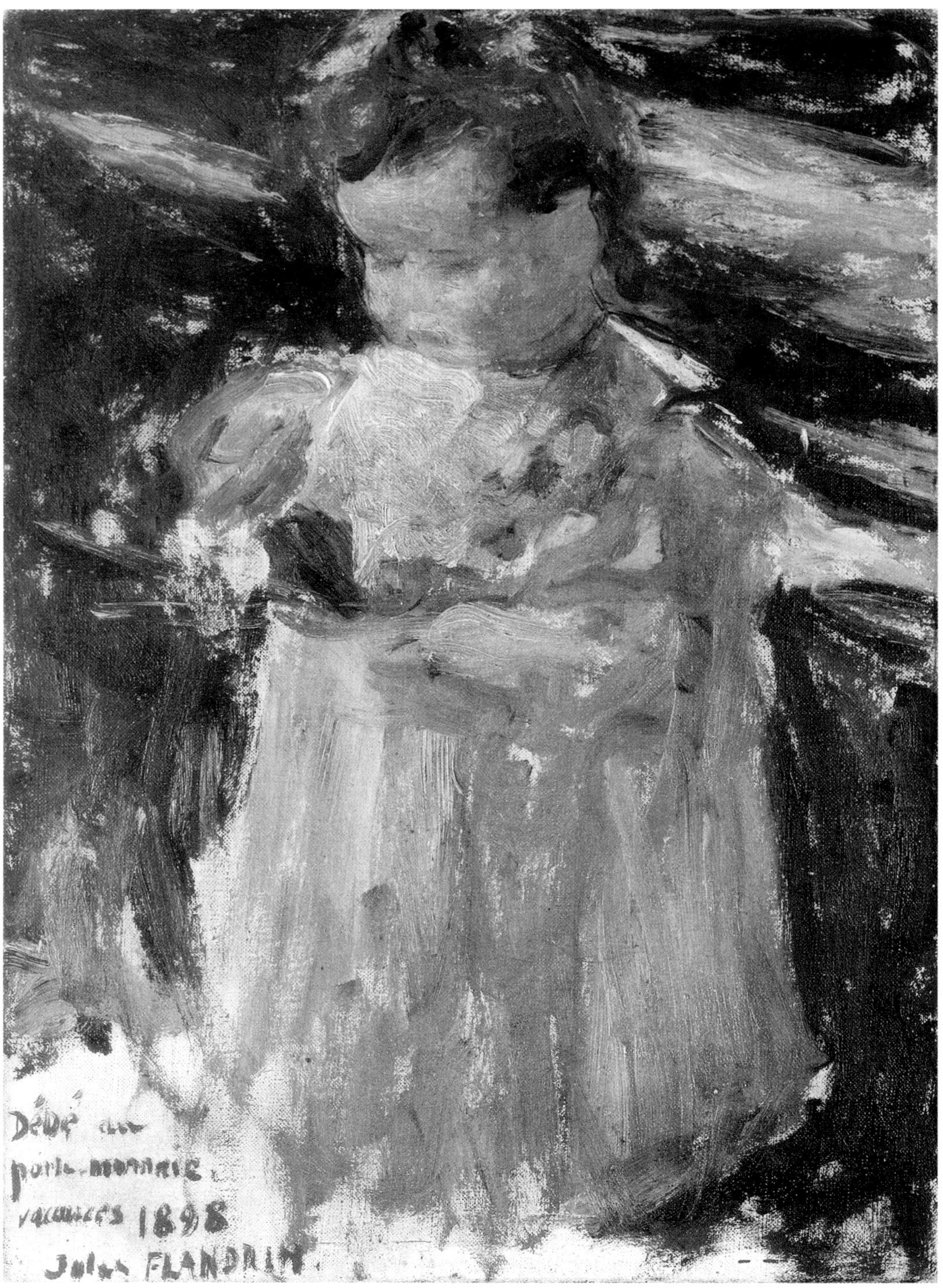

25 *Dédé with a Purse*, 1898

25 *Dédé with a Purse*

1898
Dédé au porte-monnaie

OIL ON CANVAS, 46 × 33 CMS.
INSCRIBED 'DÉDÉ AU PORTE-MONNAIE, VACANCES 1898 JULES
FLANDRIN' ON RECTO LOWER LEFT
PROV.: THE ARTIST; BY DESCENT TO THE PRESENT OWNER
LIT.: FLANDRIN AND ROUSSIER, PP.43, 50.

By the late 1890s, Flandrin was beginning to experiment with a considerable range of different artistic sources, guided by Moreau's example, and stimulated by a rich exchange of ideas with fellow Moreau students, Matisse and Marquet. The series of portraits of infants and children, which included those of his niece, Dédé, painted between 1898–1899 (see cat. 26), show him exploring colour in a way which anticipates the vigorous and 'Fauve'-style works of the early 1900s. In both paintings included here, Flandrin employs a loose Impressionist *facture*; the pervasive influence of Bonnard is also apparent in the intimism of the compositions, in which the figure of Dédé becomes almost an extension of her surroundings. But the cursorily treated forms and ragged, improvised brushwork share close similarities with Matisse's and Marquet's work of the period, in which colour is increasingly deployed for expressive rather than for representational purposes.

Private Collection, Paris

26 *Dédé in Blue**

1898
Dédé en bleu

OIL ON CANVAS, 46 × 33 CMS.
INSCRIBED 'JULES FLANDRIN' AND DATED '98' ON RECTO LOWER
LEFT
PROV.: THE ARTIST; BY DESCENT TO THE PRESENT OWNER
LIT.: FLANDRIN AND ROUSSIER, PP. 43, 51.

See cat. 25.

Private Collection, Grenoble

27 *Head of a Woman (Portrait of Jacqueline Marval)**
1899
Tête de femme (portrait de Jacqueline Marval)

Oil on canvas, 46 × 37.8 cms.
Inscribed 'J.FLANDRIN' and dated '99' on recto lower left
Prov.: The artist;... Collection Laforge, Grenoble, from
which bought by the present owner
Exh.: Paris, *Société Nationale des Beaux-Arts*, 1899
Lit.: Bernard, *Le Reveil du Dauphiné*, June 1899

This superb portrait of Marval, exhibited at the 1899 *Société Nationale*, reveals, perhaps more than any other of Flandrin's paintings, the influence of Moreau. What is initially striking about the image is its modernity: its Nabi-inspired patterning effects, and quasi abstract use of bright colour to denote flowers in the top right-hand corner. But the suggestive, almost evanescent treatment of Marval's face combined with the subject's downcast eyes, evokes an introspection and cerebrality redolent of Symbolist depictions of women such as those by Moreau, and the Belgians, Jean Delville and Fernand Khnopff.

Private Collection, Paris

28 *Horsewoman and Horseman, boulevard Montparnasse**
1899 (redated 1900)
Amazone et cavalier, boulevard Montparnasse

Oil on canvas, 41 × 33 cms.
Inscribed 'J.FLANDRIN' and dated '1900' on recto lower right
Prov.: The artist; by descent to the present owner
Exh.: Grenoble, *Salon de Grenoble*, 1931
Lit.: Flandrin and Roussier, p.59.

From his earliest days in Paris, Flandrin had been making sketches and drawings of Paris street life and scenes, observed *sur le vif*, possibly inspired by Manet and Degas but, probably more directly, by Toulouse-Lautrec in whose graphic art and paintings he took a keen interest from 1895 onwards. This important transitional work depicting an 'Amazone', a young horsewoman and her companion on a fashionable Paris boulevard, attests Flandrin's interest in the world of the late nineteenth-century 'beau monde'. Rider subjects begin to appear frequently in Flandrin's art in this period, perhaps related to his preoccupation with Impressionism, possibly connected with his constant yearning for the Dauphiné, and for the pleasures of nature and his youth. Although Flandrin, here, presents a scene from contemporary life, the riders have a still, stylized quality in sharp contrast to the lively and animated subject-matter of his drawings. The simplified figures and street buildings, and decorative colour effects again suggest the influence of Nabi art; although the use of colour for structural purposes as well as for luminosity looks ahead to the concerns of the next decade.

Private Collection, Grenoble

29 *The Nativity**

1900
Nativité

OIL ON CANVAS, 37.5 × 55 CMS.
PROV.: THE ARTIST; BY DESCENT TO THE PRESENT OWNER

Painted as a present for his small niece Dédé, and her brother Philippe (Lizambert), the two children are represented in the left hand side of the painting along with the angel, which bears Marval's features. Flandrin's interest in religious art at this period was inspired mainly by the example of Maurice Denis, whose house and private chapel (the *Prieuré*) at St. Germain-en-Laye he visited in 1904. The form of the figures, particularly of the angel, anticipates that of the 1905 decorative project (see cat. 36). The language of conscious naïveté and simplification is indebted to Denis's art (even though Flandrin's enthusiasm for Denis was eventually to wane), and possibly also to Puvis de Chavannes whose influence becomes marked for a time in Flandrin's work of the early 1900s.

Private Collection, Paris

30 *Dédé Writing**
(UNDATED) *c.*1900–2
Dédé écrivant

OIL ON CANVAS, 21 × 22 CMS.
PROV.: THE ARTIST; BY DESCENT TO THE PRESENT OWNER

See cat. 25.

Private Collection, Paris

31 *Henri Franck (François Flandrin) with a Viola*
1901
Henri Franck (François Flandrin) à l'alto

INDIAN INK AND WASH, 23.5 × 30 CMS.
INSCRIBED WITH MONOGRAM 'J.F' AND DATED '1901' ON RECTO
LOWER LEFT
PROV.: THE ARTIST; BY DESCENT TO THE PRESENT OWNER
LIT.: FLANDRIN AND ROUSSIER, P. 73.

During his years in Paris, Flandrin developed a passion for music, nurtured, in part, by his brother's talents as a musician. This lively pen and wash study, which captures François at a thoughtful moment, is characteristic of Flandrin's graphic style of the period. Like Marquet's and Camoin's contemporary graphic art, Flandrin increasingly eliminates all extraneous details from his work, concentrating instead on his subjects' essential features, conveyed by summary outlines, a few pen strokes and streaks of wash.

Private Collection, Paris

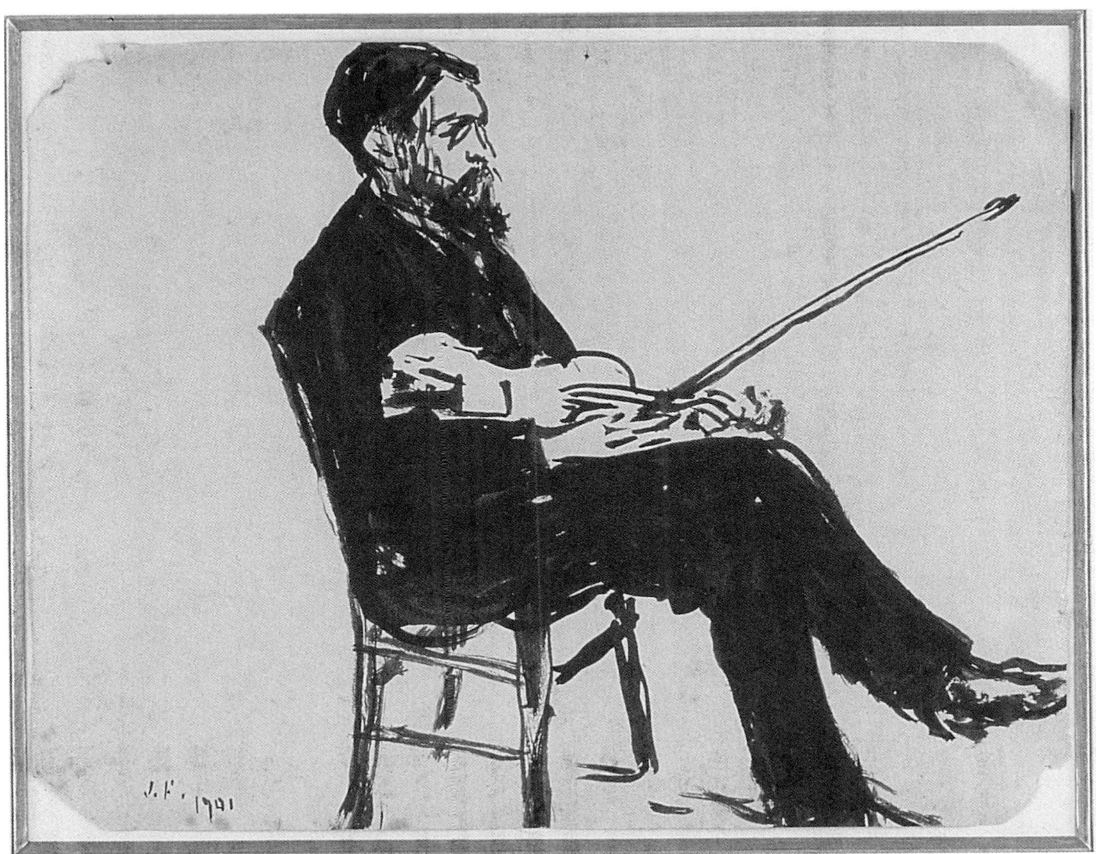

31 *Henri Franck (François Flandrin) with a Viola*, 1901

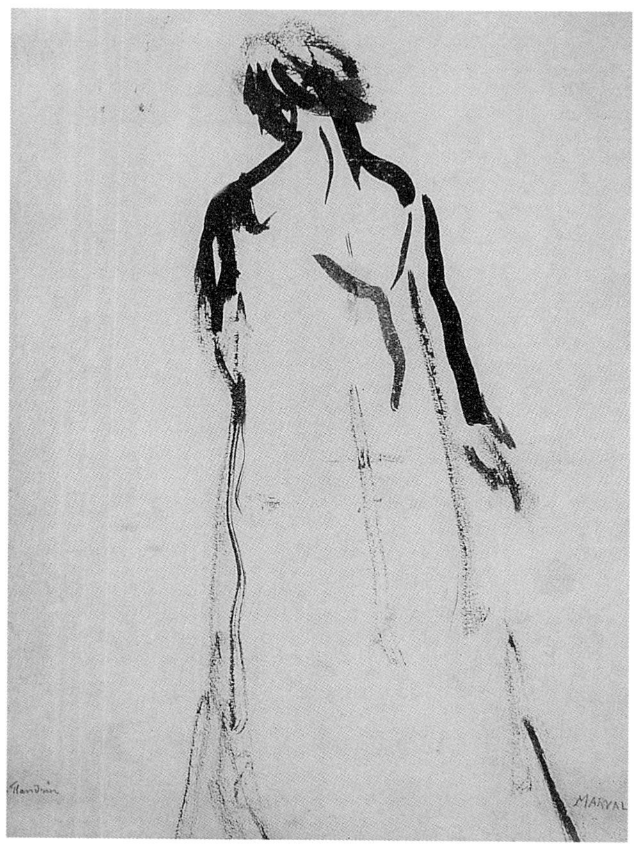

32 *Marval* (undated), *c*.1902

32   *Marval*

(UNDATED) *c*.1902
Marval

INDIAN INK, 20.5 × 29 CMS.
INSCRIBED 'FLANDRIN' ON RECTO LOWER LEFT AND 'MARVAL'
LOWER RIGHT
PROV.: THE ARTIST; BY DESCENT TO THE PRESENT OWNER

This bold and fluid sketch of Marval's silhouette is again reminiscent of
Bonnard's graphic work of the mid-to-late 1890s. But the calligraphic simplicity of execution is also close to Marquet's and Camoin's drawings in
this period, anticipating the almost abstract style of *The Smoker* (cat. 52).

Private Collection, Paris

33 *The Seine at Sunrise**

1902

La Seine au soleil levant

OIL ON CANVAS, 34 × 46 CMS.
INSCRIBED 'J.FLANDRIN' AND DATED '1902' ON RECTO LOWER
LEFT
PROV.: THE ARTIST; BY DESCENT TO THE PRESENT OWNER
LIT.: FLANDRIN AND ROUSSIER P.66.

The years 1899 to 1903, marked a period of intense collaboration between Flandrin, Marval, Matisse and Marquet. Around 1900, Matisse and Marquet became regular visitors to Flandrin's apartment at rue Campagne Première where they set up their easels in the same studio alongside Flandrin and Marval.[1] The fruits of these close partnerships were a series of paintings of familiar Paris landmarks – the Seine, Notre-Dame, the Luxembourg Gardens, the suburbs at Arcueil – in which all four artists were, to an extent, revisiting the subject-matter of Impressionism, but with a new emphasis on 'making something permanent', as Matisse put it, out of their sensations. Flandrin's *The Seine at Sunrise* is one of several views he painted between 1899 and 1900, depicting the Seine and the Luxembourg Gardens observed at different times of day. It shows him exploring the structural, expressive as well as atmospheric properties of light and colour in a manner similar to Matisse's and Marquet's series of views of Notre-Dame and the Quai St. Michel, observed from their studio windows at 19 Quai St. Michel. The stippled expanse of water and sky reflecting a luminous sunrise, blurred outlines of the river banks, and tiny barge puffing down-river, are still markedly Impressionist in character. But the intense, yellow hues which dominate the composition, together with the decorative treatment of the sky, suggest the more recent influence of Symbolism. It is possible that, via Matisse, Flandrin was also experimenting with the latest ideas on colour promoted by Paul Signac in his influential *From Eugène Delacroix to Neo-Impressionism*, published in 1899. The separate dabs and strokes of paint comprising the water in the foreground indicate an attempt to simplify his palette to achieve a greater intensity of tone as recommended by Signac, although it amounts to little more than a flirtation with Neo-Impressionist method. More important for Flandrin, as for Matisse and Marquet at this period, is the use of colour as an almost independently expressive element in its own right – a concern which was to predominate in the works of the following years.

Private Collection, Paris

[1]See Flandrin and Roussier, p.101.

34 *The Little School Boy (Philippe Lizambert)**

(UNDATED) *c*.1904

Le Petit écolier (Philippe Lizambert)

OIL ON BOARD, 27.5 × 23.5 CMS.
INSCRIBED 'J.FLANDRIN' ON RECTO LOWER LEFT, WITH
MONOGRAM 'J.F.' LOWER RIGHT
PROV.: THE ARTIST; BY DESCENT TO THE PRESENT OWNER
LIT.: FLANDRIN AND ROUSSIER, P. 74.

The earlier of a pair of works featuring the Lizambert children painted at Corenc between 1903–4 (see cat. 35), this small, striking portrait of Flandrin's nephew Philippe, is one of his boldest and most daring works of the period. Although Flandrin was not included amongst the notorious group dubbed the 'Fauves' by Louis Vauxcelles at the 1905 *Salon d'Automne*, in both spirit and style, the work shares many similarities with Matisse's and Derain's so-called Fauvist portraits of 1904–6. With its dramatically abbreviated forms, free use of colour and almost brutally worked surface, the work achieves a 'fauve'-like intensity of character and expression, also emphasized by the intimate size of the painting itself. The vigorous handling of paint scrawled and daubed onto the canvas gives an impression of great speed of execution, highlighted by the patches of canvas barely concealed by the roughly applied patchwork of strokes. Unlike the much less-robustly painted *The Masquerade* (*c*.1904: cat. 35), it is this almost aggressive assertion of texture and technique, as the critic Camille Mauclair noted, that bears the particular hallmark of Fauvism.

Private Collection, Paris

22 *The Climb up to Bert's*
(undated) *c.*1898–1900

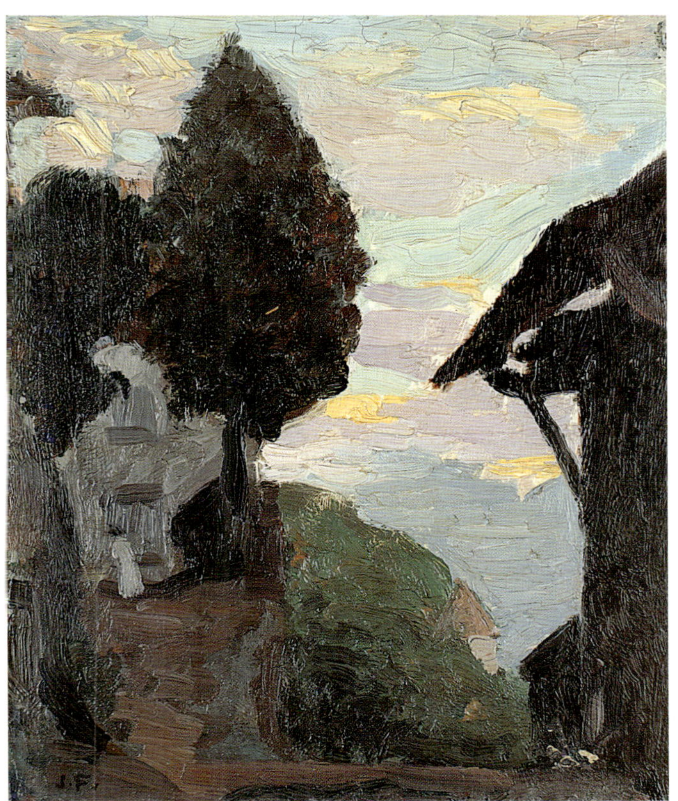

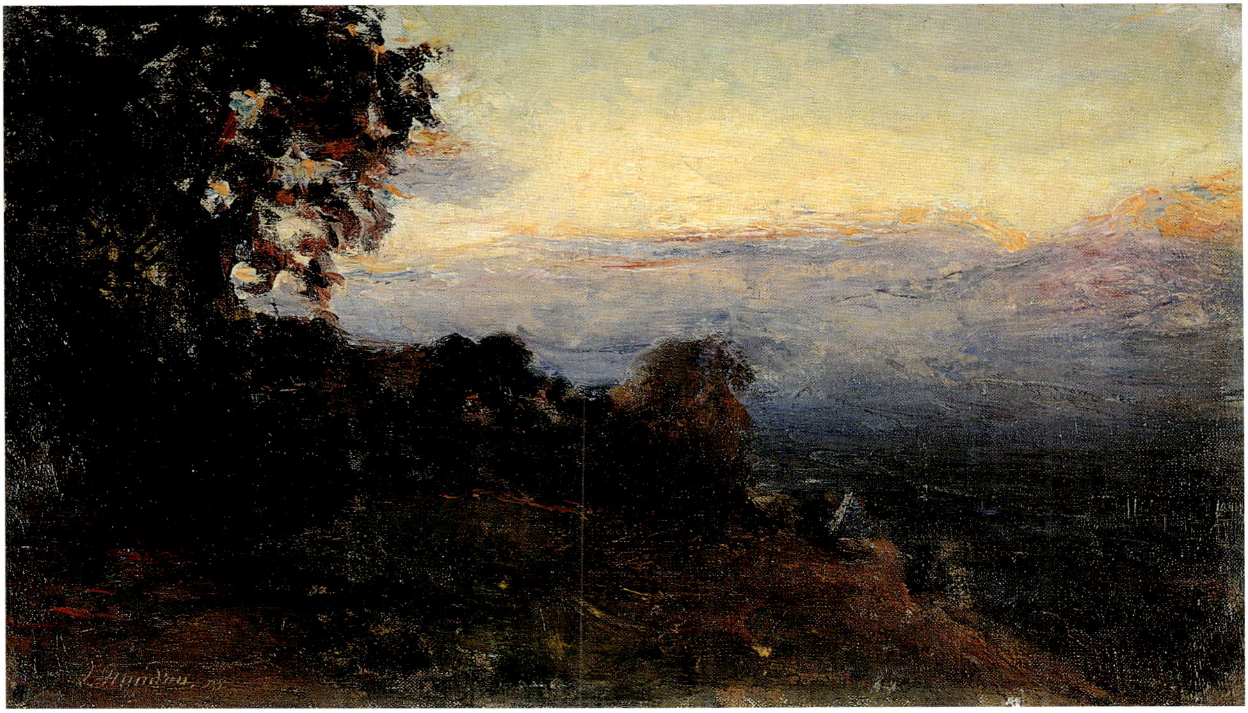

23 *The Alps at Twilight, Corenc, 1898*

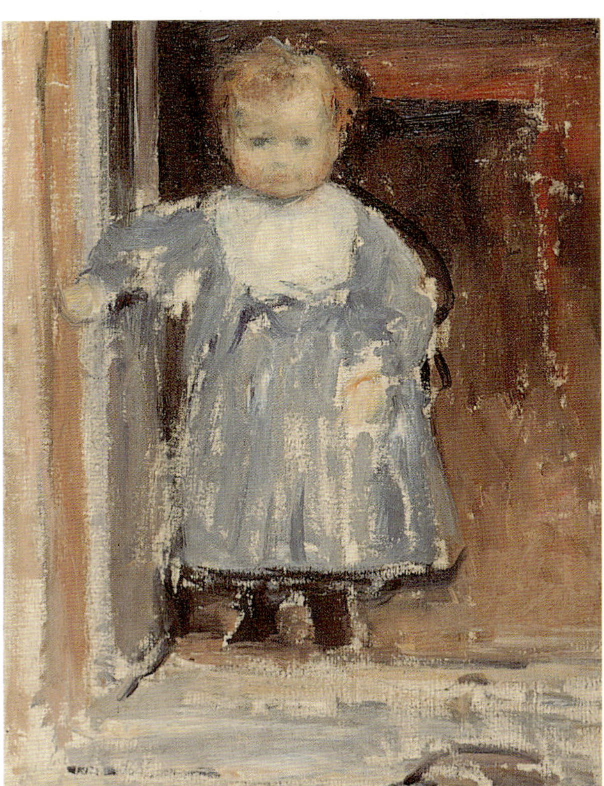

26 *Dédé in Blue, 1898*

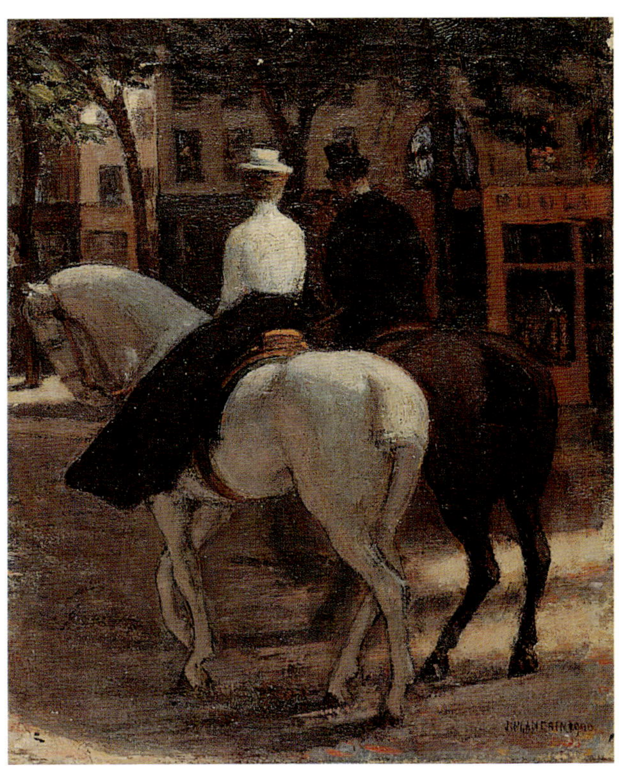

28 *Horsewoman and Horseman, boulevard Montparnasse, 1899 (redated 1900)*

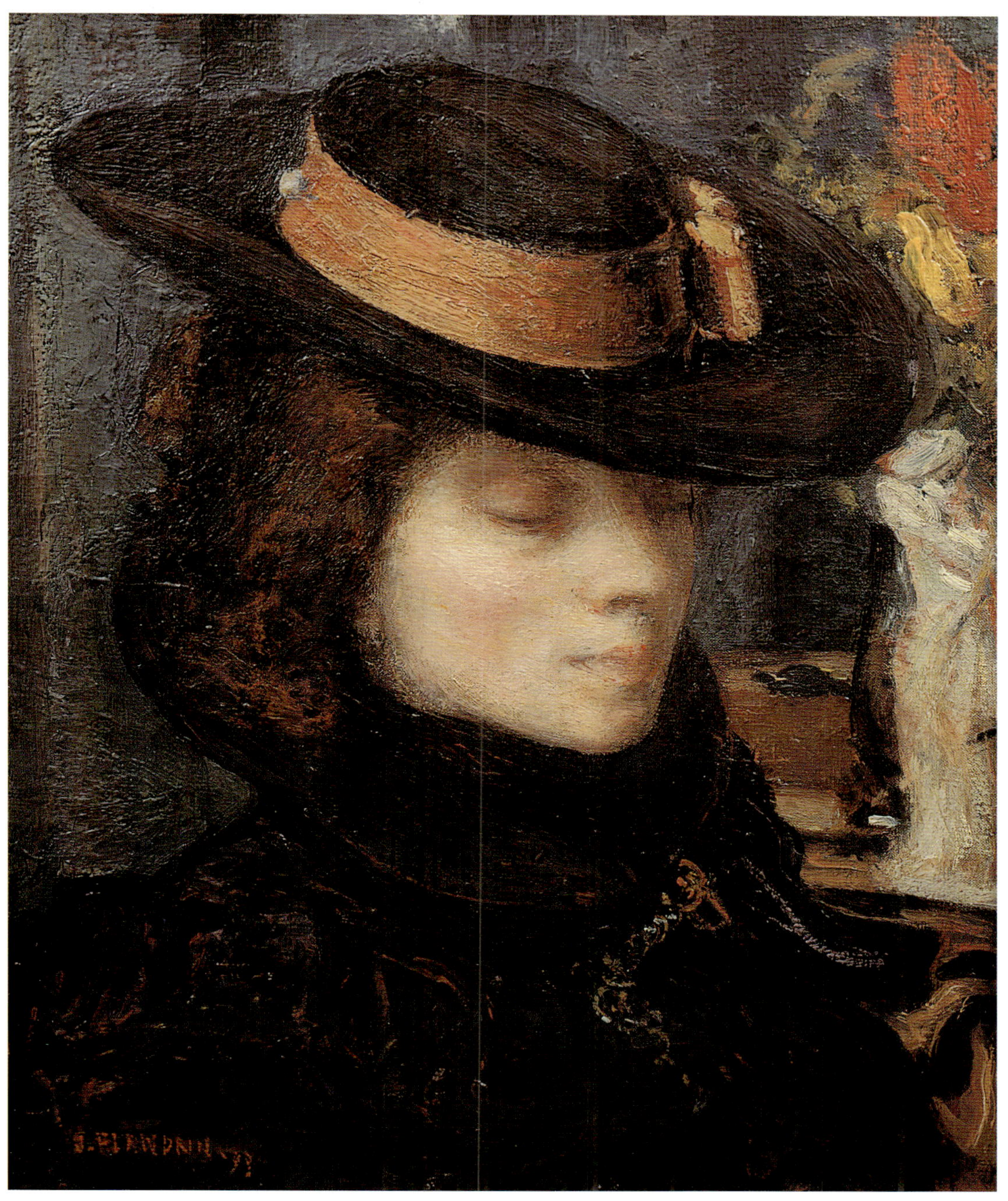

27 *Head of a Woman (Portrait of Jacqueline Marval)*, 1899

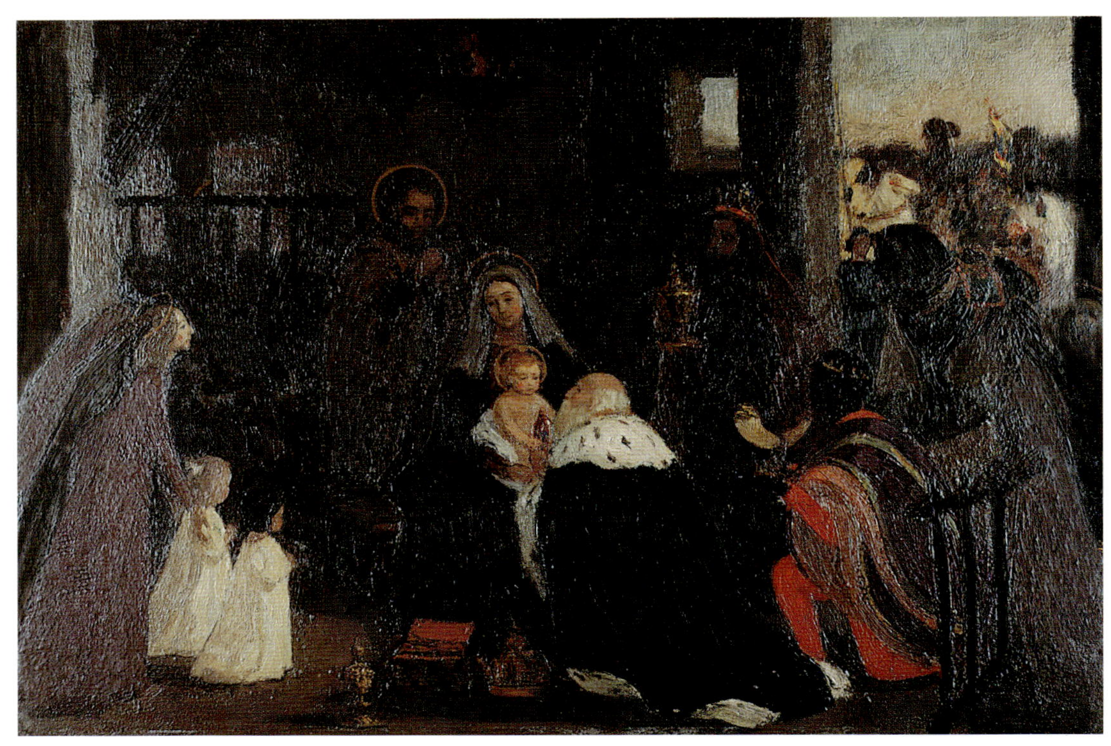

29 *The Nativity*, 1900

30 *Dédé Writing* (undated) *c.*1900–2

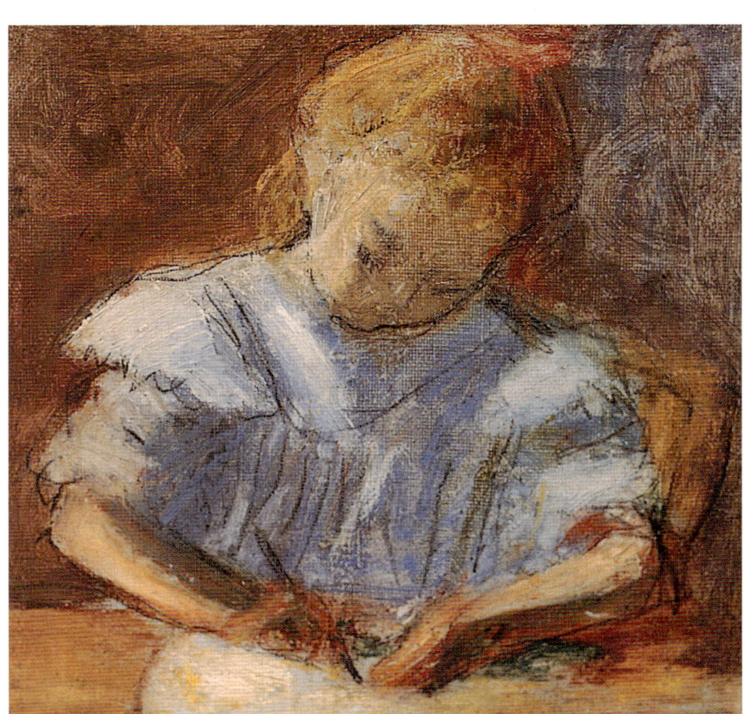

35 *The Masquerade**
    (Portraits of Children, the Lizamberts at Corenc)
    (UNDATED) *c.*1904
    La Mascarade
    (portraits d'enfants, les petits Lizamberts à Corenc)

OIL ON CANVAS, 130 × 193 CMS.
PROV.: THE ARTIST; BY DESCENT TO THE PRESENT OWNER
EXH.: PARIS, *Société Nationale des Beaux-Arts*, 1904
LIT.: BERNARD, *Le République de l'Isère*, MAY 1904; GRÉGOIRE, *Les Alpes pittoresques*, MAY-JUNE 1904; FLANDRIN AND ROUSSIER, P.76.

See cat. 34.

Private Collection, Paris

36 *An Angel, Homage to Handel**
    (Study for a Painting for the Church at Corenc)
    1905
    Un Ange, hommage à Haendel [sic]
    (étude pour le tableau de l'église de Corenc)

OIL ON CANVAS, 61 × 46 CMS.
INSCRIBED 'J.FLANDRIN.' ON RECTO LOWER RIGHT
PROV.: THE ARTIST; BY DESCENT TO THE PRESENT OWNER
LIT.: FLANDRIN AND ROUSSIER, PP. 81, 85.

This was the study version for the large-scale decorative panel painted for the church at Corenc, first exhibited at the *Société Nationale* in 1905, entitled *Un Ange, hommage à Haendel (panneau décoratif [sic])* (no. 499). It gives an accurate impression of the finished work which is still extant, and now *in situ* in Corenc. The idea for a series of decorative works on religious themes which had begun to interest Flandrin around 1900, was inspired by Denis, whose influence is clearly detectable in several of Flandrin's religious works at this time (see cat. 29), and again shows his voracious and eclectic experimentation with a variety of contemporary avant-garde tendencies. The schematic and stylized form of the angel derives from Denis's example: from his cult of a consciously naïve style to symbolize the idea of an unquestioning religious faith. But Flandrin's work also has a robustness of colour and treatment which allies it directly to his 'fauve' experiments of the same period. This helps to explain why it was roundly criticized (albeit by conservatives), when exhibited in its finished version at the *Société Nationale*. Even Matisse is alleged to have been shocked when shown the work by Flandrin, commenting 'this time, you've gone too far'.[1]

Private Collection, Paris

[1]Cited in Flandrin and Roussier, p. 81.

37 *An Audience in Venice**

1906
Une audience à Venise

OIL ON CANVAS, 59 × 80 CMS.
INSCRIBED 'J.FLANDRIN' AND DATED '1906' ON RECTO LOWER LEFT
PROV.: BOUGHT FROM THE ARTIST BY DRUET, 1906;... BT. KAPFERER COLLECTION, FROM WHICH BT. BY PRESENT OWNER
EXH.: PARIS, GALERIE DRUET, 1906
LIT.: FLANDRIN AND ROUSSIER, P.86.

Also known as *The Reception at the Palace of the Doges* (*Réception au Palais des Doges*), this was the later of two paintings of the same title, the first of which was exhibited at the Paris *Société Nationale* (no. 513) in 1903. The work is a free copy of Francesco Guardi's *The Audience given by the Doge of Venice in the Sala del Collegio of the Doge's Palace, Venice* (*L'Udienza del Doge agli ambasciatori nella sala del Collegio*) in the Louvre. The first version is now lost, but a black-and-white photograph reproduced in the 1903 *Société Nationale* catalogue shows it to be a much more faithful imitation of its source than the 1906 painting. In the later work, the scene has been dramatically simplified, including the architectural details and figures, which merge into an almost solid mass of indeterminate forms in the middle ground. Leaving aside the picturesque realism of the original, as with his earlier copies of Rubens (cat. 15) and Veronese, Flandrin has reinterpreted the scene mainly in terms of light and of vibrant colours, in accord with his main interests in this period.

Private Collection, Paris

38 *Corenc, Garden in Sunlight**

1907
Corenc, jardin au soleil

OIL ON CANVAS, 50 × 72.5 CMS.
INSCRIBED 'J.FLANDRIN' AND DATED '1907' ON RECTO LOWER
LEFT
PROV.: THE ARTIST; BY DESCENT TO THE PRESENT OWNER
EXH.: GRENOBLE, GALERIE FÉNOGLIO, 1908

One of a series of evocations of Corenc and family life painted from the
early 1900s onwards, it is likely that this was the work exhibited at the
Fénoglio Gallery in Grenoble, entitled *Coin du jardin ensoleillé* (no.19).[1] The
idyllic theme and subject-matter, developed in the series of paintings of
young girls produced between 1907 and 1913 (see cat. 39, 40, 42 and 60)
harks back to the works of the pre-Paris period. But the treatment is also
visibly affected by recent Flandrin's artistic interests and experiments,
deriving from his continuing collaboration with Marval, and from his
period spent working closely with Matisse and Marquet. The vibrant
colours and vigorous handling of paint are still Fauvist in character, as is
the consistent concern with the simplification of forms to their essentials,
stripped of unnecessary details. However, Flandrin's increasing focus on
scenes of an idyllic, sunlit world, full of pastoral pleasures, was to distance
him eventually from his association with Matisse's circle, and to ally him
more directly with the younger generation of 'intimistes' such as Henri
Lebasque and Henri Laprade.

Private Collection, Paris

[1]*Exposition de tableaux de M. Jules Flandrin* (Catalogue), 1908: *Flandrin Archives*, Paris.

39   *On the Sofa in the Salon (Corenc)**
(UNDATED) *c*.1908
Sur le canapé du salon (Corenc)

OIL ON BOARD, 24 × 24 CMS.
PROV.: THE ARTIST; BY DESCENT TO THE PRESENT OWNER
LIT.: FLANDRIN AND ROUSSIER, P.100.

See cat. 38.

Private Collection, Paris

40   *Seated Girl, Corenc (Pierrette)**
1908
Fillette assise, Corenc (Pierrette)

OIL ON CANVAS, 33 × 55 CMS.
INSCRIBED 'JULES FLANDRIN' AND DATED '1908' ON RECTO LOWER
RIGHT
PROV.: THE ARTIST; BY DESCENT TO THE PRESENT OWNER

See cat. 38.

Private Collection, Paris

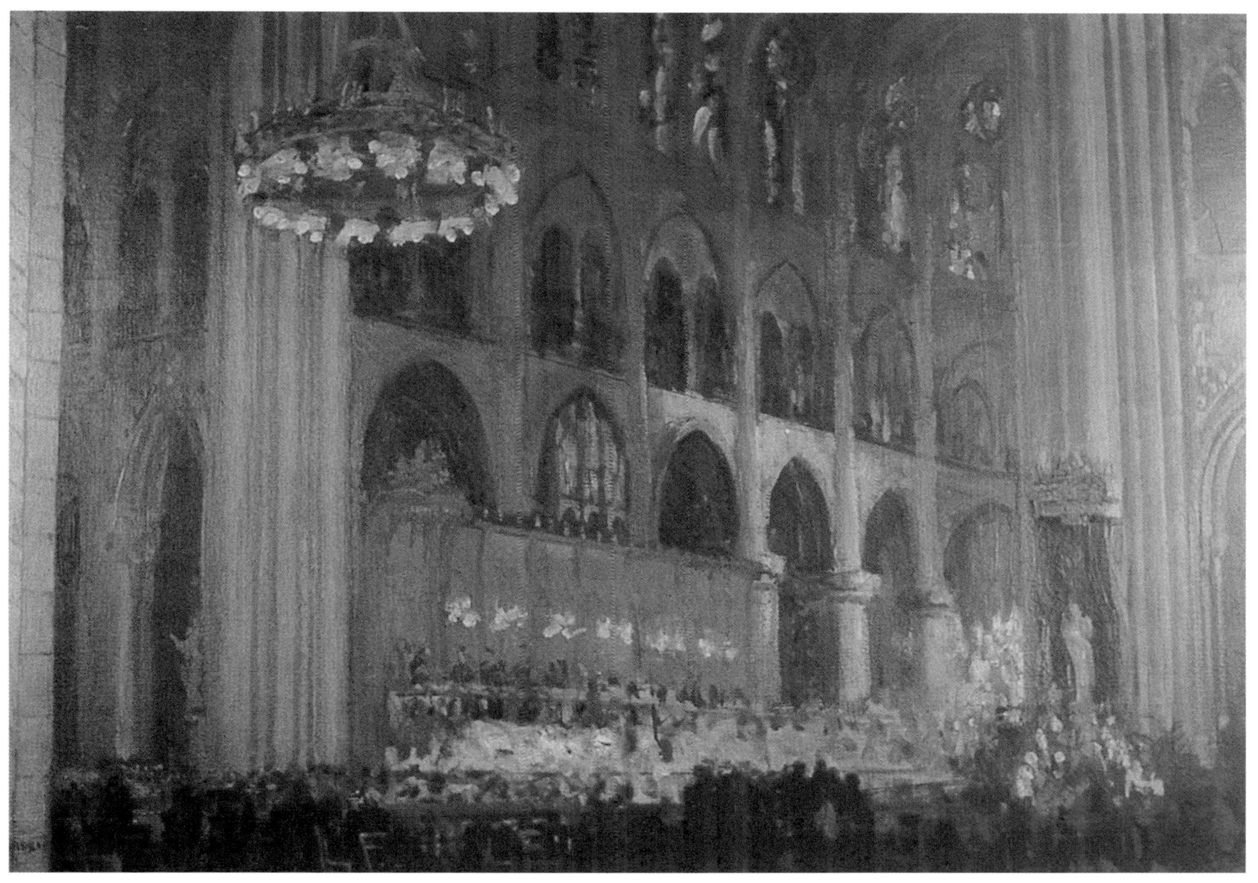

41 *Interior of the Cathedral of Notre-Dame, Paris*, 1908

41 *Interior of the Cathedral of Notre-Dame, Paris*
1908
Intérieur de la cathédrale Notre-Dame de Paris

OIL ON CANVAS, 88 × 114 CMS.
PROV.: THE ARTIST; BY DESCENT TO THE PRESENT OWNER

Following the example of Matisse and Marquet, Flandrin turned repeatedly to the subject of Notre-Dame from around this date until he left Paris in 1931. As with his *Audience in Venice* (cat. 37), the cathedral's majestic interior permits Flandrin to explore both atmospheric light effects and the massive forms of the architecture, emphasized in his boldly simplifying visual language.

Private Collection, Paris

42   *Two Young Girls, September Afternoon**
1908 (REDATED 1913)
Les Deux fillettes, après-midi de septembre

OIL ON CANVAS, 85 × 115 CMS.
INSCRIBED 'J.FLANDRIN.' AND DATED '1913' ON RECTO LOWER
LEFT
PROV.: THE ARTIST; BY DESCENT TO THE PRESENT OWNER
EXH.: GRENOBLE, GALERIE FÉNOGLIO, 1908
LIT.: FLANDRIN AND ROUSSIER, P.119.

Although part of the landscape and portrait series painted between 1907 and 1913 (see cat. 38 and 44), this striking composition also indicates an important new direction in Flandrin's work which culminated in 1913 in the monumental *Young Horsemen by a Spring* (cat. 62). The pastoral theme of young girls seated in a sun-filled Dauphinois landscape is a recurrent one in Flandrin's art, and is increasingly symbolic of his attitude to nature itself as the embodiment of harmony and plenitude. The still, rather contemplative poses of the figures, however, with their simplified, doll-like forms, suggest an unreal, dream-like atmosphere which evokes his Symbolist portraits of the *fin de siècle* (see cat. 17, 18 and 24). These tendencies may derive in part from Flandrin's adoption of the camera from 1907 to capture and 'fix' his subjects in a characteristic pose. They would be developed in the magisterial *Wooded gorge* (*Le Vallon boisé*, 1910), exhibited at the 1910 *Société Nationale*, thematically and compositionally very similar to the 1908 painting, but which now emphasizes the decorative and monumentalizing inclination of the earlier work.

Private Collection, Grenoble

43   *The Glass Fruit Bowl**
1910
La Coupe de verre

OIL ON BOARD, 33 × 44.5 CMS.
INSCRIBED 'J.FLANDRIN.' ON RECTO LOWER LEFT
PROV.: THE ARTIST; BY DESCENT TO THE PRESENT OWNER
EXH.: PARIS, GALERIE DRUET, 1910
LIT.: SALMON, *Paris-Journal*, FEBRUARY 1910; FERRY, *L'Eclair*,
FEBRUARY 1910; BAL, *The New York Herald*, FEBRUARY 1910;
FLANDRIN AND ROUSSIER, P. 114.

Still-life subjects become an important preoccupation for Flandrin around 1907, and were to remain so throughout his career. The abundant character of Flandrin's still-lifes, which depict mainly fruit and flowers, is again evocative of a bounteous and arcadian nature, linking them to his landscape and portrait subjects of the period. The style of this picture, with its clarity of colour and vigorously simplified shapes, suggests the influence of Cézanne, who was the subject of a large retrospective at the Grand Palais in 1907, following his death in 1906. In the spirit of Cézanne, Flandrin composes his painting from a few simple elements, tilting the angle of the perspective to emphasize the 'close-up' view. While the freedom of handling and colour modulations are reminiscent of Cézanne's early works, in his other still-lifes at this time the forms are modelled with an attention to structure and solidity resembling Cézanne's later style. To some degree, Flandrin's concerns, here, may be seen as part of a pervasive Cézannian tendency, identified as a marked feature of the younger generation avant-garde by critics such as Charles Morice, André Salmon and Guillaume Apollinaire. Salmon frequently links Flandrin with Cézanne between 1910 and 1913: an association which Flandrin himself exploits, although the characteristic bias of his work remains eclectic.

Private Collection, Paris

44 *Juliette in a Hat*

1910
Juliette au chapeau

OIL ON CANVAS, 65 × 50 CMS.
INSCRIBED 'J.FLANDRIN' AND DATED '1910' ON RECTO LOWER
LEFT PROV.: THE ARTIST; BY DESCENT TO THE PRESENT OWNER
EXH.: GRENOBLE, *Salon de Grenoble*, 1931
LIT.: FLANDRIN AND ROUSSIER, P. 98.

See cat. 38.

Private Collection, Grenoble

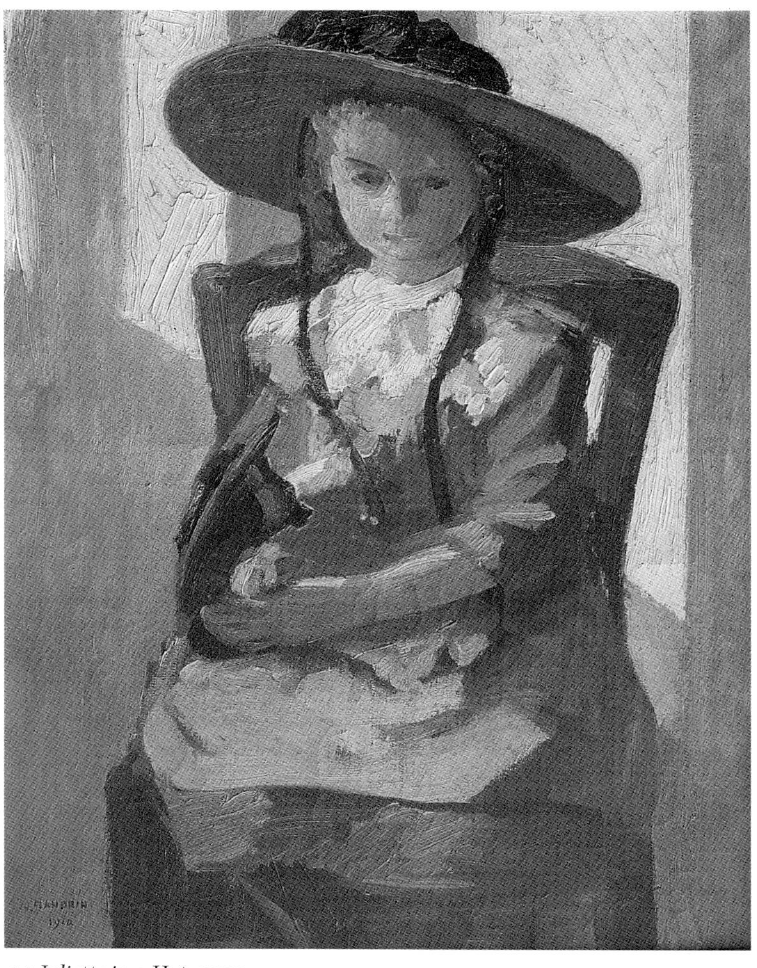

44 *Juliette in a Hat*, 1910

3

Expressing Modernity

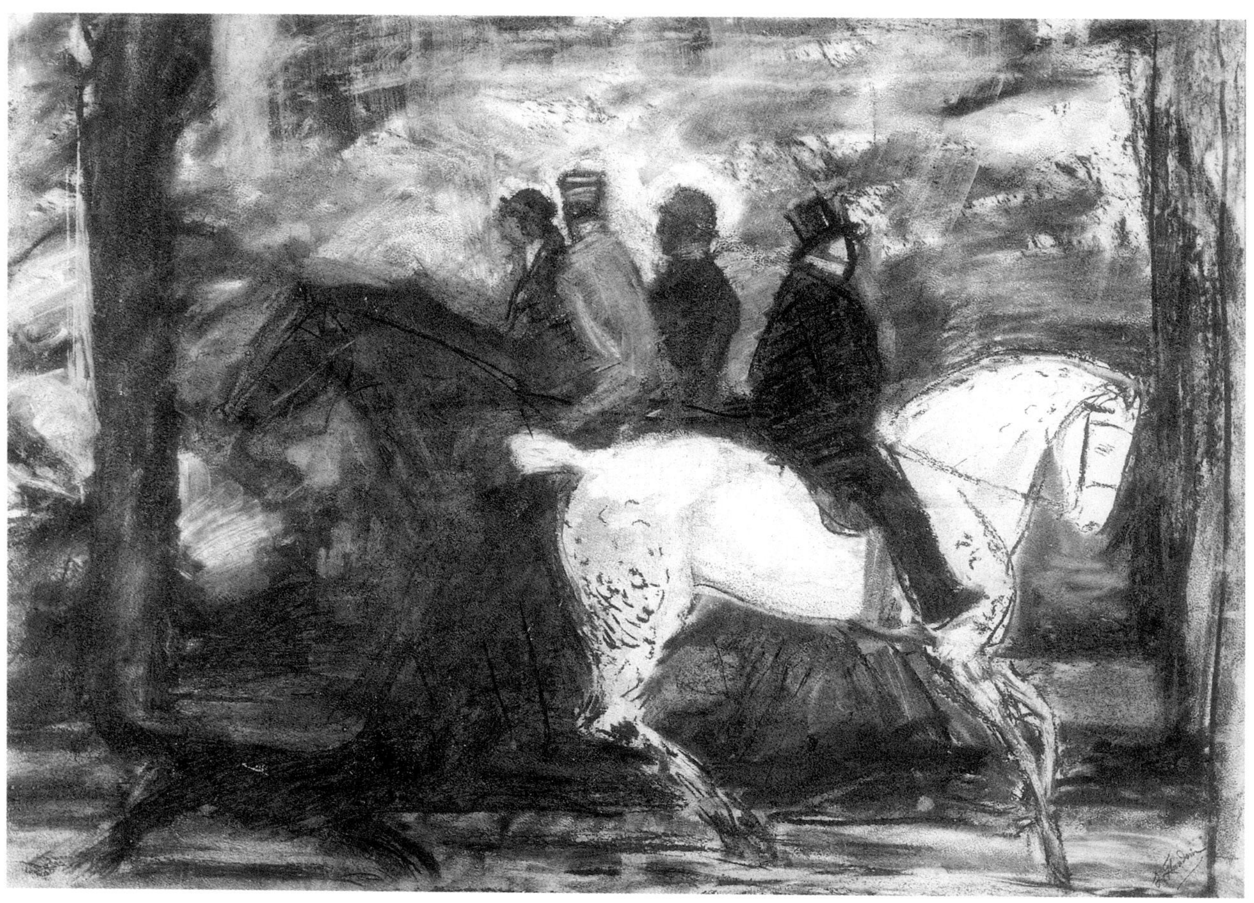

45 *The White Horse*, 1909

45 *The White Horse*

1909
Le Cheval blanc

Charcoal, 55 × 76 cms.
Prov.: The artist; by descent to the present owner
Exh.: Grenoble, Société des amis des arts, 1909; Grenoble,
Salon de Grenoble, 1931
Lit.: Flandrin and Roussier, p.95.

Flandrin's graphic work continued to provide an important outlet for his experimentation with a variety of different artistic techniques and media in the years immediately prior to 1914. This charcoal sketch, shown in Grenoble in 1931 with the title *Esquisse au cheval blanc* (no. 28), was perhaps a preparatory study for the large-scale series of *Riders in the Bois* (see cat. 47), produced between 1909 and 1912. The subject-matter and style is indebted to the work of Constantin Guys (see cat. 48), an illustrator of fashionable Second Empire Paris, and admired by Charles Baudelaire as a consummate artist of the 'heroism of modern life'. The sketchy forms of horses and riders evoke those of Guys, demonstrating Flandrin's continuing interest in the animation of modern forms: an interest which runs parallel to the decorative, monumentalizing tendencies of many of his contemporary paintings.

Private Collection, Paris

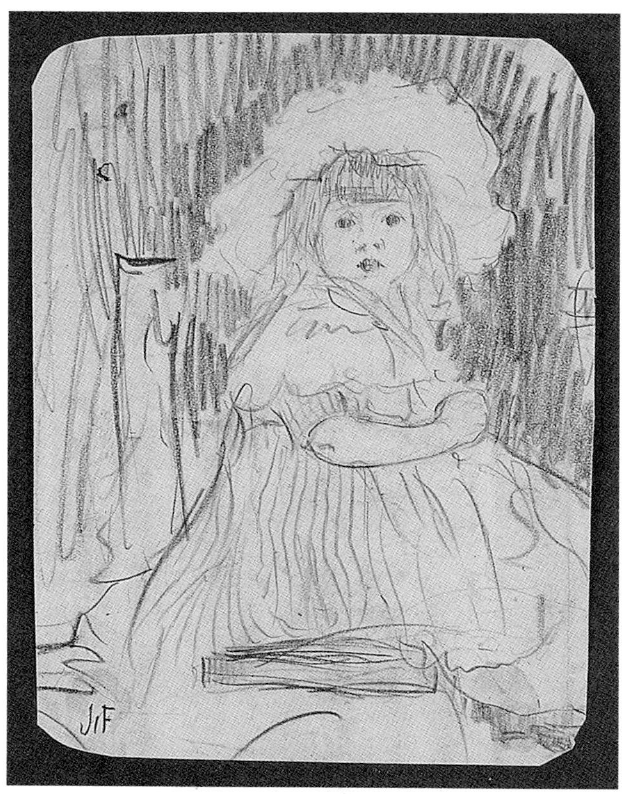

46 Girl in Blue Crayon (undated), *c.*1910

46   *Girl in Blue Crayon*

(UNDATED) *c.*1910
Fillette au crayon bleu

COLOURED PENCIL, 12.5 × 9.8 CMS.
INSCRIBED WITH MONOGRAM 'J.F' ON RECTO LOWER LEFT
PROV.: THE ARTIST; BY DESCENT TO THE PRESENT OWNER

See cat. 31.

Private Collection, Paris

47 *Riders in the Bois**

(UNDATED) *c.*1909–11
Les Cavaliers au bois

OIL ON CANVAS, 73 × 160 CMS.
INSCRIBED 'JULES FLANDRIN.' ON RECTO LOWER RIGHT
PROV.: THE ARTIST;...TO PRESENT OWNER
EXH.: PARIS, *Indépendants*, 1911; GRENOBLE, MUSÉE DE GRENOBLE,
1972
LIT.: ALEXANDRE, *Le Figaro*, APRIL 1911; SALMON, *Paris-Journal*,
APRIL 1911; BERNARD, *Le Petit Dauphinois*, JUNE 1911;
APOLLINAIRE (1911), IN *Chroniques d'art* (PARIS, 1960), P. 169;
FLANDRIN AND ROUSSIER, P. 143.

This was the smaller of the two paintings with the same title, painted
between 1909 and 1911. The work depicts a fashionable scene in the Bois
de Boulogne in the spirit of Guys's illustrations, which seem to have been
one of Flandrin's preoccupations of the period. In contrast to the much
more overtly stylized and decorative *Riders*, dated 1910,[1] the treatment of
the figures and handling is markedly Impressionist in character, recalling
Manet and Degas, and harking back to Flandrin's experiments of the early
1900s. The abbreviated, roughly-painted forms and brilliant colours,
however, once again relate to more recent concerns, showing Flandrin's
continuing filiation with the Fauvist manner (see cat. 49), and especially
with Marquet, with whom he had remained on close terms.

Private Collection, Paris

[1] In Flandrin and Roussier, p. 117.

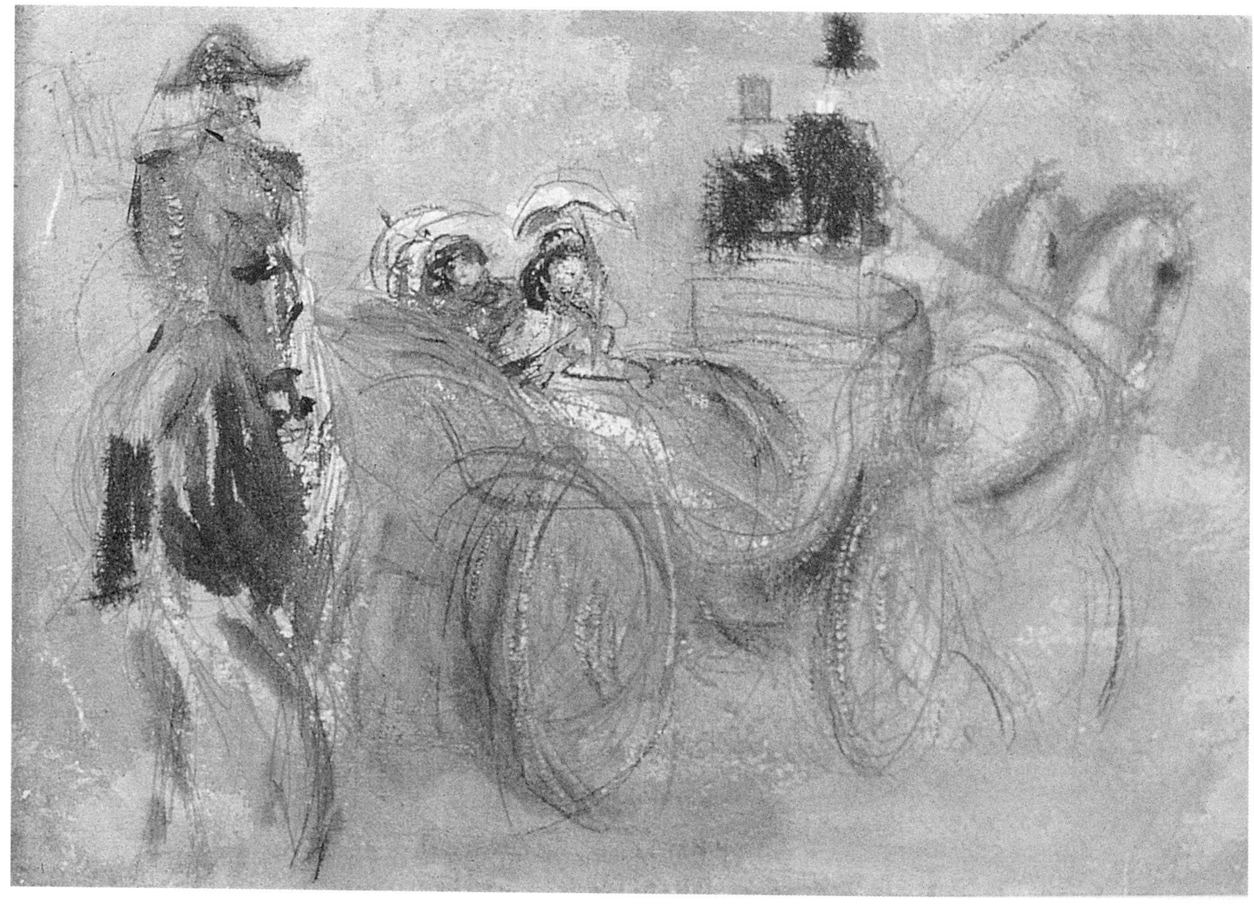

48 *Carriage and Horses in the Bois (Pastiche in the manner of Constantin Guys)* (undated), before 1914

48   *Carriage and Horses in the Bois
     (Pastiche in the manner of Constantin Guys)*
     (UNDATED) BEFORE 1914
     Attelage au bois (pastiche à la manière de Constantin Guys)

INDIAN INK AND WASH, 24 × 33 CMS.
PROV.: THE ARTIST; BY DESCENT TO THE PRESENT OWNER

See cat. 45.

Private Collection, Paris

49 *'The Firebird'**

1909
'L'Oiseau de feu'

OIL ON PANEL, 44.5 × 81 CMS
INSCRIBED 'J.FLANDRIN' ON RECTO TOP LEFT
PROV.: THE ARTIST FROM WHOM BOUGHT BY DRUET, 1910;... TO
PRESENT OWNER
EXH.: PARIS, GALERIE DRUET, 1910; GRENOBLE, MUSÉE DE
GRENOBLE, 1972
LIT.: SALMON, *Paris-Journal*, FEBRUARY 1910; MORICE, *Mercure de
France* (MARCH 1910), P. 361; FLANDRIN AND ROUSSIER, P. 274.

Dance was to become one of Flandrin's major passions following his 'discovery' of the ballet in 1905. From this date, he began to attend performances at the Paris *Ballets de l'Opéra* with Marval on a regular basis, which prompted his initial series of paintings depicting the pastoral fantasies of Gluck's *Armide*. The arrival of the *Ballets russes*, directed by Sergei Diaghilev, in 1909 for its first Paris season, however, introduced him to a vibrant and innovative concept of dance, creating, in turn, new possibilities for his art. Flandrin was captivated by the colours and exoticism of the *Ballets russes mises-en-scènes*, as well as by the grace and suppleness of its lead dancers, the great Nijinsky, Pavlova and Karsavina (see cat. 50 and 54). This scene from *The Firebird*, part of the 1909 *Ballets russes* repertoire, shows Flandrin's fascination with the energy and vitality of the spectacle, and contrasts with his evocations of the static, classical world of *Armide*. As in his graphic work of the period, Flandrin uses a language of pictorial abbreviation and dramatic simplification to convey the rhythms of the music and the dancers' bodies. But the different elements of the scene are unified in the use of vibrant colours which suggest powerful visual correlatives to the ballet's elemental subject-matter.

Private Collection, Paris

50 *Pavlova and Nijinsky**

1910

La Pavlova et Nijinsky

OIL ON CANVAS, 62 × 82 CMS.
INSCRIBED 'J.FLANDRIN' ON RECTO LOWER LEFT
PROV.: THE ARTIST, FROM WHOM BOUGHT BY DRUET, 1910;
BT. FROM DRUET BY KAPFERER; BT. FROM KAPFERER COLLECTION BY
THE PRESENT OWNER
EXH.: PARIS, GALERIE DRUET, 1910
LIT.: SALMON, *Paris-Journal*, FEBRUARY 1910; MARVAL, *L'Art
décoratif*, NO. 190 (APRIL 1913), P. 167; FLANDRIN AND ROUSSIER,
P. 112.

Flandrin's paintings of the *Ballets russes* are as much evocations of their spectacles as depictions of individual scenes and motifs. Based on a scene from *Les Sylphides* (1909 repertoire), the focus of this work is the interaction between the two dancers, expressed in the fluid rhythms of the brushwork, and in the predominantly blue and white colour harmonies.

Private Collection, Paris

51 *Two Drawings after Matisse's 'Music' and 'Dance' and Vallotton's 'Perseus Slaying the Dragon' (Letter from Flandrin to Dr Joseph Flandrin, 2 November 1910)*

1910

Lettre, 2 novembre 1910 (Matisse, 'la Musique' et 'la Danse')

PROV.: THE ARTIST; BY DESCENT TO THE PRESENT OWNER
LIT.: FLANDRIN AND ROUSSIER, PP. 120–1.

A letter to his elder brother Joseph describing his reactions to the 1910 *Salon d'Automne*, gives an important indication of Flandrin's particular artistic concerns in this period. He expresses disillusion with Denis's conception of decoration which he now finds flat and lifeless; even Bonnard comes in for similar criticism. The main focus of his interest is Valloton's work, and Matisse's two great paintings, *Music* and *Dance*, destined for the Russian Sergei Shchukin's collection. Referring tongue-in-cheek to their

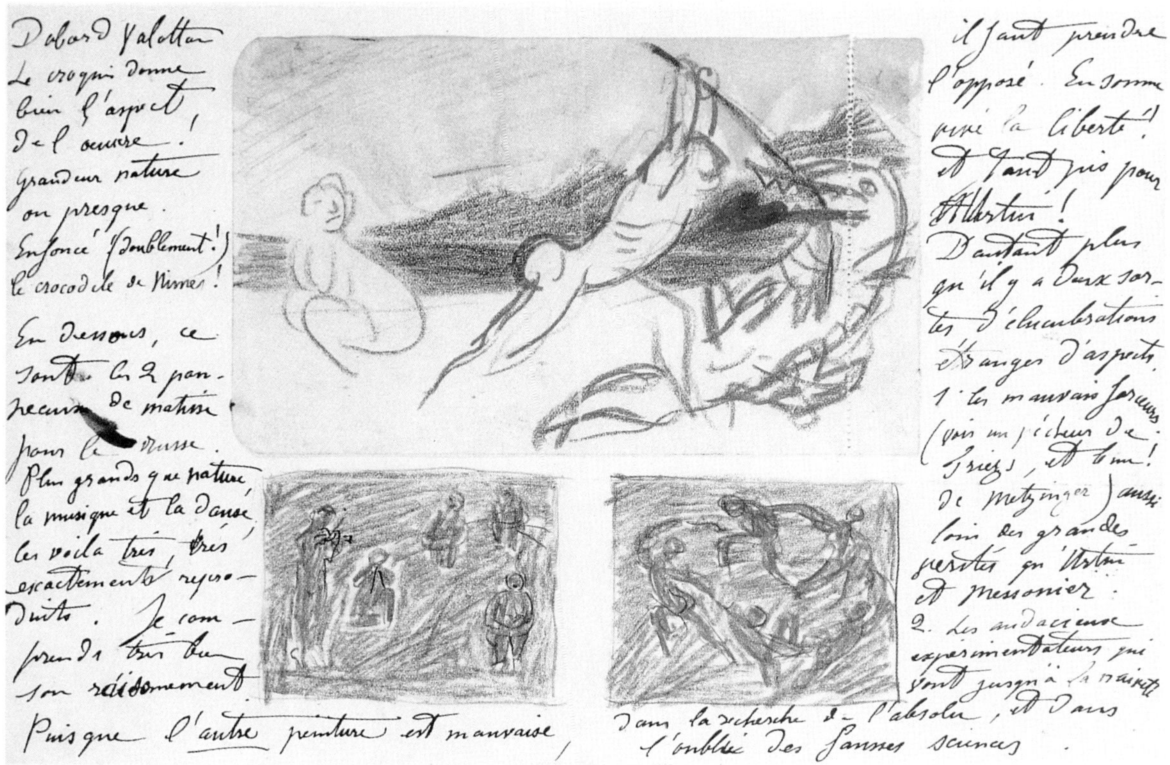

51 *Two Drawings after Matisse's 'Music' and 'Dance' and Vallotton's 'Perseus Slaying the Dragon' (Letter from Flandrin to Dr Joseph Flandrin, 2 November 1910), 1910*

primitivist style, he comments that he he has reproduced these 'very exactly'. More significant is the implicit filiation of Matisse with the art of the Old Masters which he links with the grandeur of nature itself. In Matisse's work, he perceives a universalizing element which bears the hallmark of all great art. As Flandrin's painting of the immediate pre-war period shows, the example would be of considerable significance to his own efforts to combine modernity of expression with classicism.

Private Collection, Paris

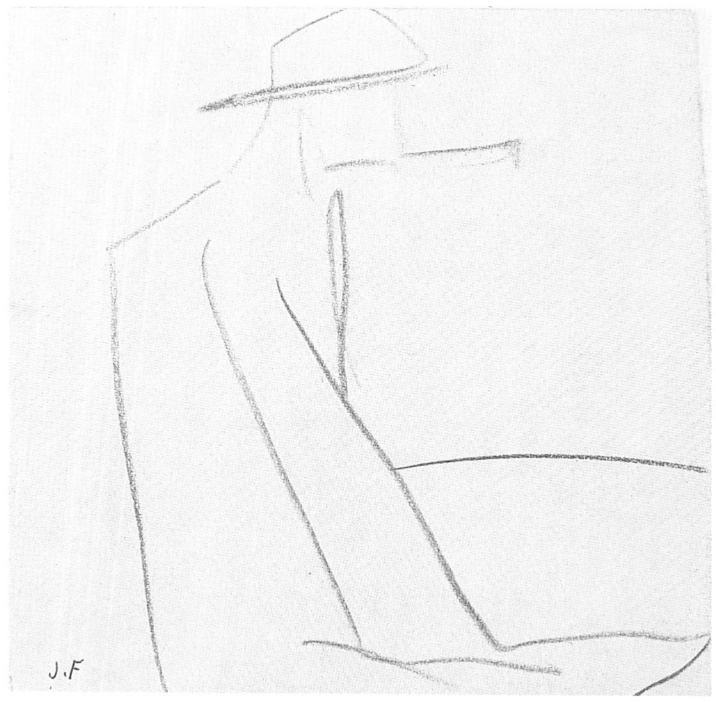

52 *The Smoker* (undated), *c.*1911–12

52 *The Smoker*

(UNDATED) *c.*1911–12
Le Fumeur

RED CHALK, 13 × 12.5 CMS.
INSCRIBED WITH MONOGRAM 'J.F' ON RECTO LOWER LEFT
PROV.: THE ARTIST; BY DESCENT TO THE PRESENT OWNER
LIT.: FLANDRIN AND ROUSSIER, P. 133.

Flandrin's graphic work of the pre-war period which included many drawings of Marval (cat. 53), corresponds with the daringly abbreviated forms and energetic rhythms in many of his contemporary *Ballets russes* paintings. In this boldly economical sketch, the figure has been reduced to a few almost abstract linear notations which corresponds with the visual shorthand developed variously by Marquet, Matisse and Camoin in the early 1900s.

Private Collection, Grenoble

53 *Marval*

(UNDATED) *c.*1912
Marval

PENCIL, 12.5 × 10 CMS.
INSCRIBED WITH MONOGRAM 'JF' ON RECTO LOWER LEFT AND
'MARVAL' LOWER RIGHT
PROV.: THE ARTIST; BY DESCENT TO THE PRESENT OWNER
LIT.: FLANDRIN AND ROUSSIER, P. 156.

See cat. 52.

Private Collection, Grenoble

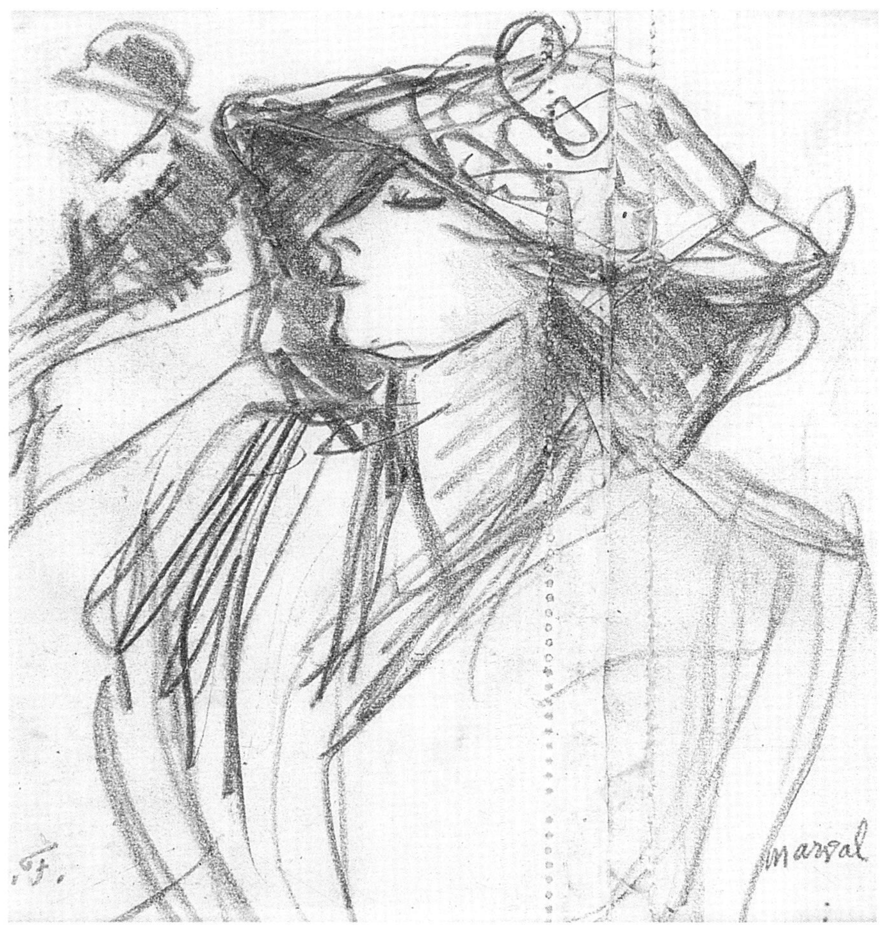

53 *Marval* (undated), *c.*1912

54   *'The Spectre of the Rose', Nijinsky and Karsavina (Opening Scene)**

1913

'Le Spectre de la rose', Nijinski et Karsavina (l'entreé en scène)

OIL ON CANVAS, 130 × 131 CMS.
INSCRIBED 'JULES FLANDRIN' ON RECTO LOWER LEFT
PROV.: THE ARTIST, FROM WHOM BOUGHT BY DRUET, *c.* 1913;
BT. FROM DRUET BY PACQUEMENT, *c.*1919; SOLD AT AUCTION, HÔTEL
DROUOT, 1936;... TO PRESENT OWNER
EXH.: PARIS, GALERIE DRUET, 1913 AND 1919; PARIS, SOCIÉTÉ DES
AMIS DU LUXEMBOURG, 1924
LIT.: MARVAL, *L'Art décoratif* (1913), P. 171; FLANDRIN AND
ROUSSIER, P. 161; KAHANE, *Nijinsky* (PARIS, 2000), P. 142.

One of two paintings depicting Nijinsky and Karsavina in the 1913 *Ballet russes* performance of the *Spectre de la rose*, this work was first exhibited at the Galerie Druet in 1913, entitled *Le Spectre de la rose (Karsavina, Nijinski)* (no.10). Between 1909 and 1913, Flandrin produced numerous works on *Ballets russes* themes and subjects. But he was most captivated by its lead dancers, Nijinsky, and the ballerinas, Pavlova and Karsavina. He painted several individual studies of Nijinsky – referred to in Marval's 1913 article on the subject[1] – concentrating on Nijinsky's fluid gestures and flowing movements, which are described in bold arabesques of paint. In the two 1913 paintings of the *Spectre de la rose*, this interest in finding painterly equivalents for rhythm, music and gesture, also evident in the earlier works (see cat. 49 and 50), is combined with his concern with decorative values, and with the visual architecture of the *mise-en-scène* as a whole. Nijinsky's and Karsavina's *pas de deux* is shown as an element within a larger decorative ensemble, suggested by the décor's broad, flat planes of colour and the dominant tonalities of mauve and blue. The doll-like features of the two dancers may have been inspired by Kees Van Dongen's work, which Flandrin had been familiar with since 1904.

Private Collection, Paris

[1] J.Marval, 'Les Danseurs de Flandrin', *Revue de l'art décoratif*, no. 190 (April 1913), pp. 165–76.

55 *Marval in Disguise at the Van Dongen Ball*

1914

Marval déguisée au bal chez Van Dongen

PASTEL, 21 × 13 CMS.
INSCRIBED 'J. FLANDRIN' AND DATED '1914' ON RECTO LOWER
RIGHT
PROV.: THE ARTIST; BY DESCENT TO THE PRESENT OWNER
LIT.: FLANDRIN AND ROUSSIER, P. 167.

This striking pastel of Marval in her costume for the masked ball organized by Van Dongen in March 1914 shows Flandrin's continuing debts to Toulouse-Lautrec – a major influence in his graphic work of the pre-war period.

Private Collection, Paris

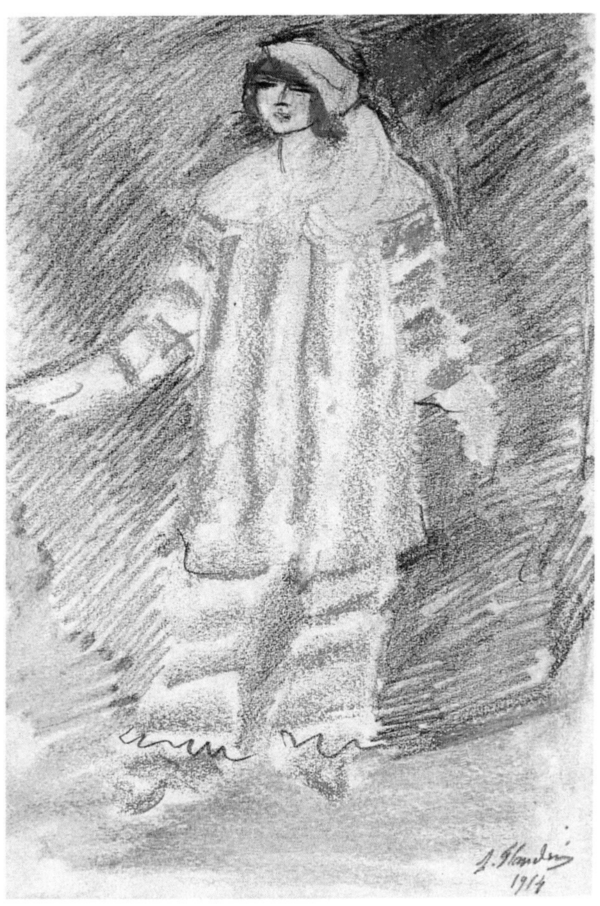

55 Marval in Disguise at the Van Dongen Ball, 1914

56 *Face of a Young Girl*
(UNDATED) BEFORE 1914
Visage de petite fille

PENCIL, 9 × 12.5 CMS.
INSCRIBED WITH A MONOGRAM 'J.F.' ON RECTO LOWER RIGHT
PROV.: THE ARTIST; BY DESCENT TO THE PRESENT OWNER

Possibly a sketch of one of the Lizambert children, it demonstrates the freedom of treatment and economy of means increasingly characteristic of Flandrin's mature graphic style.

Private Collection, Paris

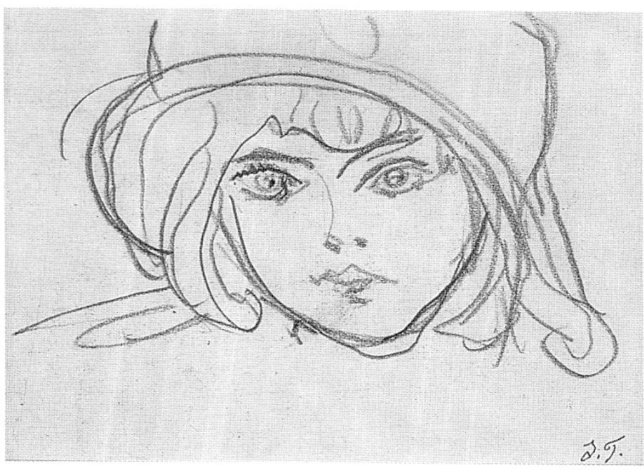

56 *Face of a Young Girl* (undated), before 1914

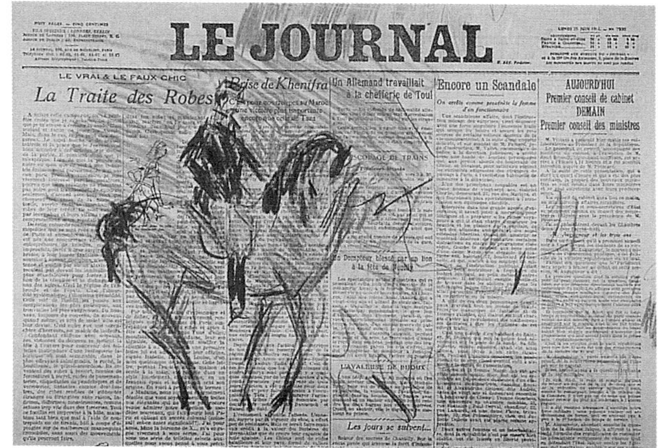

57 *'Le Journal', Drawing of Cavalry Officer on Horseback*, 1914

57 *'Le Journal', Drawing of Cavalry Officer on Horseback*
1914
'Le Journal', Officier de cavalerie à cheval

PASTEL, 32 × 45 CMS.
PROV.: THE ARTIST; BY DESCENT TO THE PRESENT OWNER

See cat. 45.

Private Collection, Paris

4

Towards a New Classicism

58   *Square in Venice**
1910
Place à Venise

OIL ON CANVAS, 54 × 73 CMS.
INSCRIBED 'J.FLANDRIN' ON RECTO LOWER LEFT
PROV.: THE ARTIST; BY DESCENT TO THE PRESENT OWNER
EXH.: PARIS, GALERIE DRUET, 1910; PARIS, SOCIÉTÉ DES AMIS DU
LUXEMBOURG, 1924[1]
LIT.: FLANDRIN AND ROUSSIER, P. 106.

In September 1909, Flandrin made the first of what would be many visits to Italy, travelling initially to Milan and thence to Bologna, Venice, Florence and Rome. Earlier in the same year, he had expressed his desire to set foot on the 'sacred soil of Italy' in a letter to his brother Joseph (April 1909)[2] – a long-nourished aim to see at first hand the Masters he had copied in his youth. This Venetian scene was included amongst his Italian paintings, first shown at the Galerie Druet in 1910, which comprised landscapes and views of Italian cities, their architecture and their inhabitants. These 'views' were profoundly influenced by Flandrin's response to the art of the Italian Masters: to Leonardo and to fifteenth-century Florentine and Venetian masters. But they also show his concern to make connections between such traditions and the interests of contemporary art. In the *Square in Venice*, Italian light and colour as much as memories of Carpaccio are the guiding inspiration in this vision of a bustling Venetian piazza. The clarity of the light compels Flandrin, as in his earlier work, to simplify and synthesize forms to their essentials of line, shape and colour. Architectural details are schematized, modelled simply in broad tonal masses of light and shade, while the crowds are picked out in a series of cursory colour notations. This combination of expressive, decorative and classicizing elements would be developed further in Flandrin's paintings of the immediate pre- and post-war period.

Private Collection, Paris

[1]Exhibited with the title *La piazetta à Venise* [*sic*] (no.6).
[2]Cited in Flandrin and Roussier, pp. 96–7.

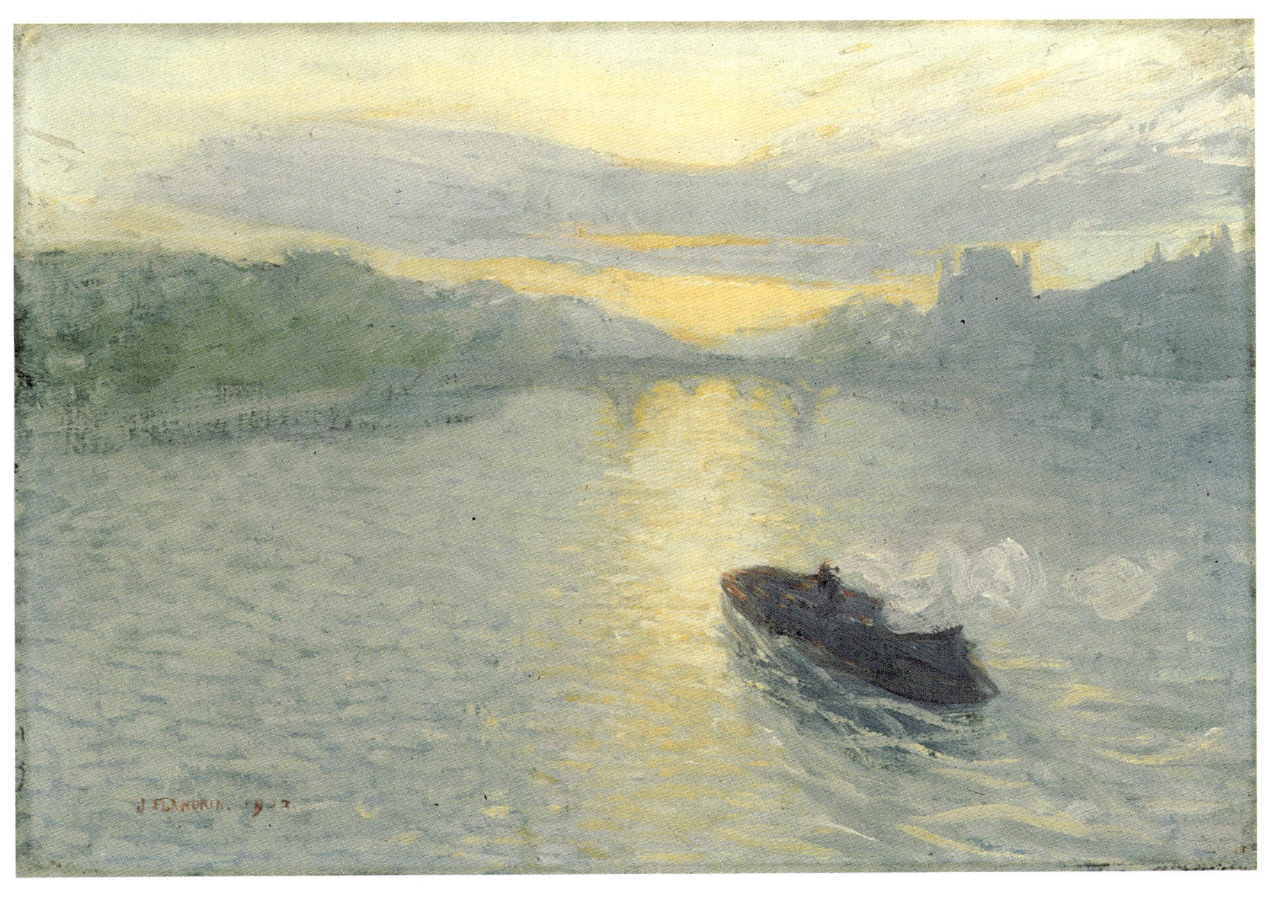

33 *The Seine at Sunrise,* 1902

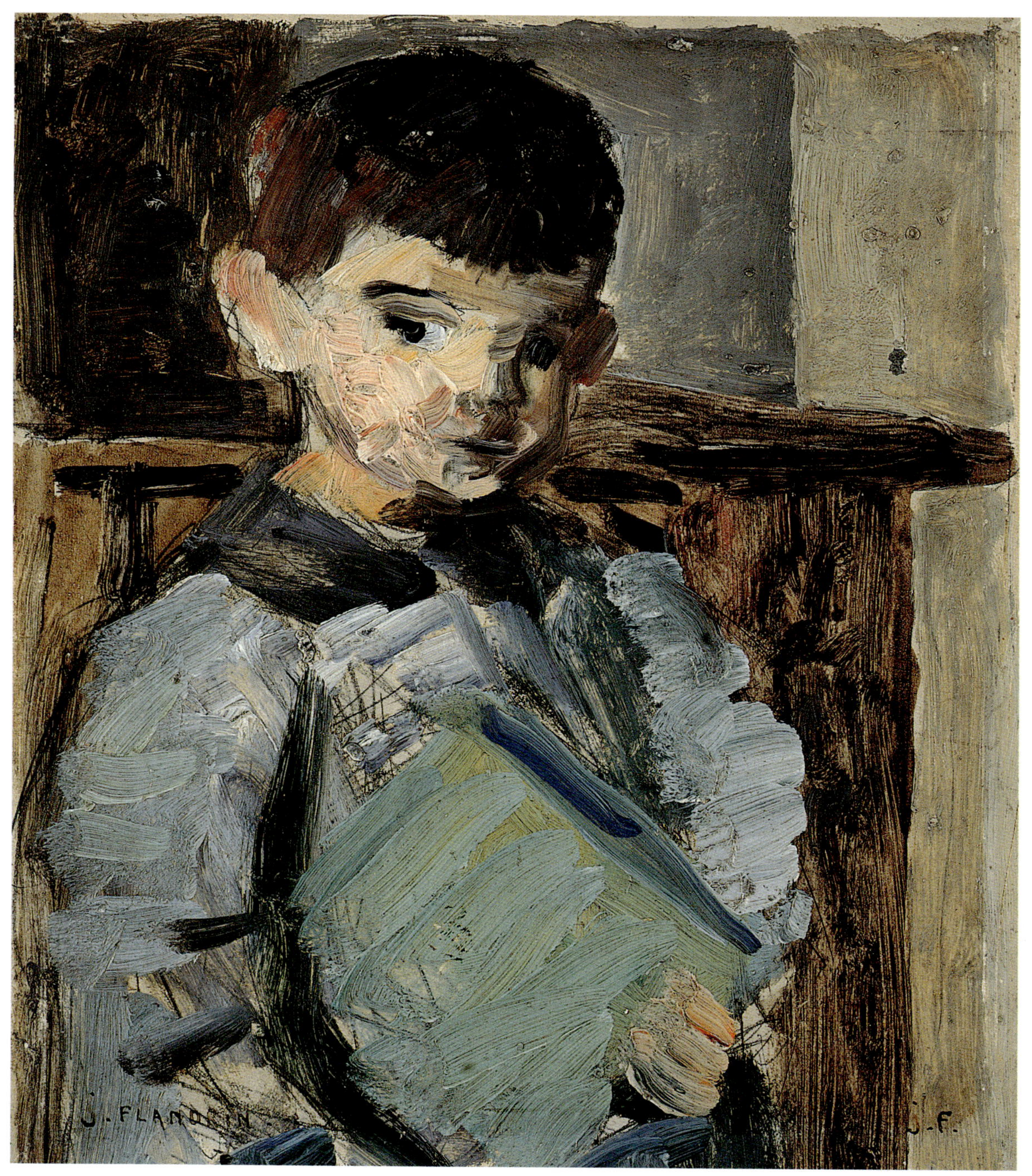

34 *The Little School Boy (Philippe Lizambert) (undated)* c.1904

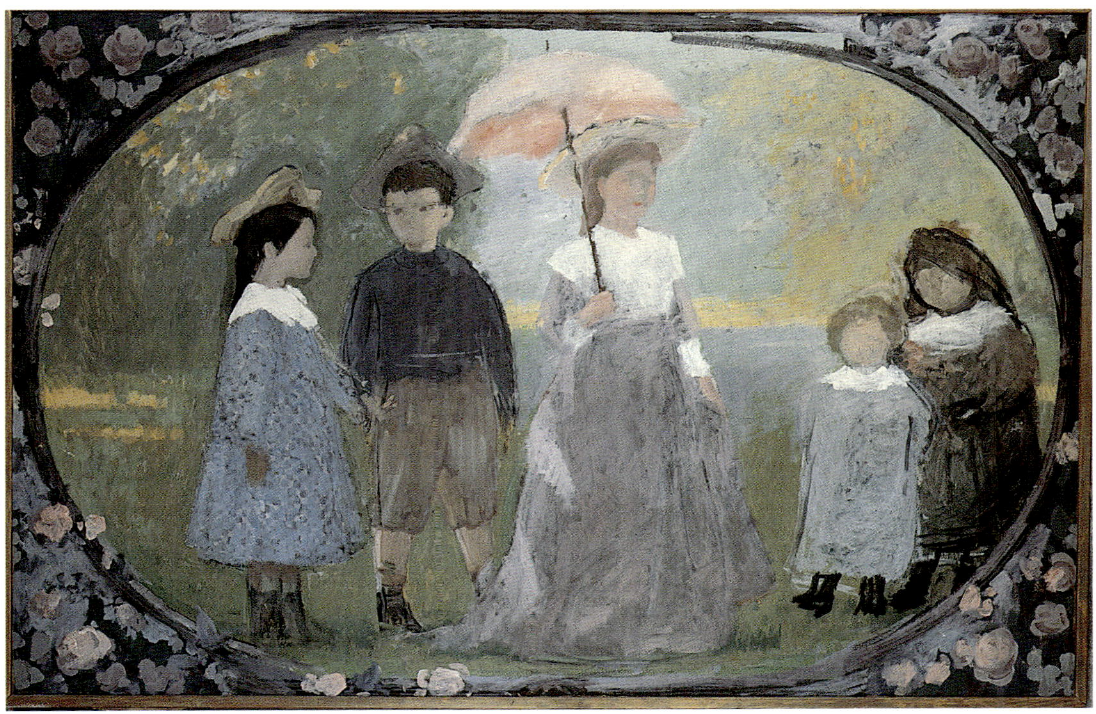

35 *The Masquerade (Portraits of Children, the Lizamberts at Corenc)* (undated) *c.*1904

37 *An Audience in Venice,* 1906

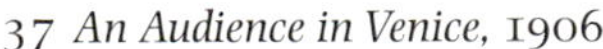

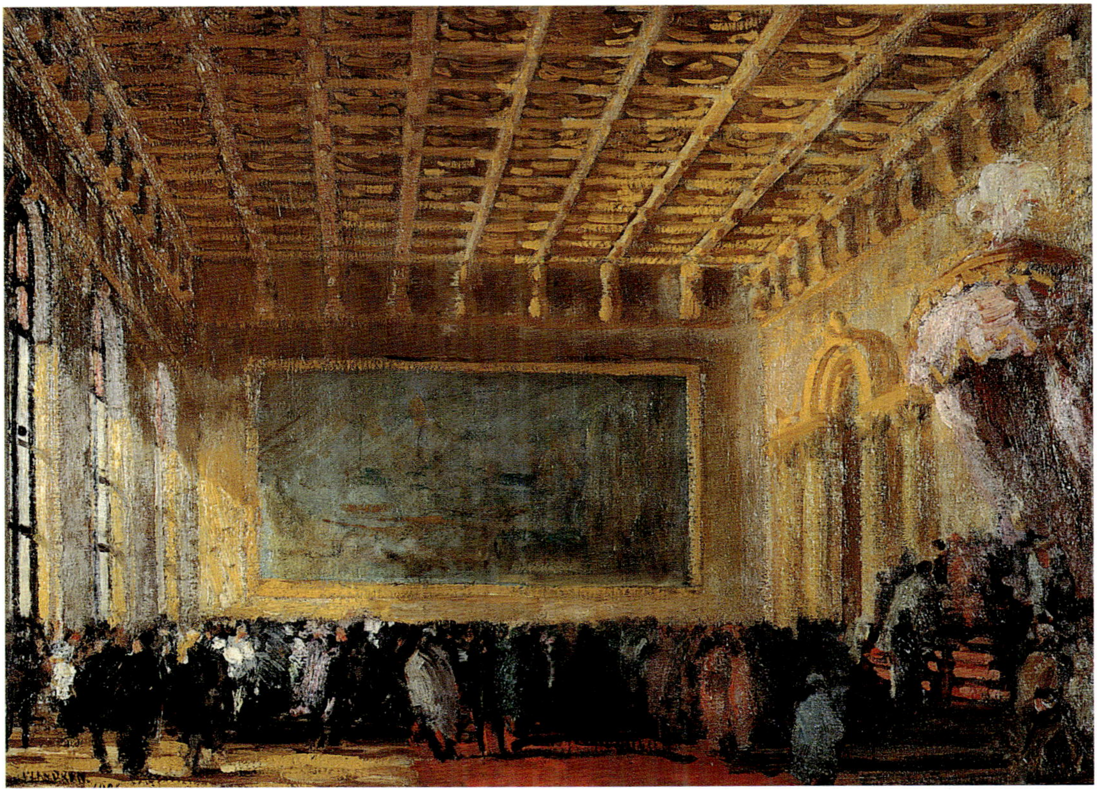

36 *An Angel, Homage to Handel*
(Study for a Painting for the
Church at Corenc), 1905

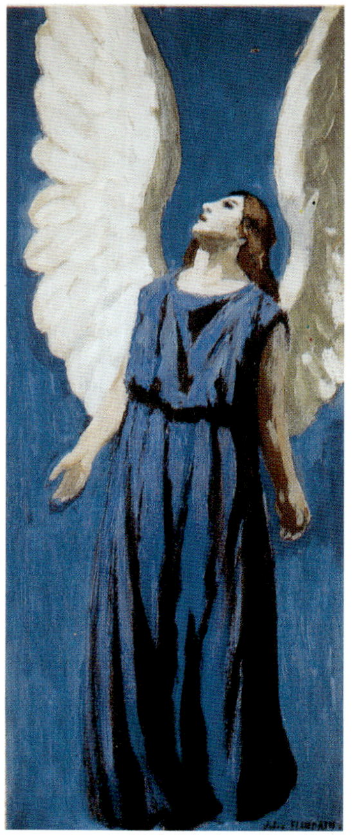

39 (OPPOSITE) *On the Sofa in the
Salon (Corenc)* (undated) *c.*1908

38 *Corenc, Garden in Sunlight,* 1907

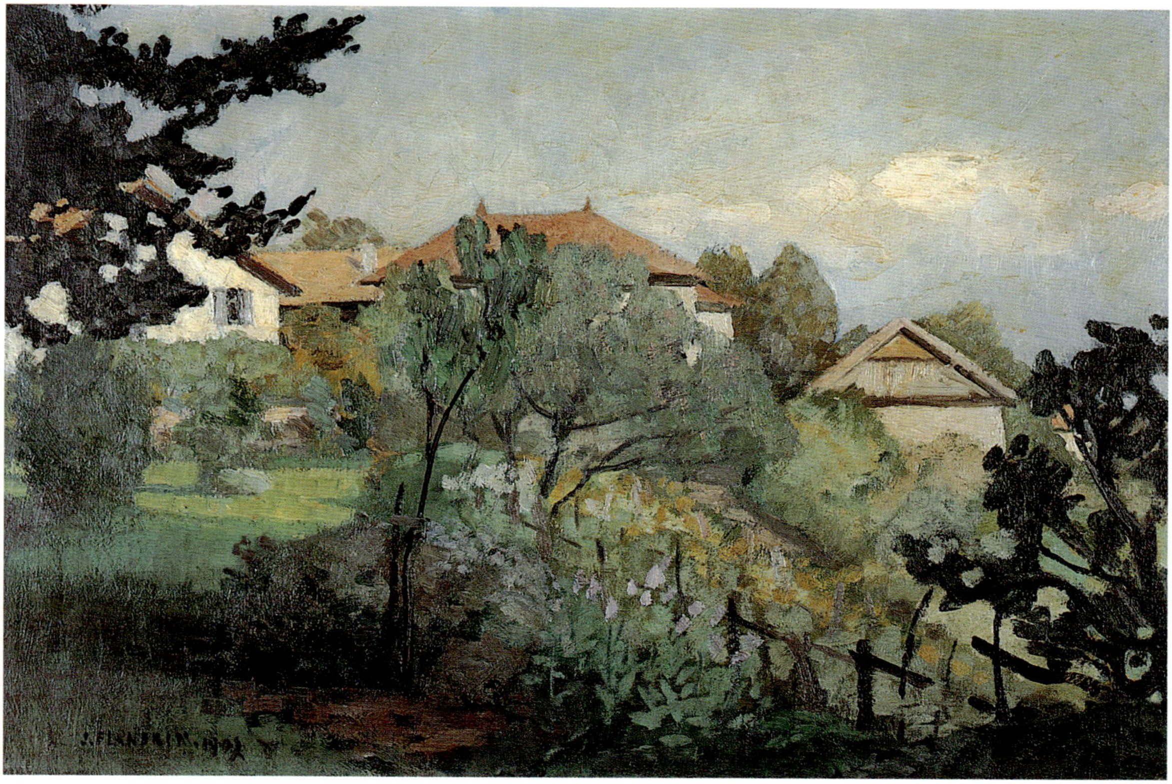

40 (OPPOSITE BELOW)
Seated Girl, Corenc (Pierrette), 1908

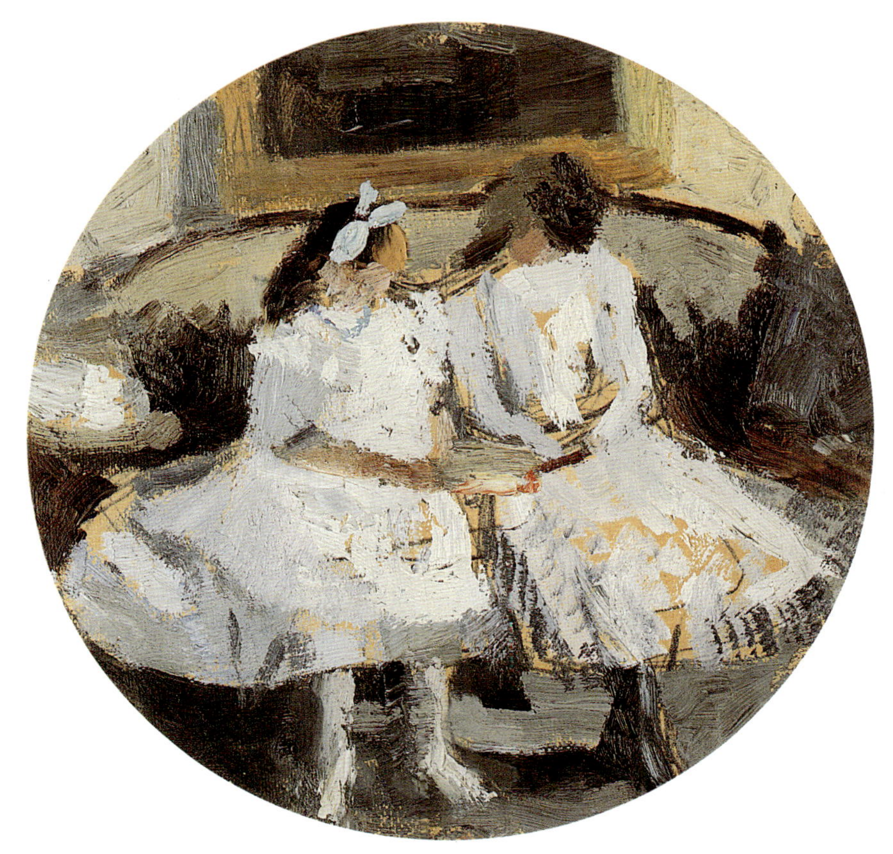

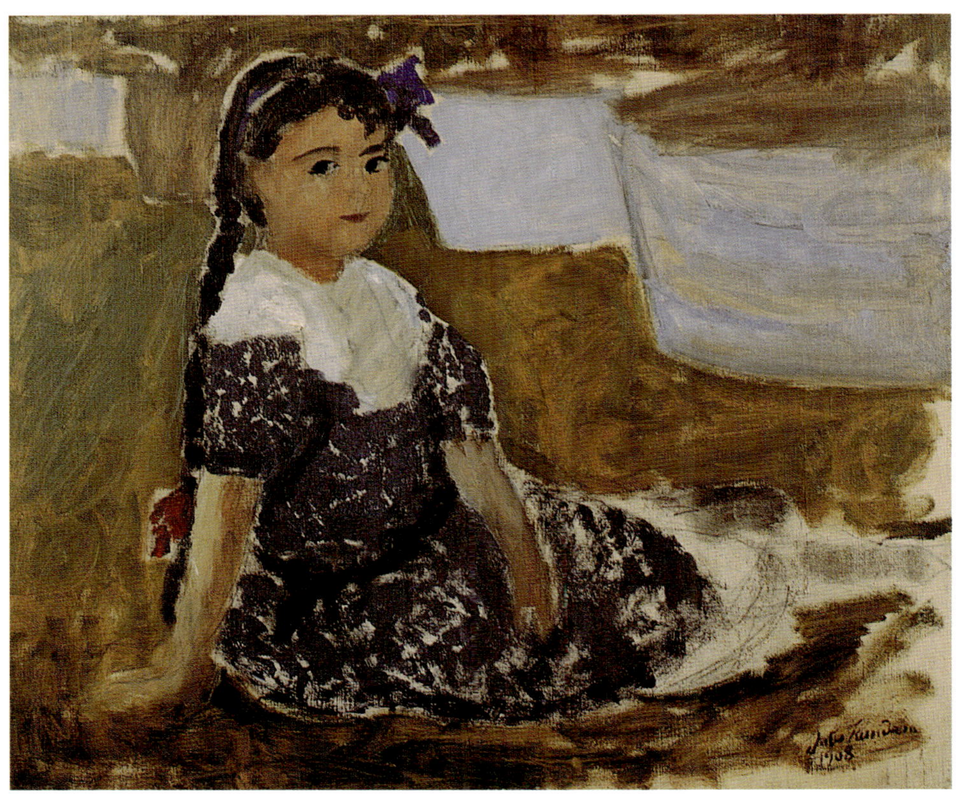

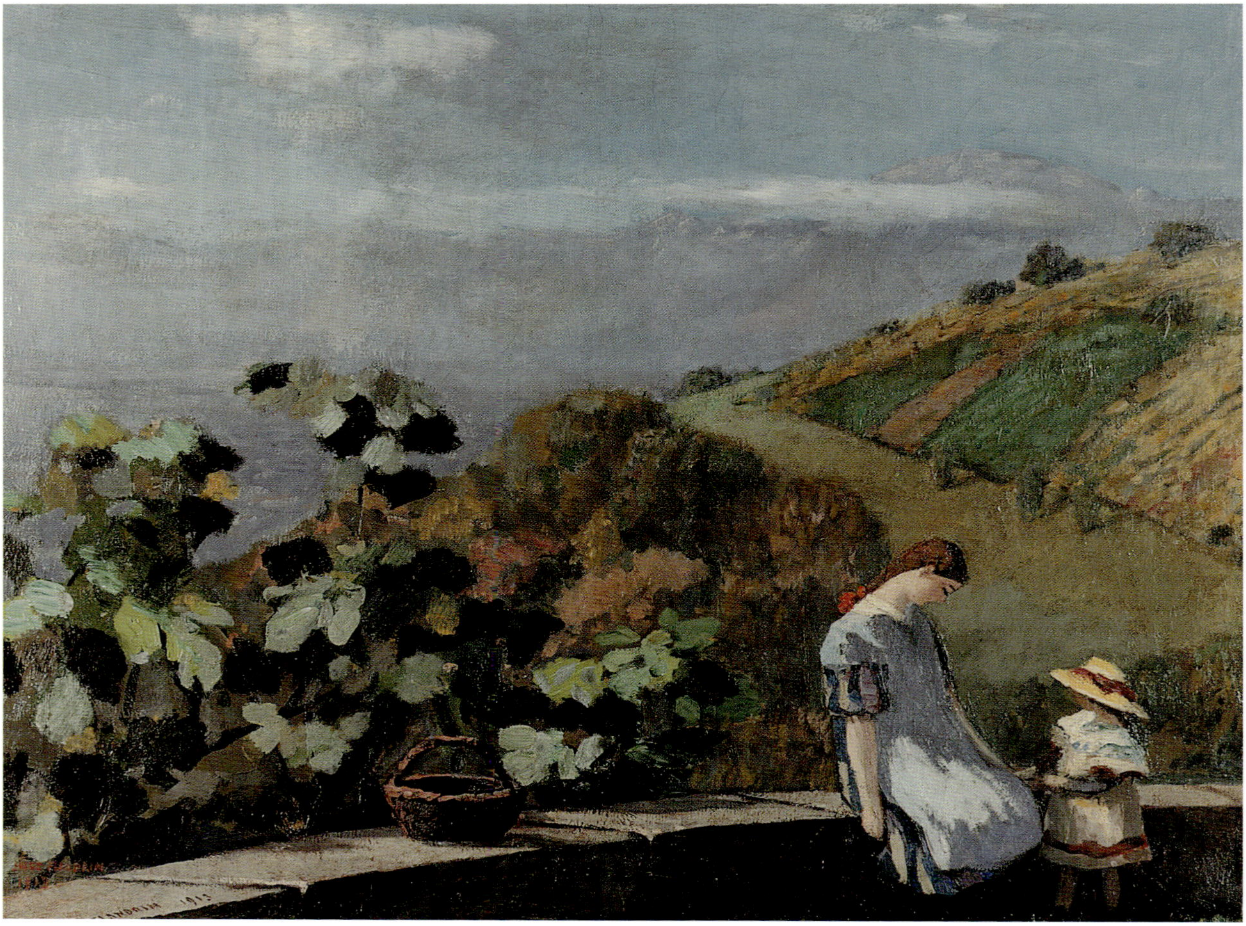

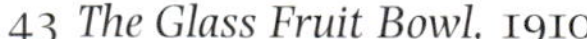

42 *Two Young Girls, September Afternoon,* 1908

43 *The Glass Fruit Bowl,* 1910

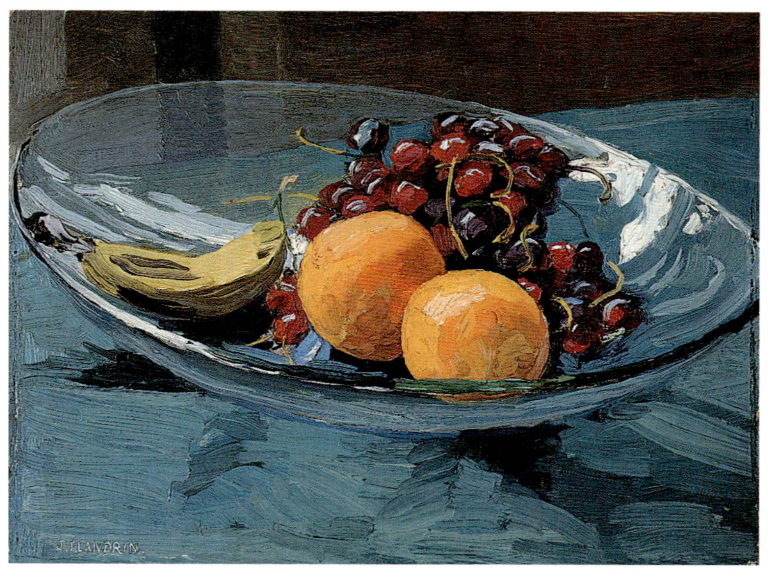

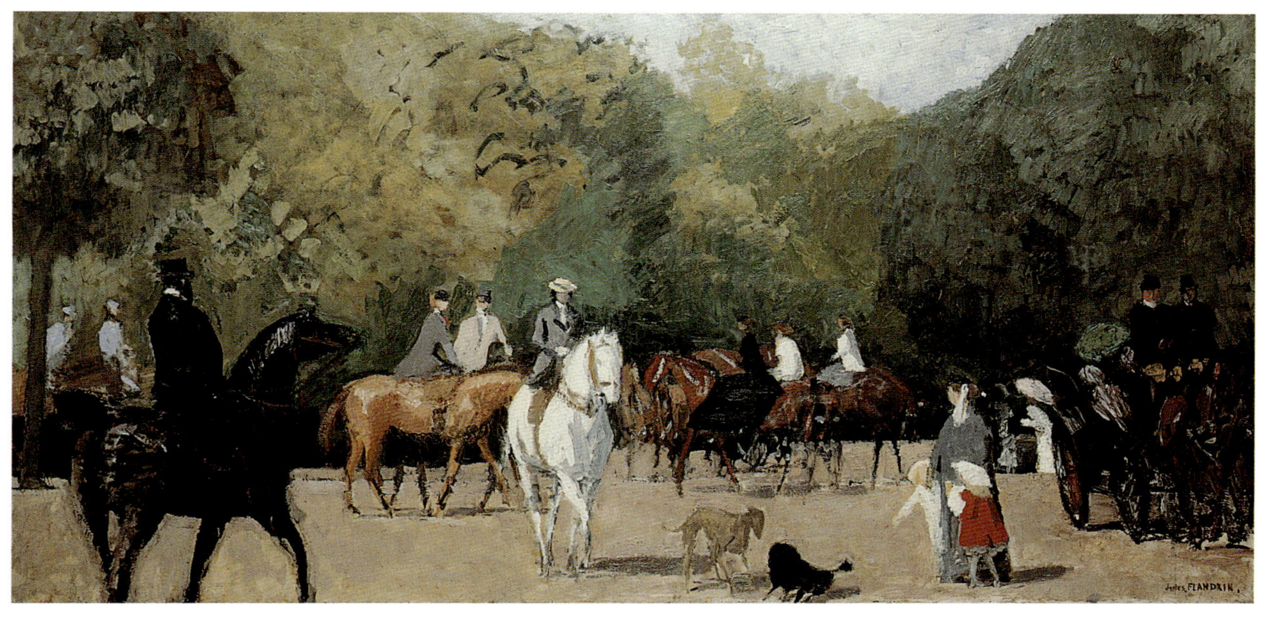

47 *Riders in the Bois* (undated) *c.*1909–11

49 *'The Firebird'*, 1909

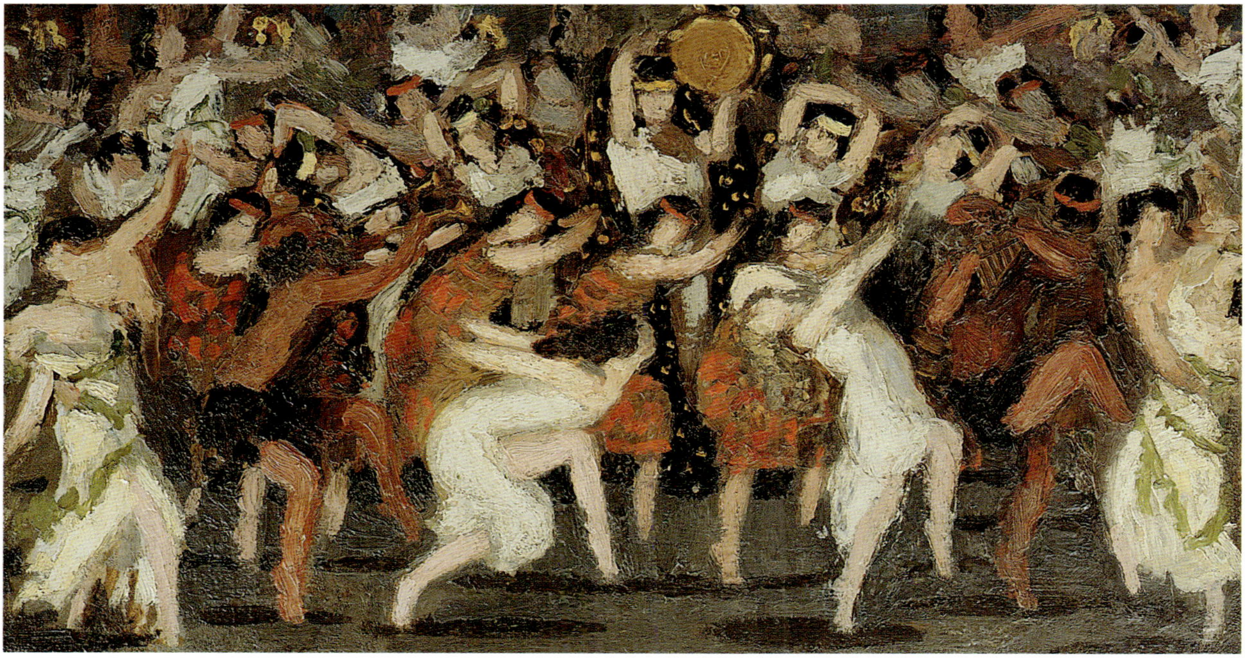

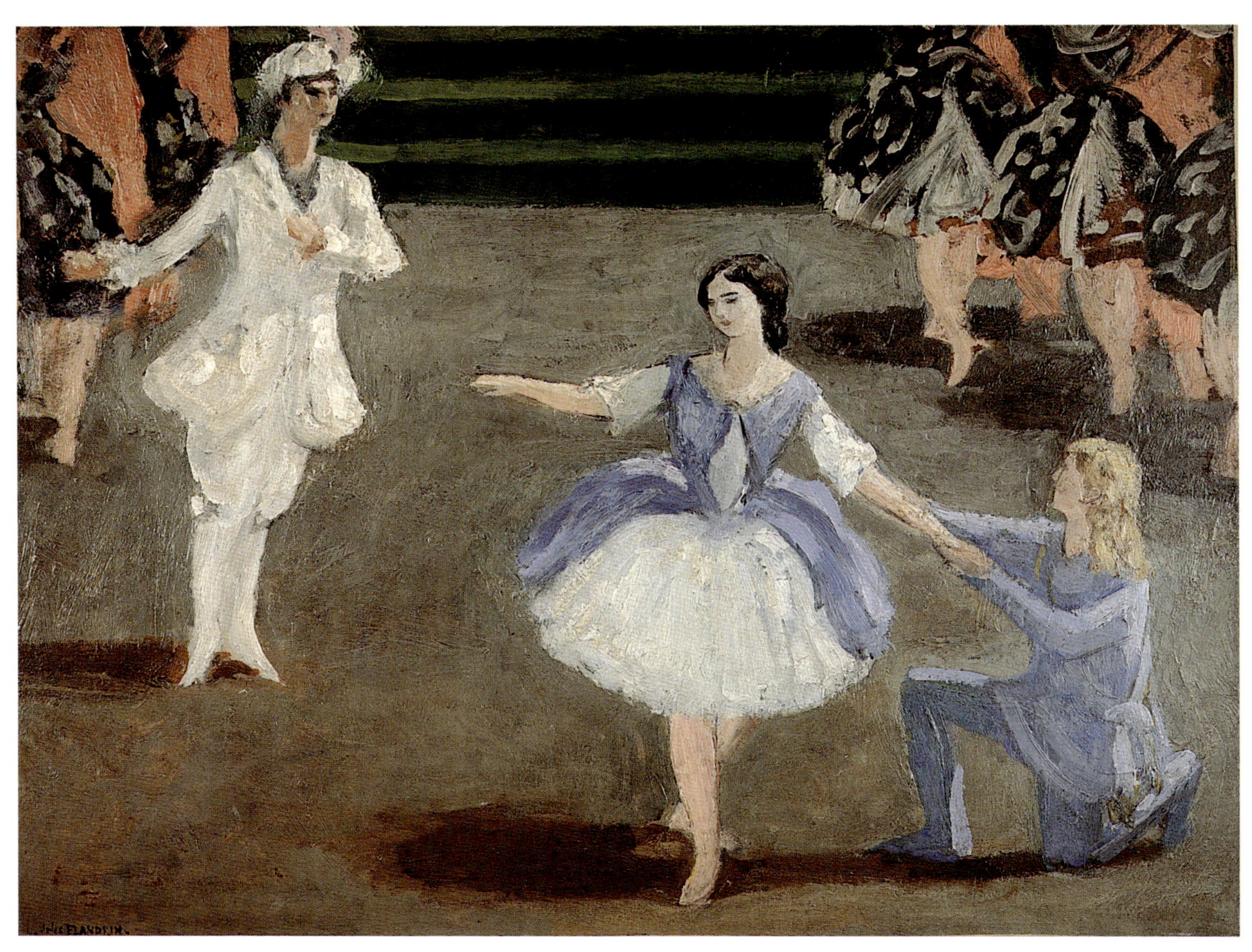

50 *Pavlova and Nijinsky,* 1910

59 *Young Italian Woman**

1912

La Jeune italienne

OIL ON CANVAS, 116.5 × 81 CMS.
INSCRIBED 'J.FLANDRIN' ON RECTO MIDDLE LEFT
PROV.: THE ARTIST; BY DESCENT TO THE PRESENT OWNER
EXH.: GRENOBLE, GALERIE ST. LOUIS, MUSÉE CARRAND-JONGKIND,
1929
LIT.: FLANDRIN AND ROUSSIER, P. 104.

The model for this portrait is not known; it is likely to have been based on a drawing made during Flandrin's Italian visit of 1909. The style, somewhat in the manner of Denis's later work, is reminiscent of the Florentine Primitives, especially of Masaccio whose work Flandrin had copied in 1909. The daring and free Fauve manner of his earlier portraits, notably *The Little School Boy* (cat. 34), has been replaced by clarity of form, a greater sense of modelling, and more structured brushwork, indicating Flandrin's interest in classical values and principles which become dominant characteristics in his art in this period.

Private Collection, Paris

60 *Girl in a Large Hat**

1913

La Fillette au grand chapeau

OIL ON CANVAS, 100 × 73 CMS.
INSCRIBED 'J.FLANDRIN' AND DATED '1913' ON RECTO LOWER
LEFT
PROV.: THE ARTIST, FROM WHOM BOUGHT BY DRUET, 1913;
BT. FROM DRUET BY CARTIER-MILLION, BY WHOM BEQUEATHED TO
THE PRESENT OWNER
EXH.: PARIS, GALERIE DRUET, 1913; BASLE, KUNSTHALLE, 1917;
GRENOBLE, MUSÉE DE GRENOBLE, 1972
LIT.: 'LA PALETTE' (SALMON), *Le Gil blas*, FEBRUARY 1913;
ALEXANDRE, *Comoedia*, OCTOBER 1913; FLANDRIN AND ROUSSIER,
P. 145.

Between 1910 and 1913, Flandrin was working on an increasingly large scale, consistent with his interest in decorative art, and expressive of his attempts to develop a style which combined modern and classical tendencies. At this time his work was also eliciting considerable and favourable commentaries from a number of leading contemporary critics, including Salmon and Apollinaire, who were consciously allying it to the emergence of a new classical spirit in French art. Reviewing Flandrin's *The Wooded Gorge* exhibited at the 1910 *Société Nationale*, Salmon had praised it highly, observing that 'the exhibition of Flandrin's work places this artist amongst the Masters of previous generations'.[1] The painting of a young girl in a large straw hat, probably produced during one of his periods spent at Corenc in 1913, combines the lyrical and monumental qualities which begin to emerge around 1908 in his landscapes and portraits, notably in *Two Young Girls* (cat. 42), and are further developed in the striking *Wooded Gorge*, the subject of much critical attention in 1910. Although the young girl's meditative pose and gaze shares affinities with the inwardness of *Two Young Girls* and the *Wooded Gorge*, it lacks the lapidary stillness which characterizes many of the works inspired by Flandrin's 1909 Italian visit, notably the *Young Italian Woman* (cat. 59). Here, the treatment of the subject is noticeably freer and more animated, shown in the warm colours and patchwork of swift brushstrokes describing the girl's dress, hat, hair and the interior, recalling the intimacy of Flandrin's Nabi-influenced paintings of the late 1890s.

Private Collection, Grenoble

[1] A. Salmon, 'Le Salon de la Société Nationale des Beaux-Arts', *Paris-Journal*, 14 April 1910.

61 *Riders on the Corenc Road*

1913
Les Cavaliers, chemin de Corenc

OIL ON CANVAS, 60 × 72.5 CMS.
INSCRIBED 'J.FLANDRIN.' AND DATED '1913' ON RECTO LOWER LEFT
PROV.: THE ARTIST; BY DESCENT TO THE PRESENT OWNER
EXH.: GRENOBLE, GALERIE FÉNOGLIO, 1914
LIT.: FLANDRIN AND ROUSSIER, P. 158.

The subject-matter of this work relates to several paintings of the previous years, featuring riders in a landscape setting (see cat. 45 and 47). However, Flandrin's main preoccupation here is with nature, as suggested by the small figures on horseback which are almost dwarfed by the impressive wooded landscape of the Dauphiné. By 1912, the arcardian themes of Flandrin's landscapes, and their monumental scale, were eliciting frequent comparisons with Puvis, Cézanne and Poussin. With Moreau's guidance always in mind, Flandrin was certainly making increasingly explicit links between tradition and nature, demonstrated to some extent in his attempts to create compositions which display a Poussinesque harmony and unity of form. Yet the silhouetted figures of the riders and stylized landscape setting have a poster-like simplicity which recalls more modern interests, indicating Flandrin's concern at this time, with developing a modern equivalent to the 'grand oeuvre' of the past.

Private Collection, Paris

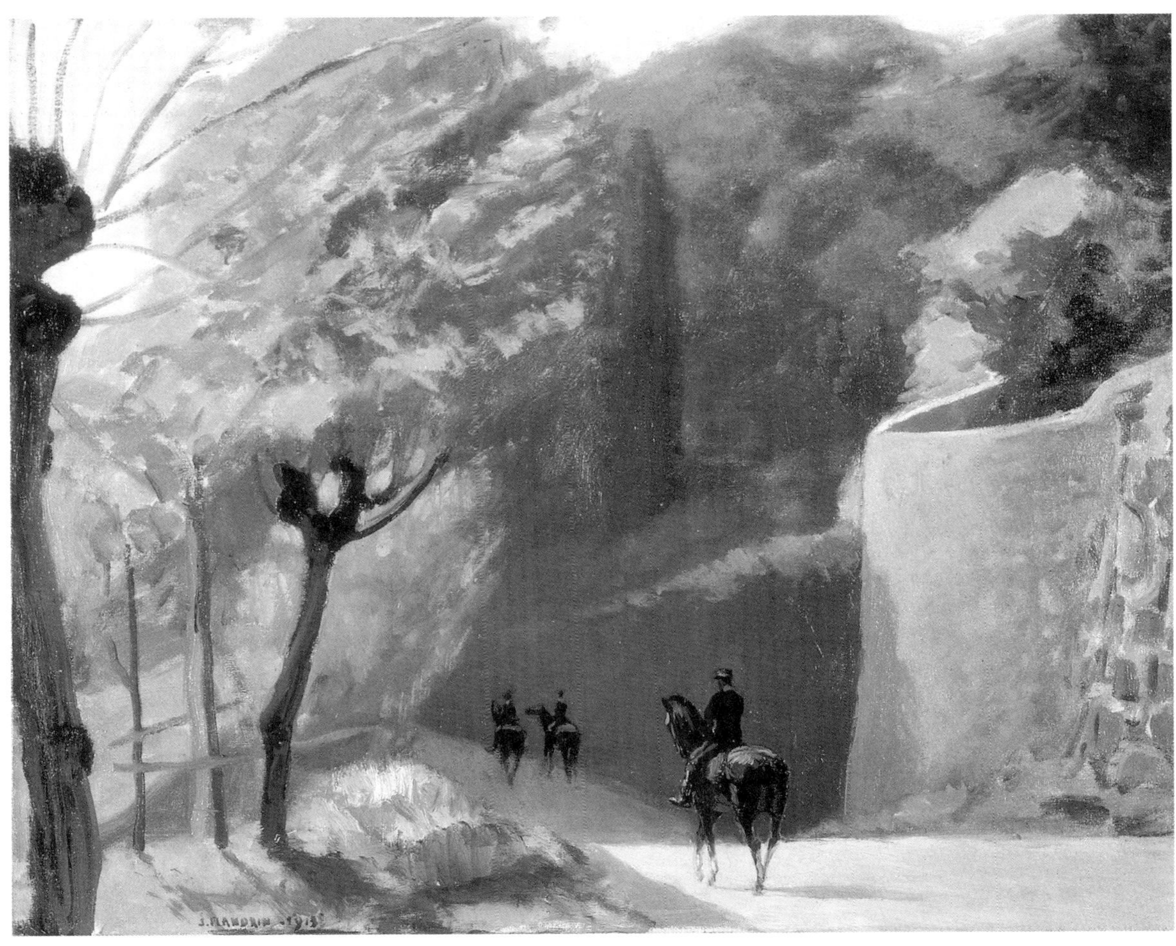

61 *Riders on the Corenc Road*, 1913

62   *Young Horsemen by a Spring**
1913, REWORKED 1923
Jeunes cavaliers près d'une source

OIL ON CANVAS, 241 × 176 CMS.
INSCRIBED 'JULES FLANDRIN' ON RECTO LOWER LEFT
PROV.: THE ARTIST; BY DESCENT TO THE PRESENT OWNER
EXH.: PARIS, *Société Nationale des Beaux-Arts*, 1913; PARIS, GALERIE
DRUET, 1919; PARIS, *Salon des Tuileries*, 1923 (REWORKED VERSION);
BRISTOL, ROYAL WEST OF ENGLAND ACADEMY, 1930 (REWORKED
VERSION)
LIT.: VAUXCELLES, *Le Gil blas*, APRIL 1913; MOUREY, *Le Journal*,
APRIL 1913; SARRADIN, *Journal des débats*, APRIL 1913; GENET,
L'Opinion, APRIL 1913; CHARLES, *La Liberté*, APRIL 1913; GOTH,
Hommes du jour, MAY 1913; APOLLINAIRE (1913), IN *Chroniques
d'art* (1960), P. 314; KAHN, *Le Quotidien*, 1923; FLANDRIN AND
ROUSSIER, PP. 124, 136–7, 207.

Flandrin regarded this particular work as representing the culmination of
his art prior to the outbreak of the First World War. Exhibited four times in
his lifetime, it was reworked in 1923 with alterations made to the right and
left-hand figures and to the landscape setting, and shown in 1923 at the
Salon des Tuileries, entitled *Jeunes cavaliers (projet de Tapisserie)* (no.374).
Thereafter, the reworked painting was the model for the tapestry version
completed in 1929. The pastoral subject, with its three loosely antique male
horsemen, and arcadian landscape, recalls the allusive and dream-like
paintings of Puvis, with their evocations of a mythical realm of peace, harmony and plenty. Several commentators also saw resonances of the
'Poussinesque tradition' in both the painting's theme and treatment.
Writing in *Le Gil blas*, Louis Vauxcelles, for example, suggested that
'Flandrin is amongst those young artists who will have contributed to the
revival of the taste for the style and cadence of classical art'. The two concerns are certainly consistent with Flandrin's other major works of the
period, where he attempts to synthesize a Symbolist-type evocation of
mood and other-worldliness with a pastoral and essentially harmonious
nature, harking back to the Arcadia of antiquity. However, as Vauxcelles
also noted, the style of *The Young Horsemen* is also strikingly and rigorously contemporary, with its shallow space, its schematized landscape, and
flatly-painted figures with their abstracted expressions. Indeed this rather
introspective and stylized classicism, which is in no sense academic, parallels Derain's contemporary efforts to rediscover the principles of the great
masters of the past in relation to contemporary art.

Private Collection, Paris

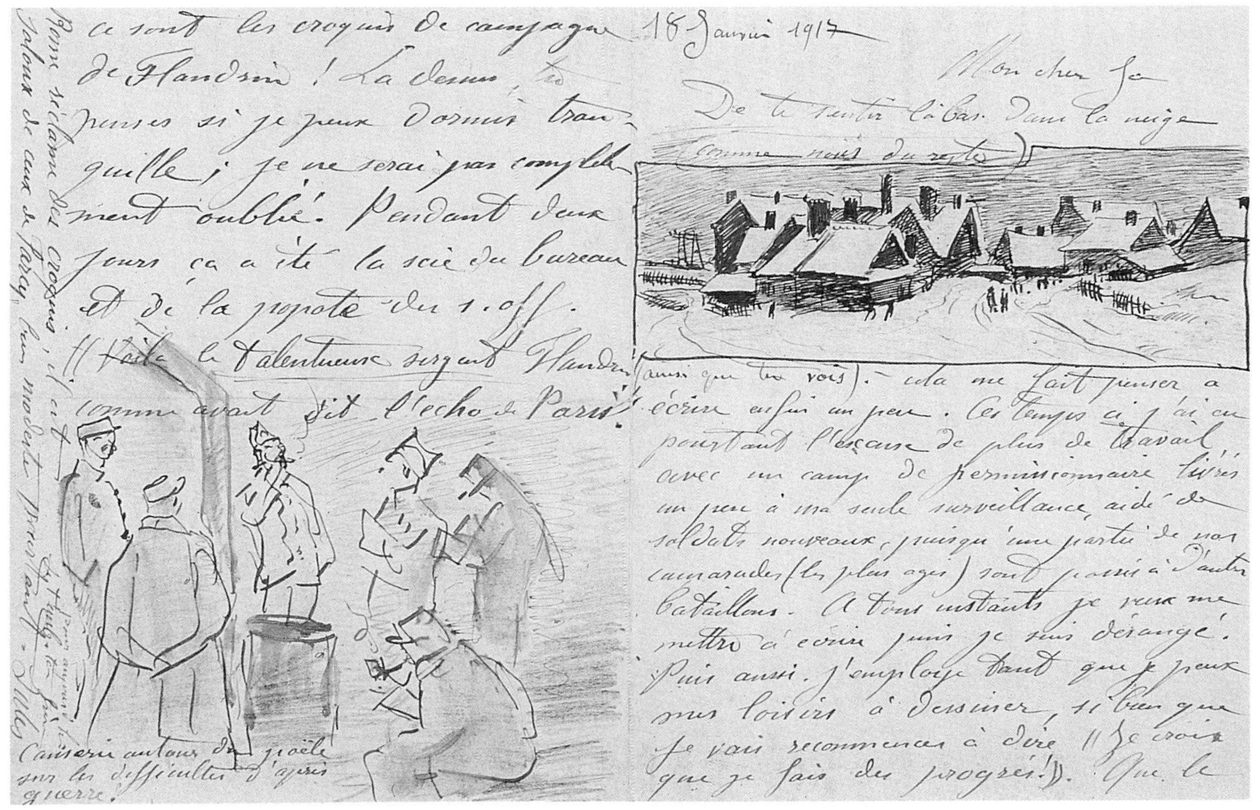

63 *Letter from Flandrin to Dr Joseph Flandrin dated 18 January 1917 showing sketches of*
soldiers smoking and a village under snow

63 *Letter from Flandrin to Dr Joseph Flandrin dated 18 January 1917 showing sketches of soldiers smoking and a village under snow*
Lettre, 18 janvier 1917 (village sous la neige)

Flandrin was enlisted in the territorial army in August 1914 and billeted in
the Seine-et-Oise region for the duration of the war years. He spent much
of this period, when not on duty, producing numerous sketches of army
life, many of which illustrated letters to his family. A number of these were
exhibited at the War Salon in Paris, *Le Salon des Armées de la République* in
1917.

Private Collection, Paris

64 *The House at Corenc*
(UNDATED) *c.*1919–20
La Maison de Corenc

BLUE CRAYON, 24 × 30.5 CMS.
INSCRIBED WITH MONOGRAM 'JF' ON RECTO LOWER RIGHT
PROV.: THE ARTIST; BY DESCENT TO THE PRESENT OWNER

The family house at Corenc increasingly came to represent an idyllic and tranquil haven for Flandrin, particularly in the immediate aftermath of the war. This view was produced at a time when Flandrin was beginning to spend considerable periods in the Dauphiné. The immediacy and liveliness of the sketch with its swift, incisive lines and abbreviated forms is consistent with innovations in Flandrin's graphic art of the pre-war years.

Private Collection, Paris

64 *The House at Corenc* (undated), *c.*1919–20

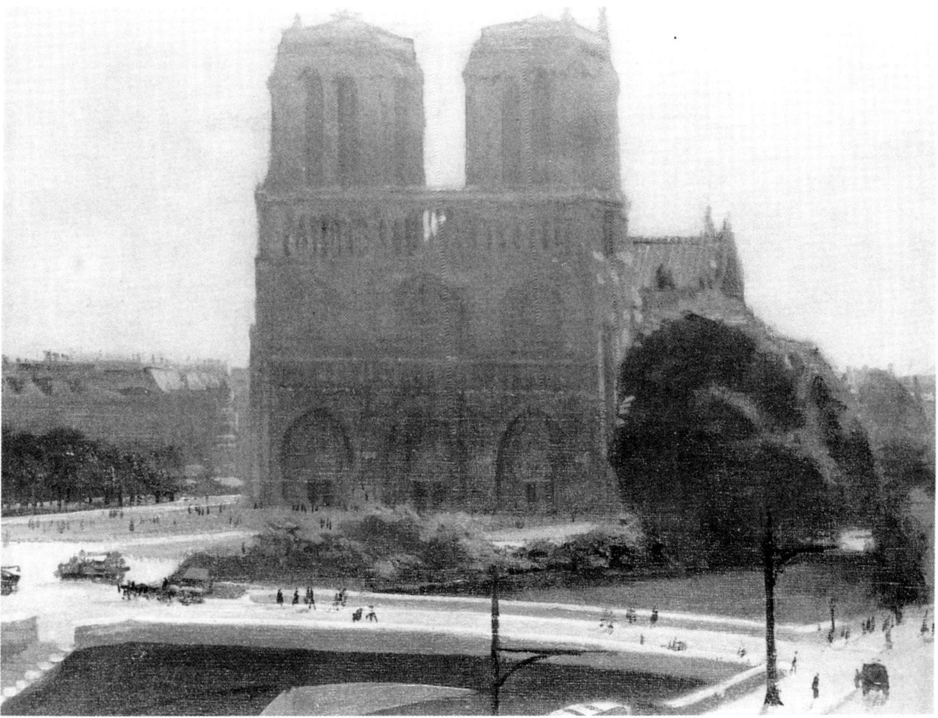

65 *Notre-Dame, Fine Afternoon*, 1919

65   *Notre-Dame, Fine Afternoon*

1919

Notre-Dame, bel après-midi

OIL ON CANVAS, 44 × 53 CMS.
PROV.: THE ARTIST;... TO CARTIER-MILLION, *c.* 1922, BY WHOM
BEQUEATHED TO THE PRESENT OWNER
EXH.: PARIS, GALERIE DRUET, 1919
LIT.: FLANDRIN AND ROUSSIER, P. 198.

In 1919 Flandrin and Marval moved to Matisse's former home at 19 Quai St. Michel, where they now occupied separate studios. This painting of Notre-Dame was the first of a series of views of Notre-Dame and the Seine, based directly on views observable from Flandrin's studio windows which overlooked the Quai St. Michel. The majestic presence of the cathedral, depicted at different times of day and under varying light conditions, shows a return to the themes and stylistic preoccupations of the turn of the century. The concern with the simplification and schematization of form to the essentials of shape, mass and colour harks back to Matisse's and Marquet's Notre-Dame series of the early 1900s. However, the planar geometries of the bridges and surrounding boulevards, are evidence of Flandrin's more recent concern with the decorative and the monumental, which had found a new outlet in 1919 in his series of murals on patriotic themes commissioned by the restaurant des Tourelles in the boulevard Delessert, and in his tapestry workshop, opened in Grenoble in the same year.

Private Collection, Paris

66 *Notre-Dame, Morning Sun**
1921
Notre-Dame, soleil du matin

OIL ON CANVAS, 80 × 100 CMS.
INSCRIBED 'JULES FLANDRIN' ON RECTO LOWER LEFT
PROV.: THE ARTIST;... TO THE PRESENT OWNER
EXH.: PARIS, GALERIE DRUET, 1922
LIT.: FLANDRIN AND ROUSSIER, P. 217.

See cat. 65.

Private Collection, Grenoble

67 *Reading (Pierre Flandrin Reading in the Studio)**
1922
La Lecture (Pierre Flandrin lisant à l'atelier)

OIL ON CANVAS, 130 × 96 CMS.
INSCRIBED 'JULES FLANDRIN' ON RECTO LOWER RIGHT
PROV.: THE ARTIST; BY DESCENT TO THE PRESENT OWNER
EXH.: PARIS, GALERIE DRUET, 1922
LIT.: FLANDRIN AND ROUSSIER, P. 194.

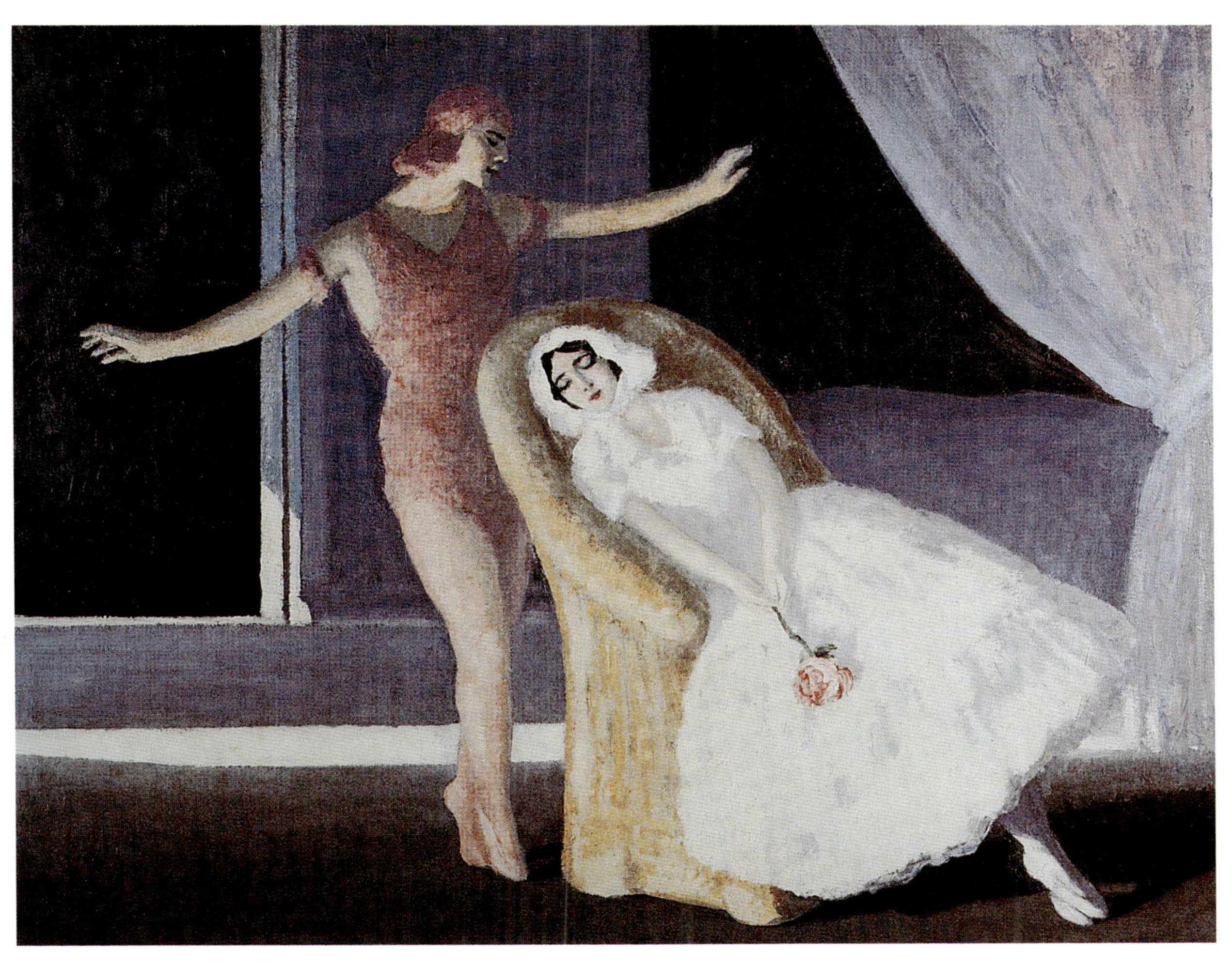

54 *'The Spectre of the Rose', Nijinsky and Karsavina (Opening Scene)*, 1913

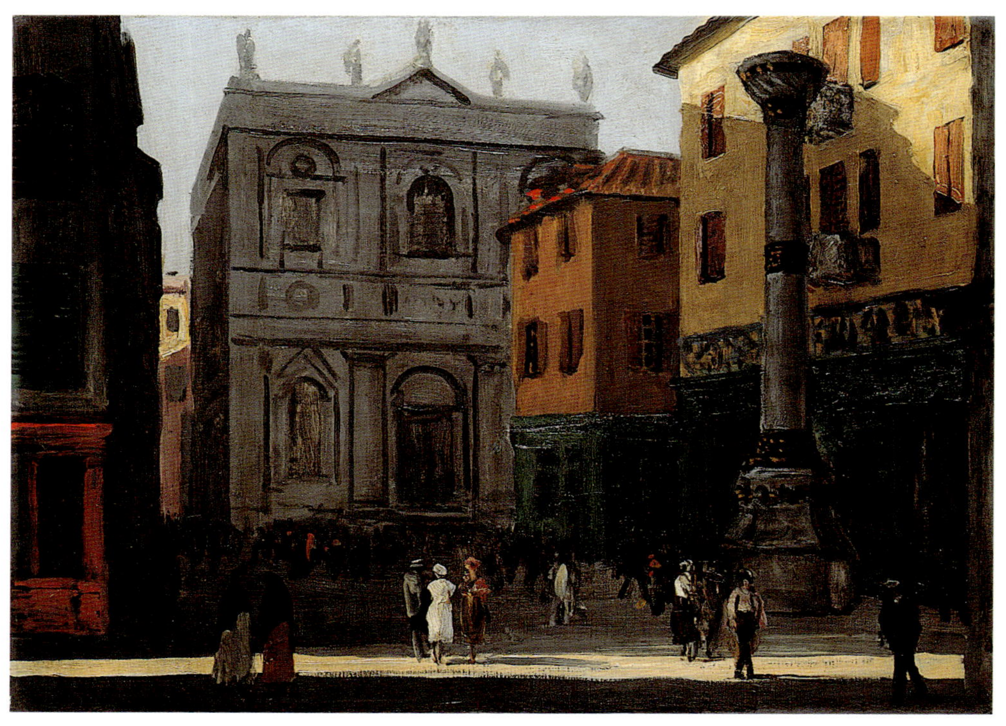

58 *Square in Venice,* 1910

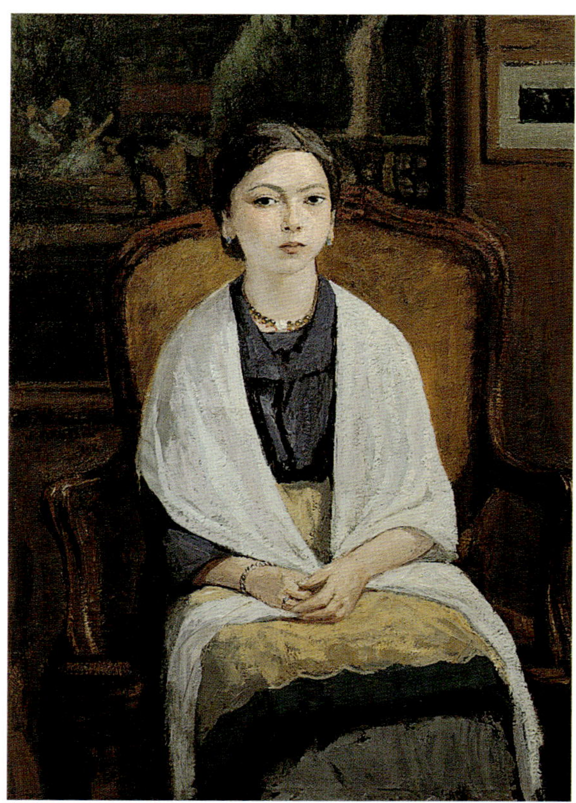

59 *Young Italian Woman,* 1912

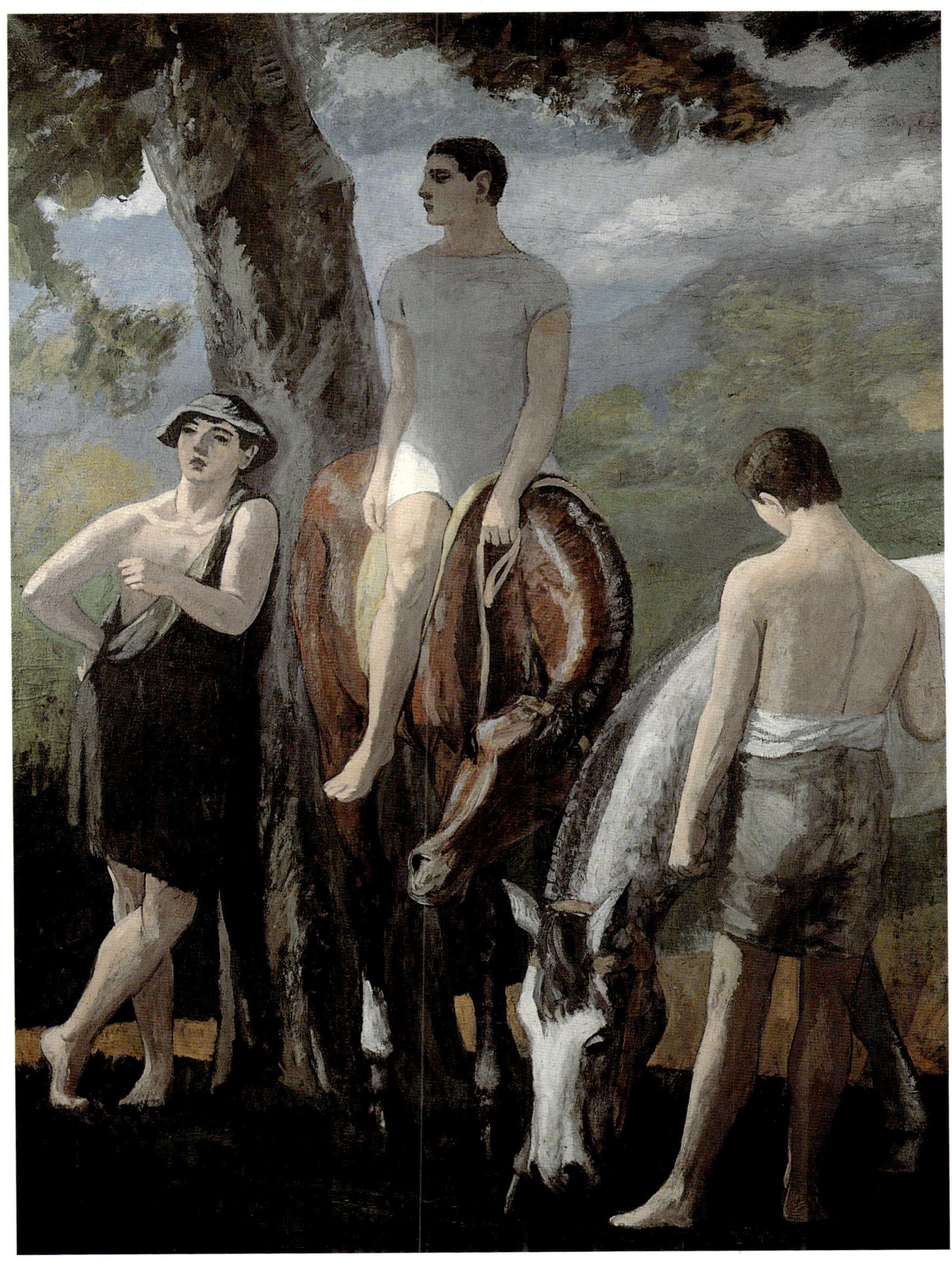

62 *Young Horsemen by a Spring*, 1913, reworked 1923

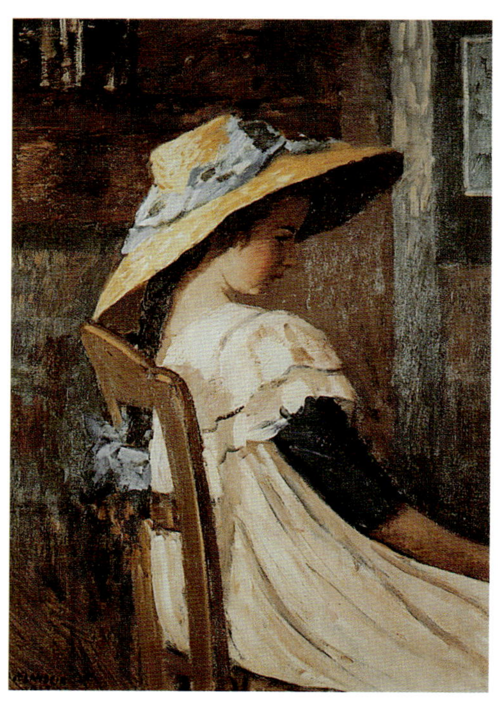

60 *Girl in a Large Hat,* 1913

66 *Notre-Dame, Morning Sun.* 1921

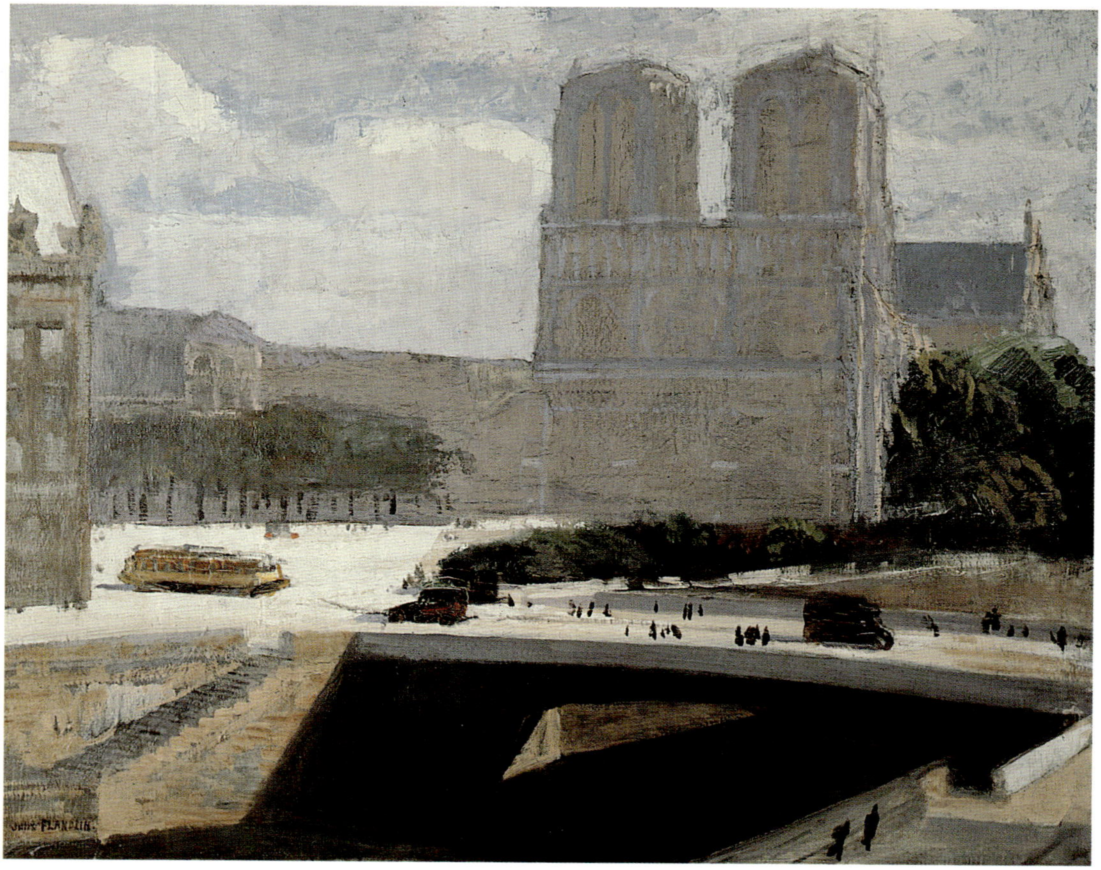

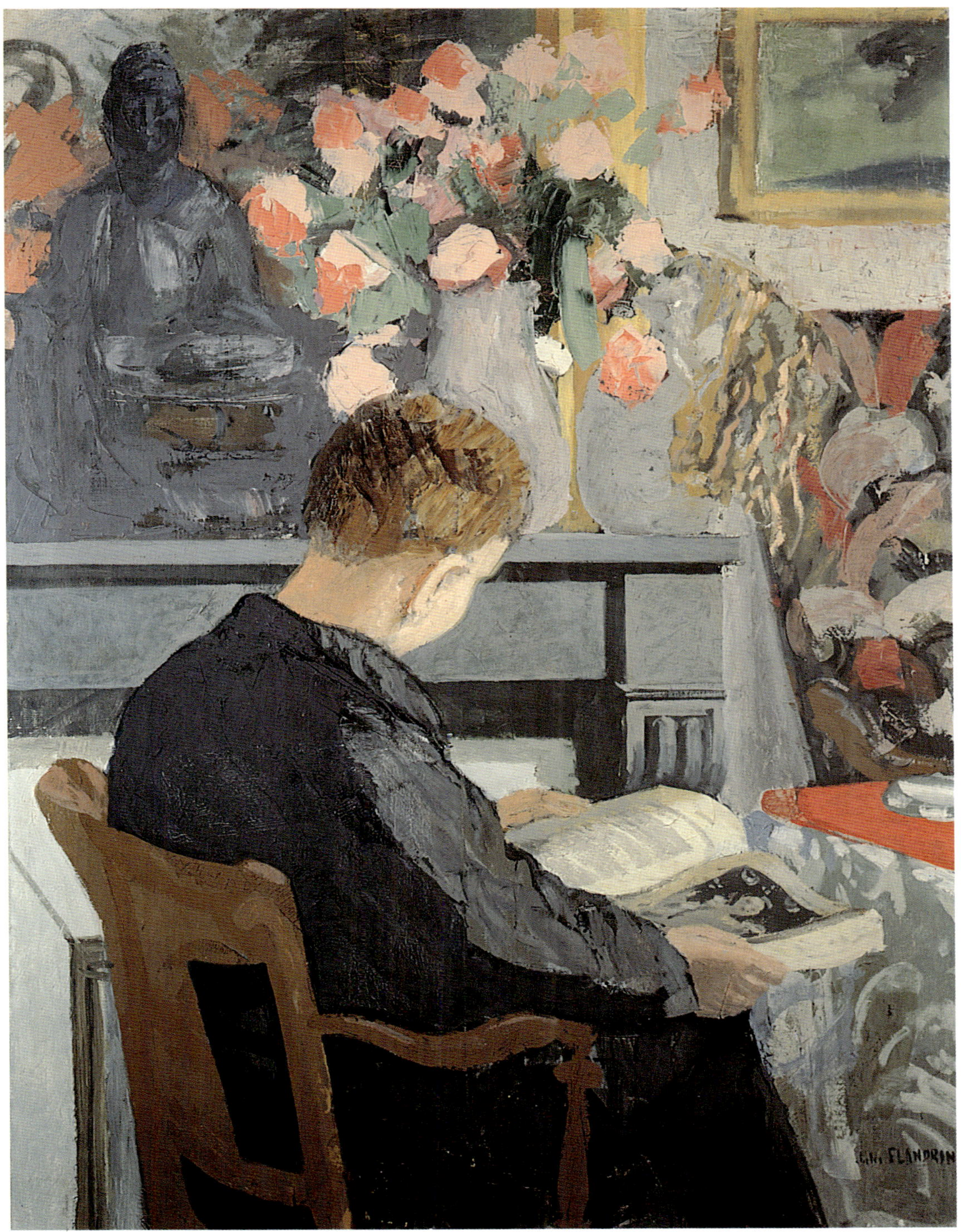

67 *Reading (Pierre Flandrin Reading in the Studio)*, 1922

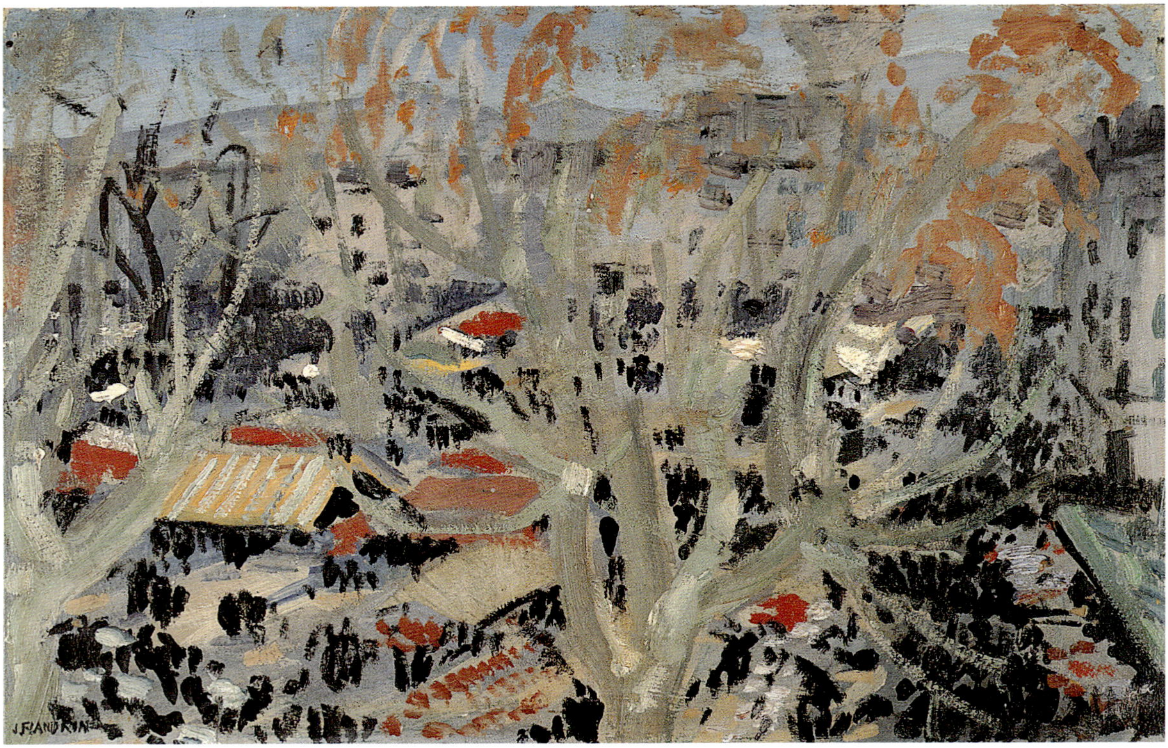

J. FLANDRIN

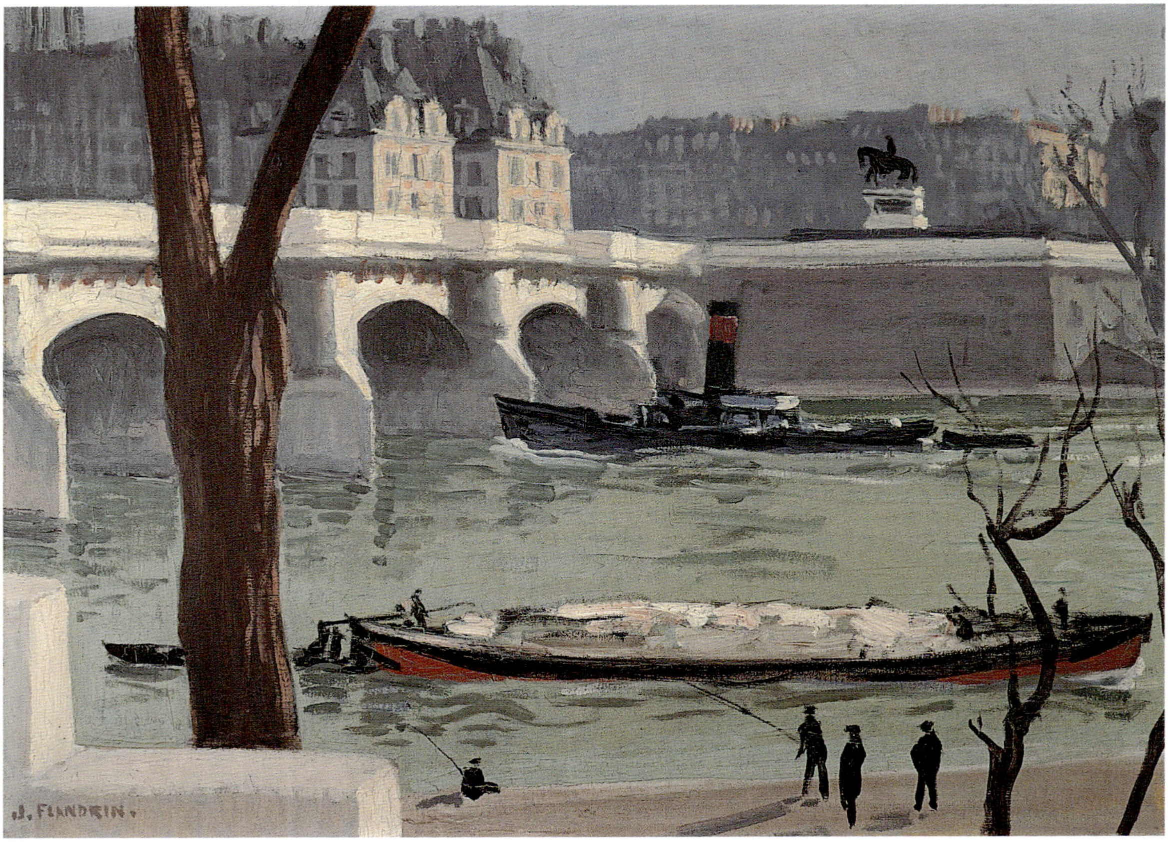

J. FLANDRIN.

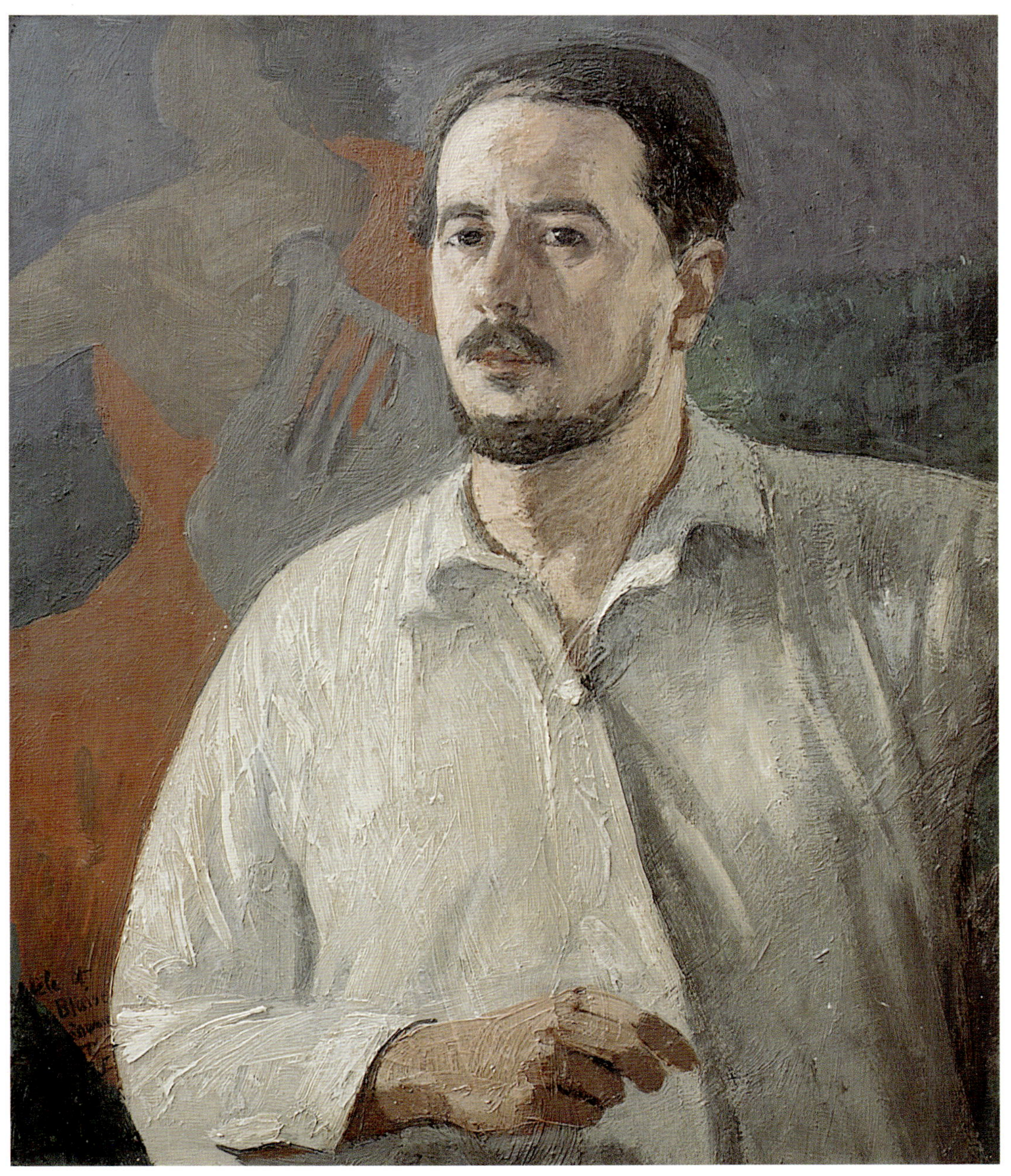

70 *Portrait of the Artist*, 1924

68 (Opposite above) *Vaison, Market Day*, 1923

69 (Opposite below) *Pont-Neuf, Winter Afternoon*, 1924

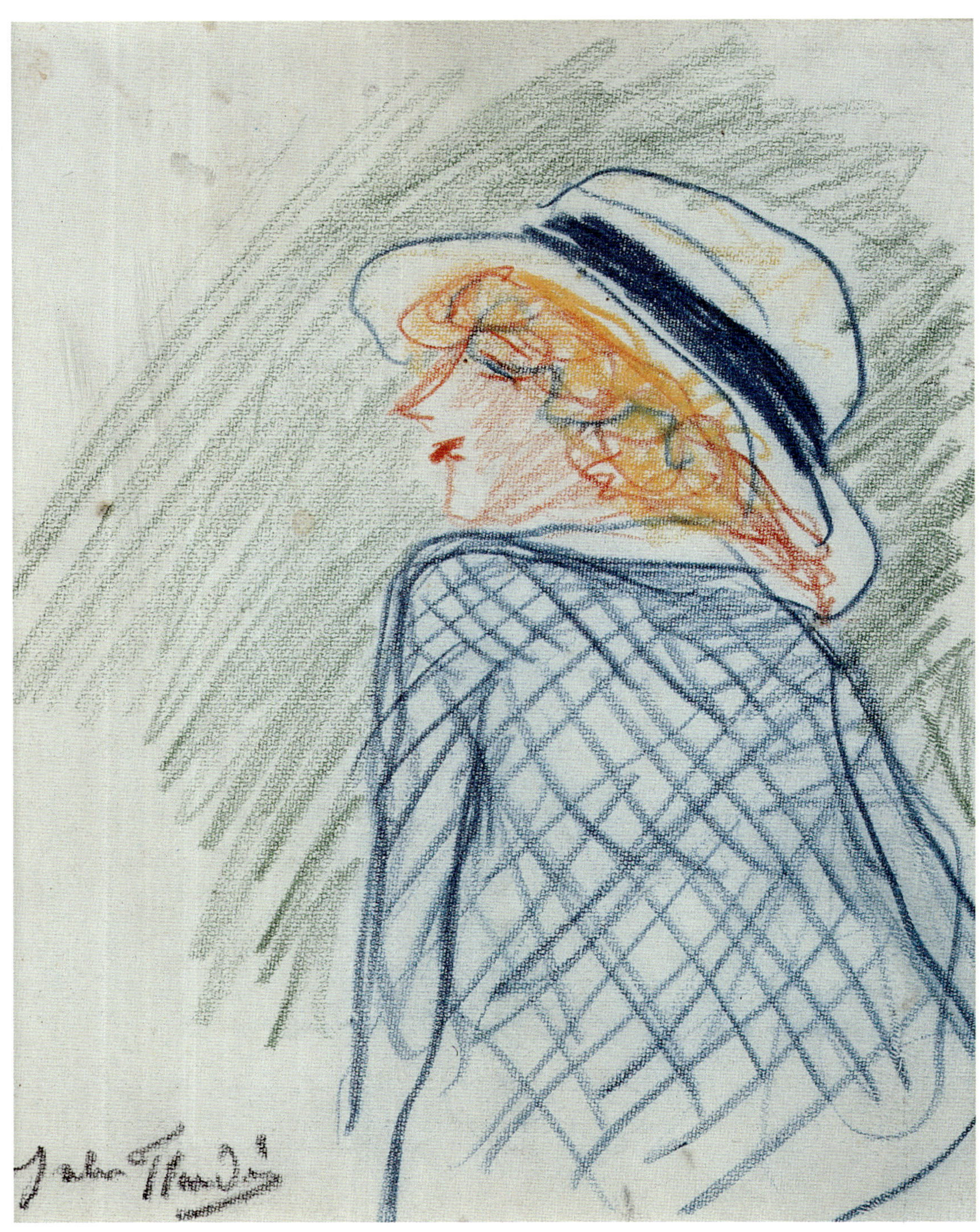

76 *Henriette Deloras, 1930*

A portrait of Flandrin's nephew, Pierre in the studio at 19 Quai St. Michel shows him reading a copy of Charles Morice's 1920 monograph on Gauguin.[1] Together with the large buddha on the mantlepiece to the left of Pierre's head, the paintings's style, with its exotic colours and simplified, stylized forms may be seen as a conscious effort on Flandrin's part to recreate a Gauguinesque manner.

Private Collection, Paris

[1]Charles Morice, *Paul Gauguin: Avec trente-trois planches hors-texte, dont un bois original en fac-simile* (nouvelle éd.), Paris, 1920.

68   *Vaison, Market Day**

1923
Vaison, jour de marché

OIL ON BOARD, 34 × 52 CMS.
INSCRIBED 'J FLANDRIN' ON RECTO LOWER LEFT
PROV.: THE ARTIST; BY DESCENT TO THE PRESENT OWNER
LIT.: FLANDRIN AND ROUSSIER, P.218.

The dominant theme in Flandrin's art of the 1920s is a concern with both recovery and rediscovery of the past. Alongside his increasingly prolific output of still-lifes and landscapes depicting an idyllic Dauphiné, he produced numerous works, including portraits and views of Paris, which show him constantly revisiting and reworking subjects and stylistic innovations of the pre-war period in the light of current preoccupations. Late in 1923, he travelled to Vaison, a location of the war years, staying incognito at a hotel in order to renew his memory of the village which had enchanted his eyes even in the midst of conflict. This striking image of animation presents a bustling and vibrant scene of village life, far removed from the conditions under which Flandrin had first visited it. The style shows a conscious debt to Marquet's manner, with its boldly abbreviated forms picked out in brilliant splashes of colour, and extremely free and improvised brushwork. It recalls, perhaps, the sense of optimism and discovery which had characterized the artistic camaraderie of the early 1900s.

Private Collection, Paris

69   *Pont-Neuf, Winter Afternoon**
1924
Pont-Neuf, après-midi d'hiver

OIL ON CANVAS, 60 × 81 CMS.
INSCRIBED 'J.FLANDRIN.' ON RECTO LOWER RIGHT
PROV.: THE ARTIST; BY DESCENT TO THE PRESENT OWNER
EXH.: PARIS, GALERIE DRUET (*Deuxième groupe*), 1925
LIT.: FLANDRIN AND ROUSSIER, P. 199.

Once again, the subject and style of this painting is reminiscent of Marquet's works of the pre-1914 period. The wintry scene, unusual in Flandrin's work, relates to his painting of Vaison (cat. 68), likewise characterized by a mood of nostalgia, despite the animation it depicts. The pattern of boats, bridge and buildings, the bare forms of trees and tiny silhouetted figures on the quayside, recall Marquet's lively views of the Seine of 1900–1911 with their simplified outlines of boats, bridges and figures, as well as the stylization of a Japanese print, which again may be seen as another allusion to Marquet's interests and to the preoccupations of the early Paris years.

Private Collection, Paris

70   *Portrait of the Artist**
1924
Portrait de l'Artiste

OIL ON BOARD, 55 × 46 CMS.
PROV.: THE ARTIST; BY DESCENT TO THE PRESENT OWNER

See cat. 16.

Private Collection, Grenoble

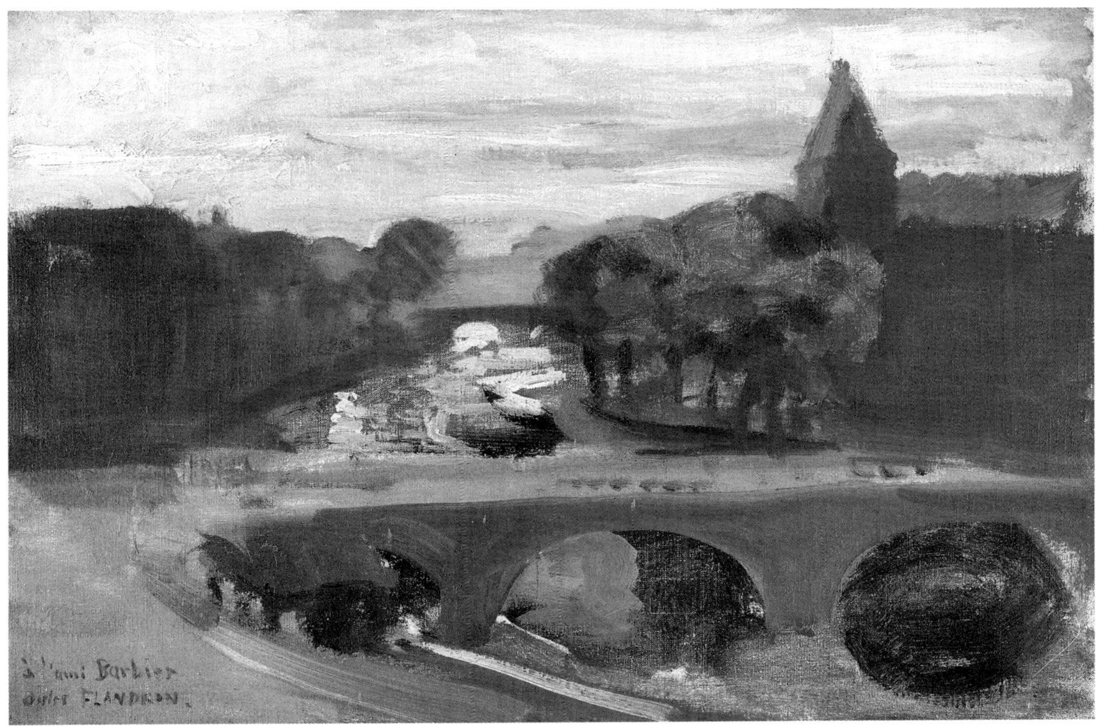

71 *Pont Saint-Michel* (undated), *c.* 1926–7

71 *Pont Saint-Michel*

(UNDATED) *c.*1926–7
Pont Saint-Michel

OIL ON CANVAS, 38 × 55 CMS.
INSCRIBED 'À L'AMI BARBIER JULES FLANDRIN.' ON RECTO LOWER
LEFT
PROV.: THE ARTIST; BY DESCENT TO THE PRESENT OWNER
EXH.: PARIS, GALERIE DRUET, 1927
LIT.: FLANDRIN AND ROUSSIER, P. 215.

Based on another view from Flandrin's studio at 19 Quai St. Michel, this
small painting is dedicated to the painter André Barbier whom Flandrin
had met in the early 1900s. Although no more than a *pochade*, like *Vaison,
Market Day* (cat. 68), it shows a conscious return to Flandrin's manner of
the 1900–1905 period. The daubs of colour and rapidly improvised brushwork convey a sense of the immediacy of the scene and of Flandrin's
sensations, suggesting, yet again, an effort to reinvest his work with the
energy and expressiveness associated with Fauvism at its peak.

Private Collection, Paris

72   *Cupola in Rome*
1929
Coupole à Rome

BLUE CRAYON, 16 × 25.5 CMS.
INSCRIBED WITH MONOGRAM 'JF' ON RECTO LOWER RIGHT
PROV.: THE ARTIST; BY DESCENT TO THE PRESENT OWNER

In 1926, Flandrin embarked on another series of rediscoveries. Setting out to renew his acquaintance with Italy and Italian art, which had been curtailed by war, he made the first of what were to become annual visits between 1926 and 1930. This time, Flandrin was drawn mainly to the monuments of antiquity, to Rome and to the Roman *campagna*. One of numerous drawings and paintings of Roman landmarks and architecture, this view of a church shows Flandrin's interest in capturing the architectural variety of the classical inheritance: a concern reflected in the several travel journals he kept during his Italian sojourns, filled with sketches, watercolours, notes and photographs which attest Flandrin's preoccupation with the scenery, light and atmosphere of Italy as well as with reminders of the classical world.

Private Collection, Paris

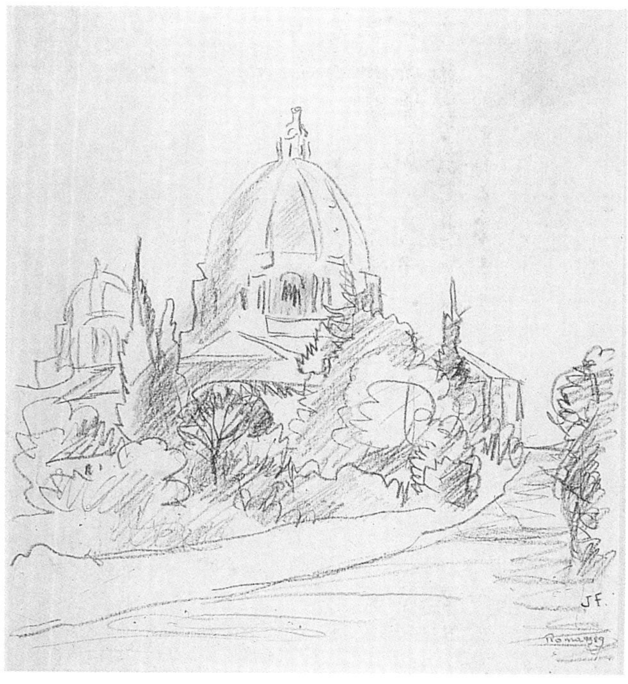

72 Cupola in Rome, 1929

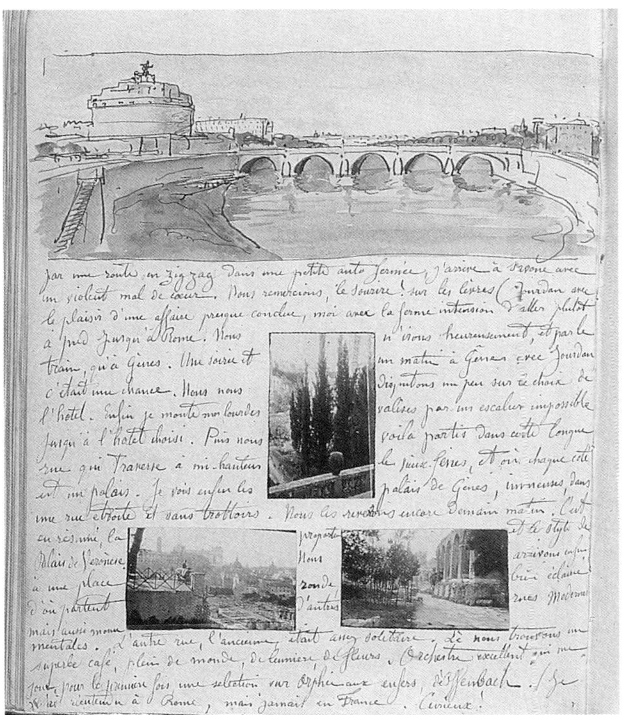

73 *Travel Journal showing views of Italy*, 1927

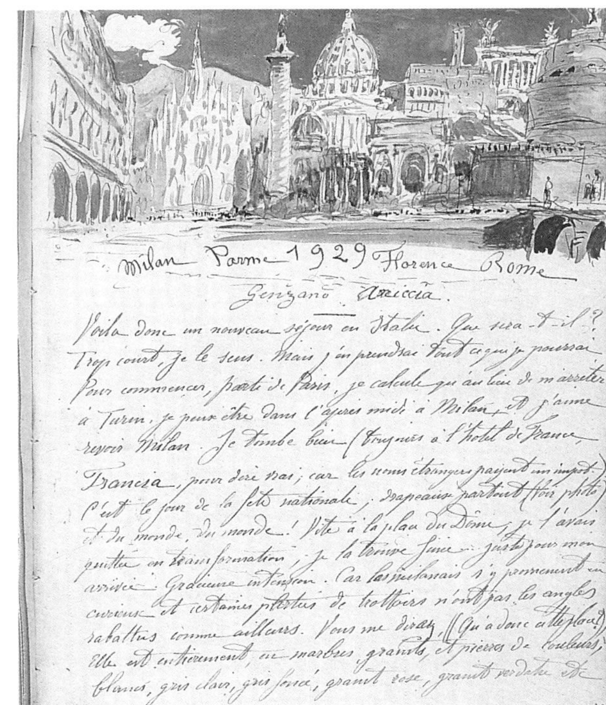

74 *Travel Journal showing views of Italy*, 1929

73–4 *Travel Journals showing views of Italy*

1927 AND 1929
Cahiers des Vacances

PROV.: THE ARTIST; BY DESCENT TO THE PRESENT OWNER

See cat. 72.

Private Collection, Paris

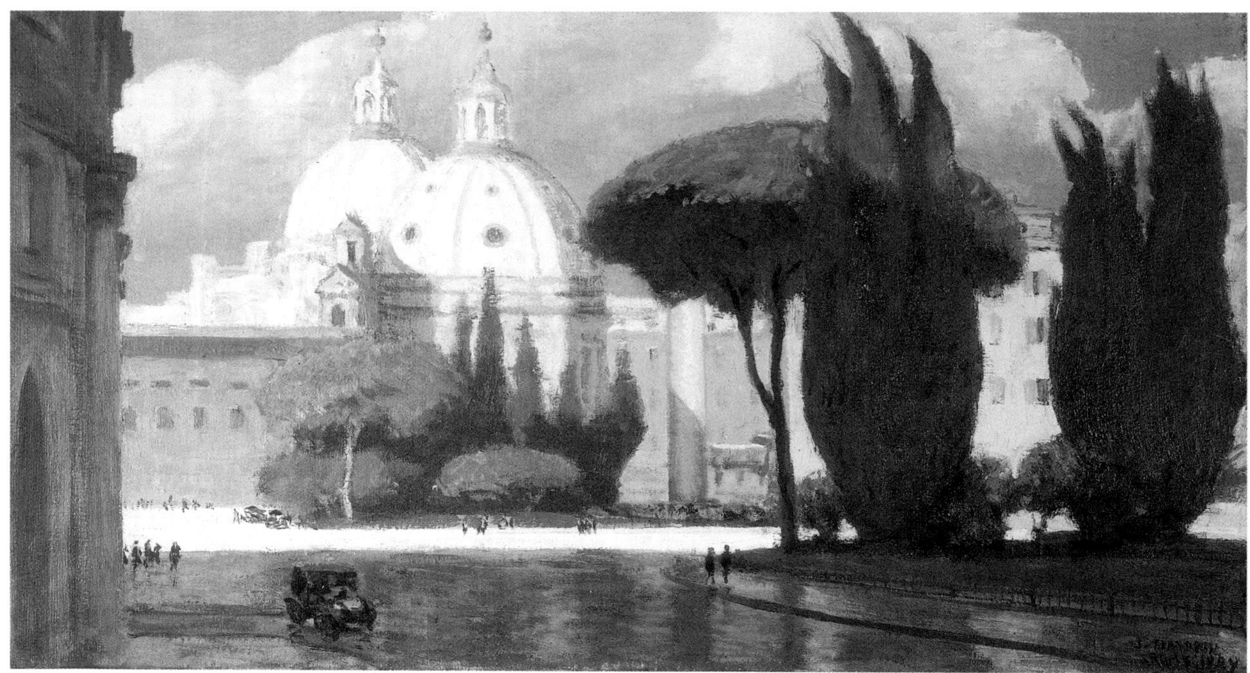

75 *Sun after Rain, Place de Venise, Rome*, 1929

75   *Sun after Rain, Place de Venise, Rome*
1929
Soleil après la pluie, Place de Venise à Rome

Oil on canvas, 45 × 81 cms.
Inscribed 'J.FLANDRIN. ROME' and dated '1929' on recto
lower right
Prov.: The artist; by descent to the present owner
Exh.: Paris, Galerie Druet, 1929
Lit.: Flandrin and Roussier, p. 232.

Exhibited at the Galerie Druet in 1929 entitled *Soleil après la pluie* (no.9), this was one of a number of panoramic city views Flandrin painted between 1927 and 1929. As the tiny figures in the foreground suggest, the main focus of interest, here, is the Roman architecture, its sculptural solidity reflected in the forms of the surrounding trees. The attention to light and weather effects echo Flandrin's Impressionist experiments of the turn of the century. But the rendering of the scene in intense blocks of colour which convey the brilliance of the Mediterranean sun may also be seen as an attempt to find equivalents for the weighty presence of the past and of the classical tradition. It is interests such as these which were eventually to draw Flandrin away from Paris and towards the landscapes of his native Dauphiné, which from 1931 until his death in 1947, he was to rework through the lens of Italy and of the classical inheritance.

Private Collection, Paris

76 *Henriette Deloras**

1930
Henriette Deloras

COLOURED CRAYON, 13.5 × 11.5 CMS.
INSCRIBED 'JULES FLANDRIN' ON RECTO LOWER LEFT
PROV.: THE ARTIST; BY DESCENT TO THE PRESENT OWNER
LIT.: FLANDRIN AND ROUSSIER, P. 21.

In 1921, Flandrin began corresponding with a young Grenoblois artist, Henriette Deloras, then only twenty-one years of age, who had been one of his childhood neighbours in Corenc. Much to Marval's fury and dismay, Henriette was to become his new idol and his passion for much of the rest of the decade. This spirited sketch executed with Flandrin's characteristic swiftness, freedom and economy of expression, suggests the pert, confident young woman who was draw him permanently back to Corenc, shortly to become his wife in 1931 and the mother of his only child, Jules.

Private Collection, Paris

Select Bibliography

The bibliography includes all sources referred to in the essays and catalogue, including unpublished sources and exhibition catalogues.

UNPUBLISHED SOURCES

Flandrin Archives (A collection of newspapers, press cuttings, reviews, journals, sketchbooks, notebooks, drawings and paintings relating to the family, life and work of Jules Flandrin), Paris and Corenc.

Archives Gustave Moreau, Inv. 16096 (*Léon Bonnat papers*); Inv. nos.318 (51/64–89) and 319 (51/64–87); Inv. 320 (51/64–88), and 321 (51/64–84) (Matisse/Rouault donations – Collection du Musée de la littérature tchèque à Prague).

Archives nationales, Doc. AJ 52 284, 15–19 (list of inscriptions for the *atelier* Gustave Moreau at the École des Beaux–Arts); Doc. F/21/4909B; dossier 10; pièce 20, 22, 65, 98 [série cahiers des musées] (registers of State purchases by museums); Doc. F/21/4500B; dossier 2; pièce 14 [série cahiers des musées] (registers of State purchases by museums); Doc. F/21/4208 [série artistes] (registers of State purchases); Doc.F/21/2133 [série artistes] (registers of State purchases).

Walsh, Philip, *The Atelier of Gustave Moreau at the École des Beaux-Arts*, unpublished Ph.D. dissertation (Harvard), 1995.

PUBLISHED SOURCES

Albert, Aristide, *Le Peintre Blanc-Fontaine (1819–1897)*, Grenoble, 1902.

Alexandre, Arsène, 'Supplément du vernissage', *Le Figaro*, 30 April 1898.

– 'La Vie artistique – Les Indépendants', *Le Figaro*, 20 April 1911.

– 'Exposition du deuxième groupe', *Comoedia*, 6 October 1913.

Apollinaire, Guillaume, *Chroniques d'art (1902–1918)*, Paris, 1960.

– *Meditations esthétiques: Les peintres cubistes*, ed. Leroy C. Breunig and Jean-Claude Chevalier, Paris, 1965.

Bal, Georges, 'Le Peintre Jules Flandrin exposé dans les Galeries Druet [*sic*]', *The New York Herald* (Paris), 9 February 1910.

Barr, Alfred H. Jr., *Matisse: His Art and His Public*, New York, 1951, repr. 1966.

Benjamin, Roger, 'Recovering Authors: The Modern Copy, Copy Exhibitions and Matisse', *Art History*, 12, no.2 (June 1989), pp. 176–201.

– 'Ingres chez les Fauves', *Art History*, vol. 23, no.5 (2000), pp. 743–77.

Bernard, Henri, 'Le Dauphiné au Salon', *Le Reveil du Dauphiné*, 21 June 1898.

– 'Le Dauphiné au Salon – M. Flandrin', *Le Reveil du Dauphiné*, 9 June 1899.

– 'Le Dauphiné au Salon', *Le République d'Isère*, 2 May 1904.

– 'Le Dauphiné aux Salons', *Le Petit Dauphinois*, 6 June 1911.

Besson, Georges, *Marquet*, Paris, 1920.

Blanc 'la Goutte', *Poésies en patois du Dauphiné*, dessins de D. Rahoult, gravures de E. Dardelet, préface de George Sand, Grenoble, 1864.

Boime, Albert, 'Le Musée des copies', *Gazette des Beaux-Arts*, vol. 64 (October 1964), pp. 237–47.

– *The Academy and French Painting in the Nineteenth Century*, London, 1971.

Cachin, Françoise, and Rosenberg, Pierre, *et al.*, *De Corot aux Impressionnistes, donations Moreau-Nélaton* (exh. cat., Grand Palais, Paris, 1991), Paris, 1991.

Carco, Francis, *L'Ami des peintres* (2nd ed.), Paris, 1953.

Charles, Étienne, 'Le Salon de la Nationale', *La Liberté*, 21 April 1913.

Chipp, Herschel B., *Theories of Modern Art: A Source Book by Artists and Critics*, Berkeley, Los Angeles and London, 1968.

Clerc, Marianne, *Jacques-André Treillard, 1712–1794, peintre dauphinois*, Grenoble, 1995.

Cuzin, Jean-Pierre, *et al.*, *Copier Créer: De Turner à Picasso, 300 oeuvres inspirées par les maîtres du Louvre* (exh. cat., Musée du Louvre, Paris, 1993), Paris, 1993.

D'Agen, Boyer, 'Au Salon de la Société Nationale', *Le Figaro illustré*, July 1899.

Delaborde, Henri, *Ingres*, Paris, 1870.

Désiré-Lucas, 'Comment j'ai connu Gustave Moreau', *L'Art*, September–October, 1929.

Desvallières, Georges, 'Préface du catalogue de l'Exposition Gustave Moreau et quelques-uns de ses élèves', Galerie Georges Petit, Paris, April 1926.

Druick, Douglas W., 'Gustave Moreau and the Symbolist Ideal', in Lacambre, *et al.*, *Gustave Moreau* (Paris, Princeton, 1998), pp. 33–9.

Dupuy, Marie-Anne, 'Les Copistes à l'oeuvre', in *Copier Créer* (exh. cat., Paris, 1993), pp. 42–51.

Evenepoël, Henri, *Lettres à mon père*, 2 vols, Brussels, 1994.

Feinberg, Larry J., 'Gustave Moreau and the Italian Renaissance', in Lacambre, *et al.*, *Gustave Moreau 1826–1898* (exh. cat. Paris and Princeton, 1998), pp. 5–13

Ferry, R.-M., 'Petits notes d'art', *L'Eclair*, 12 February 1910.

Flam, Jack D., *Matisse: the Man and his Art, 1869–1918*, London, 1986.

Flandresy, Jean de, *La Gravure, les graveurs Dauphinois*, Grenoble, 1901.

Flandrin, Georges (Preface), in *Les Ballets russes par Jules Flandrin 1871–1947*, exh. cat., Galerie Thomire, Le Louvre des Antiquaries, Paris, October–November, 1990.

Flandrin, Georges and Roussier, François, *Jules Flandrin (1871–1947): Un élève de Gustave Moreau témoin de son temps*, La Tronche, 1992.

Genet, Henri, 'Le Salon de la Nationale', *L'Opinion*, 19 April 1913.

Goth, Max, 'Le Salon de la Société Nationale', *Les Hommes du jour*, no.279, 24 May 1913.

Grégoire, Félicien, 'Le Dauphiné aux Salons de 1904 – Société Nationale des Beaux-Arts', *Les Alps pittoresques*, no.79, 31 May – 1 June 1904.

Grenoble, *Catalogue des tableaux* (ville de Grenoble), Grenoble, 1901.

Grenoble, *Maître Pierre Blache*, Hôtel des Ventes (sale catalogue), 12 December 2000.

Hyslop, Francis E. (ed.), *Henri Evenepoël à Paris: Letters choisies, 1892–1899*, Brussels, 1971.

– *Henri Evenepoël: Belgian Painter in Paris 1892–1899*, University Park, Penn., 1975.

Jamot, Paul, *Auguste Ravier (1814–1895)*, Lyon, 1911.

Jensen, Robert, *Marketing Modernism in Fin-de-Siècle Europe*, Princeton, 1994.

Kahane, Martine, *et al.*, *Nijinsky 1889–1950* (exh. cat., Musée d'Orsay, Paris, 2000–2001), Paris, 2000.

Kahn, Gustave, *L'Esthétique de la rue*, Paris, 1901.

– 'Le Salon des Tuileries', *Le Quotidien*, 31 October 1923.

Kennedy, Janet, *The 'Mir Iskusstva' Group and Russian Art*, New York, 1977.

Lacambre, Geneviève, *Gustave Moreau e l'Italia* (exh. cat., Accademia di Francia a Roma, Villa Medici, Rome, 1996–1997), Milan, Rome, 1996.

– *et al.*, *Gustave Moreau 1826–1898: Between Epic and Dream* (exh. cat., Grand Palais, Paris, 1998–9; Art Institute of Chicago, Chicago, 1999; Metropolitan Museum of Art, New York, 1999), Paris and Princeton, 1998.

Lebensztejn, Jean-Claude, 'Tournant', in Pagé, *et al.*, *Le Fauvisme ou 'l'épreuve du feu'* (exh. cat., Paris, 1999), pp. 26–45.

Lee, Jane, *Derain*, Oxford, 1990.

Lobstein, Dominique, 'Antony Roux: Portrait d'un collectionneur et mécène', in *Gustave Moreau, le rêve symbolique, Dossier de l'art*, no.51 S (October 1998), pp. 58–64.

Loisel, Philippe, *et al.*, *Simon Bussy (1870–1954): L'Esprit du trait, du zoo à la gentry* (exh. cat., Musée Départementale de l'Oise, Beauvais, 1996), Paris, 1996.

Magne, Émile, 'L'Esthétique de la rue', *Mercure de France*, vol. LVI (July 1905), pp. 161–81.

Maignien, Édmond, *Les Artistes Grenoblois*, Grenoble, 1887.

Marval, Jacqueline, 'Les Danseuses de Flandrin', *L'Art décoratif*, no. 190 (April 1913), pp. 165–76.

– *Vente des tableaux de la collection Jacqueline Marval*, Hôtel Drouot, Paris, 21 December 1932.

Matisse, Henri, *Écrits et propos sur l'art*, Paris, 1972.

Mauclair, Camille, *La Farce de l'art vivant*, Paris, 1929.

Monnier, Gérard, *L'Art et ses institutions en France: de la Révolution à nos jours*, Paris, 1995.

Moreau, Gustave, *Gustave Moreau et ses élèves* (exh. cat., Musée Cantini, Marseille, 1962), Marseille, 1962.

– *Peintures, cartons, aquarelles, etc. exposés dans les galeries du Musée Gustave Moreau*, Paris, 1990.

Morice, Charles, 'Le XXIème Salon des Indépendants', *Mercure de France*, vol. LIV, no. 188 (April 1905), pp. 536–56.

– 'Enquête sur les tendances actuelles des arts plastiques', *Mercure de France*, vols LVI and LVII, nos 195–7 (August–September, 1905), pp. 346–59; 538–55 and 61–85.

– 'Le Salon d'Automne', *Mercure de France*, vol. LVIII, no.203 (December 1905), pp. 379–80.

– 'Art moderne – Jules Flandrin', *Le Mercure de France*, vol. LXXXIV, no.306 (March 1910), pp. 360–1.

– *Paul Gauguin: Avec trente-trois planches hors-texte, dont un bois original en facsimile* (nouvelle éd.), Paris, 1920.

Mourey, Gabriel, 'Au Salon de la Société Nationale', *Le Journal*, 14 April 1913.

Pagé, Suzanne, *et al.*, *Le Fauvisme ou 'l'épreuve du feu': Éruption de la modernité en Europe* (exh. cat., Musée d'Art moderne de la Ville de Paris, 1999–2000), Paris, 1999.

Prache, Anne, 'Souvenirs d'Arthur Guéniot sur Gustave Moreau et sur son enseignement à l'École des Beaux-Arts', *Gazette des Beaux-Arts*, vol.67 (April 1966), pp. 229–40.

Perrin, Abbé H.-J., *Histoire du Pont-de-Beauvoisin*, Paris, 1897.

Raymond, Marcel, *Jean Achard (1807–1884)*, Paris, 1887.

Reymond, Marcel, *Étude sur le Musée de Tableaux de Grenoble*, Grenoble, 1879.

Romains, Jules, *La Vie unanime*, Paris, 1908.

– *Puissances de Paris* (1911), repub. Paris, 2000.

Rouault, Georges, *Souvenirs intimes*, Paris, 1926.

– *Sur l'art et sur la vie*, Paris, 1971.

– *Rouault: Première période, 1903–1920* (exh. cat., Musée national d'Art moderne, Paris, 1992), Paris, 1992.

Salmon, André, 'Les Expositions de Peinture – Jules Flandrin (Galerie Druet)', *Paris-Journal*, 9 February 1910.

–'Les Indépendants', *Paris-Journal*, 20 April 1911.

– *La Jeune peinture française*, Paris, 1912.

– ('La Palette'), 'Exposition du deuxième groupe – Galerie Druet', *Le Gil blas*, 18 February 1913.

Schneider, Pierre, *Les Dialogues du Louvre*, Paris, 1967, repr. 1972.

– *Matisse*, Paris, 1984.

– *Matisse*, transl. Michael Taylor and Bridget Strevens Romer, London, 1984.

Sarradin, Édmond, 'Escaliers et paliers – MM. Flandrin, Hanicotte, Milcendeau', *Journal des débats*, 16 April 1913.

Serrano, Véronique, *et al.*, *Charles Camoin: Rétrospective, 1879–1965* (exh. cat., Lausanne, Fondation de l'Hermitage, 1997; Marseille, Musée Cantini, 1997–1998), Paris, 1997.

Société Nationale des Beaux-Arts, Catalogue illustré du Salon de 1898, Paris, 1898.

– *Catalogue illustré du Salon de 1899*, Paris, 1899.

– *Catalogue illustré du Salon 1903*, Paris, 1903.

– *Catalogue illustré du Salon 1904*, Paris, 1904.

– *Catalogue illustré du Salon 1905*, Paris, 1905.

– *Catalogue illustré du Salon 1906*, Paris, 1906.

– *Catalogue illustré du Salon 1913*, Paris, 1913.

Spurling, Hilary, *The Unknown Matisse: Man of the North, 1869–1908*, London, 1998.

Stevens, MaryAnne, *et al.*, *Alfred Sisley* (exh. cat., Royal Academy of Arts, London, 1992; Musée d'Orsay, Paris, 1992–1993; The Walters Art Gallery, Baltimore, 1993), New Haven and London, 1992.

Suarès, André, *Correspondance*, Paris, 1960.

Ternois, Daniel, *Montauban – Musée Ingres: Peintures Ingres et son temps*, Paris, 1965.

Thiébault-Sisson, 'Le Salon du Champ-de-Mars', *Le Petit temps*, 23 April 1897.

Tison-Braun, Micheline, *La Crise de l'humanisme*, vol. II (1914–1939), Paris, 1967.

Vauxcelles, Louis, 'Le Salon de la Société Nationale', *Le Gil blas*, 13 April 1913.

Vellein, G., *Le Poète Blanc-la-Goutte*, Grenoble, 1907.

Von Holten, Ragnar, *et al.*, *Gustave Moreau* (exh. cat., Musée du Louvre, Paris, 1961), Paris, 1961.

Weber, Eugene, *France Fin de Siècle*, Cambridge, Mass., and London, 1986.

Werth, Léon, 'Le mois du peintre, d'après les Maîtres', *La Phalange*, 20 May 1910.

Zavie, Émile, 'Galerie Bernheim – Copies "d'après les Maîtres"', *Le Feu*, no. 62, 1 June 1910.

List of Exhibitions of and including Jules Flandrin's Works

Months of the exhibition are given where known.

1890 Grenoble, Galerie Roux, *Oeuvres de Jules Flandrin*

1895 Grenoble, Galerie Roux, *Oeuvres de Jules Flandrin*

Grenoble, Société des amis des arts, *Salon de Grenoble*, 1 July–30 August

1896 Paris, Champ-de-Mars, *Salon de la Société Nationale des Beaux-Arts*, April

1897 Grenoble, Librarie Falque et Perrin, *Oeuvres de Jules Flandrin*

Paris, Champ-de-Mars, *Salon de la Société Nationale des Beaux-Arts*

1898 Paris, Champ-de-Mars, *Salon de la Société Nationale des Beaux-Arts*

1899 Paris, Champ-de-Mars, *Salon de la Société Nationale des Beaux-Arts*

Grenoble, Société des amis des arts, *Salon de Grenoble*, 18 July–30 August

1900 Paris, Grand Palais, *Exposition Internationale Universelle de 1900*, 15 April–15 October

1901 Paris, Grand Palais, *Société Nationale des Beaux-Arts*, Xème exposition, 22 April–30 June

Grenoble, Galerie Fénoglio, *Exposition Jules Flandrin*, July

1902 Paris, Galerie Berthe Weill, *Exposition de Groupe*, February

Paris, Grand Palais, *Société Nationale des Beaux-Arts*, XIIème exposition, 20 April–30 June

Grenoble, Galerie Fénoglio, *Exposition de tableaux par M. Jules Flandrin*, July

1903 Paris, Grand Palais, *Société Nationale des Beaux-Arts*, XIIIème exposition, 16 April–30 June

Grenoble, Galerie Fénoglio, *Exposition de tableaux de M. Jules Flandrin*, October

Paris, Petit Palais, *Salon d'Automne*, 1ère exposition, 31 October–6 December

1904 Paris, Grand Palais, *Société Nationale des Beaux-Arts*, XIVème exposition, 17 April–30 June

Grenoble, Société des amis des arts, *Salon de Grenoble*, 18 July–30 August

Grenoble, Galerie Fénoglio, *Exposition de tableaux par M. Jules Flandrin*, August

1905 Paris, Grandes Serres de la ville de Paris, *Société des Artistes Indépendants*, 24 March–30 April 1905

Paris, Grand Palais, *Société Nationale des Beaux-Arts*, XVème exposition, 15 April–30 June

Paris, Grand Palais, *Salon d'Automne*, 18 October–25 November

Grenoble, Galerie Fénoglio, *Exposition Jules Flandrin*

1906 Paris, Galerie Druet, *Exposition de peinture de M. Jules Flandrin*, 15–27 January

Paris, Grandes Serres de la ville de Paris, *Société des Artistes Indépendants*, 20 March–30 April

Paris, Grand Palais, *Société Nationale des Beaux-Arts*, XVIème exposition, 15 April–30 June

Paris, Grand Palais, *Salon d'Automne*, 6 October–15 November

1907 Paris, Grandes Serres de la ville de Paris, *Société des Artistes Indépendants*, 20 March–30 April

Paris, Grand Palais, *Société Nationale des Beaux-Arts*, 14 April–30 June

Paris, Palais de Bagatelle (Bois de Boulogne), *Portraits de femmes, rétrospective de la Société Nationale des Beaux-Arts*

Grenoble, Galerie Fénoglio, *Exposition de tableaux de M. Jules Flandrin*

1908 Paris, Galerie Berthe Weill, *Aquarelles et peintures*, 6–31 January

Grandes Serres de la ville de Paris, *Société des Artistes Indépendants*, 20 March–2 May

Paris, Galerie Druet, *Exposition de peinture de M. Jules Flandrin*, 2–11 April

Paris, Grand Palais, *Société Nationale des Beaux-Arts*, April–June

Paris, Galerie Druet, *Exposition de tableaux modernes*, 3–20 July

Paris, Galerie Druet, *Exposition d'aquarelles et de dessins*, 21 December 1908–16 January 1909

Grenoble, Galerie Fénoglio, *Exposition Jules Flandrin*

Grenoble, *Société Dauphinois des Beaux-Arts, Salon de 1908*

1909 Brussels, *La Libre esthétique*, 16ème exposition, 7 March–12 April

Paris, Jardin des Tuileries, Serres de l'Orangerie, *Société des Artistes Indépendants*, 27 March–2 May

Paris, Grand Palais, *Société Nationale des Beaux-Arts*, 15 April–30 June

Grenoble, Société des amis des arts, *Salon de Grenoble*, 19 April–15 June

Le Havre, Hôtel de Ville, *Cercle de l'Art Moderne*, June

Paris, Galerie Eugène Blot, *Natures mortes et fleurs (peintures)*, 13 November–4 December

Paris, Galerie Druet, *Dessins de trente cinq artistes contemporains, terres vernissées et grès de M. André Methey*, 20 December 1909–8 January 1910

Grenoble, Galerie Fénoglio, *Exposition Jules Flandrin*

1910   Paris, Galerie Druet, *Exposition de peintures de M. Jules Flandrin*, 7–9 February

Brussels, *La Libre esthétique*, 12 March–17 April

Paris, *Société des Artistes Indépendants*, Cours la Reine (Pont des Invalides), 18 March–1 May

Paris, Grand Palais, *Société Nationale des Beaux-Arts*, 15 April–30 June

Paris, Galerie Bernheim-Jeune, *D'après les Maîtres*, 18–30 April

London, Stafford Gallery, *Exposition de peinture de M. Jules Flandrin*, 3–10 November

Paris, Galerie Druet, *Dessins et aquarelles (trente sept artistes)*, 19–31 December

Interlaken, *Exposition Internationale des Beaux-Arts*

Paris, *Exposition de Bienfaisance, les inondations de Paris*

Buenos Aires, *Exposition Internationale du Centenaire*

Grenoble, Galerie Fénoglio, *Exposition Jules Flandrin*

1911   Paris, Galerie Druet, *Exposition annuelle du deuxième groupe*, 13–25 March

Brussels, *La Libre esthétique*, 18 March–23 April

Paris, Grand Palais, *Société Nationale des Beaux-Arts*, 16 April–30 June

Paris, Quai d'Orsay (Pont de l'Alma), *Société des Artistes Indépendants*, 21 April –13 June

Munich, *Kunstausstellungsgebaüde Secession, München*, 16 May–31 October

Paris, *Exposition d'ensemble organisée par les élèves de Gustave Moreau*

Grenoble, Galerie Fénoglio, *Exposition de tableaux de M. Jules Flandrin*

Paris, Galerie Ch. Hesséle, *Exposition, les églises de France*

Paris, Galerie Druet, *Dessins et aquarelles*, 26 December 1911–6 January 1912

1912   St. Petersburg, Palais Youssoupoff, *Exposition Centenale de l'art français (1812–1912)*, 15 January–30 March

Paris, Galerie Druet, *Exposition annuelle du deuxième groupe*, 5–17 February

Paris, Grand Palais, *Société Nationale des Beaux-Arts*, 14 April–30 June

Marseille, ateliers du quai Rive-Neuve, *Le Salon de Mai*, 1–15 May

Paris, Galerie Druet, *Exposition de peintures de M. Jules Flandrin*, 13–25 May

Paris, Grand Palais, *Société du Salon d'Automne*, 1 October–8 November 1912

Paris, Galerie Manzi et Joyant, *Exposition d'art contemporain*, October 1912

Paris, Galerie Druet, *Exposition de dessins et aquarelles*, 23 December 1912–4 Januuary 1913

Grenoble, Galerie Fénoglio, *Exposition Jules Flandrin*

1913   New York, the Armory of the Sixty-Ninth Infantry, *International Exhibition of Modern Art*, 15 February–15 March; Chicago, the Art Institute of Chicago, 24 March–16 April; Boston, Copley Hall, 28 April–19 May

Paris, Galerie Druet, *Exposition annuelle du deuxième groupe*, 17 February–1 March

Paris, Grand Palais, *Société Nationale des Beaux-Arts*, 14 April–30 June

Munich, *L'Art Français*, July

Gand, *Oeuvres modernes, section française des beaux-arts*, summer

Grenoble, Société des amis de Grenoble, *Salon de Grenoble*, 5 August–20 September

Geneva, Galerie Moos, *Paris, ses peintres*, 1–30 September

Paris, Galerie Druet, *Exposition d'affiches originales*, 20–29 October

Paris, Grand Palais, *Société du Salon d'Automne*, 15 November 1913–5 January 1914

Paris, Galerie Druet, *Exposition de peinture de M. Jules Flandrin*, 1–13 December 1913

Paris, Galerie Manzi et Joyant, *Exposition d'art contemporain*, December

Paris, Galerie Druet, *Exposition de dessins et aquarelles*, 29 Decembe 1913–10 January 1914

1914   Paris, Galerie Druet, *Exposition annuelle du deuxième groupe*, 9–21 February 1914

Grenoble, Galerie Fénoglio, *Exposition Jules Flandrin*, 26 February–10 March 1914

Paris, Champ-de-Mars, *Société des Artistes Indépendants*, 1 March–30 April

Paris, Hôtel Drouot, *La Peau d'ours*, 2 March

Brussels, *La Libre esthétique*, 7 March–13 April

Venice, *XI. Expositione internationale d'arte della città di Venezia*, 23 April–31 October

Brussels, Galerie Giroux, *Salon des Artistes Indépendants de Paris*, 16 May–7 June

Paris, Galerie Levesque, *Troisième réunion des oeuvres d'un groupe de peintres, sculpteurs, graveurs*

Lyon, *Exposition internationale des beaux-arts*

1915   Paris, Galerie Druet, *Exposition annuelle du deuxième groupe*, 27 May–7 June

Paris, Galerie Bernheim-Jeune, *Tombola artistique au profit des artistes polonais victimes de la Guerre*, 28 December 1915–January 1916

1916   Paris, Salle du Jeu de Paume, *Exposition d'art français, la Triennale*, 2 March–16 April

Winterthur, Kunstverein, *Ausstellung französischer Malerei*, 29 October–26 November

1917   Basel, Kunsthalle, *Exposition de peinture française*, 10 January–4 February

Paris, Galerie Numès et Fiquet, *Exposition vente de l'oeuvre du prêt d'honneur aux aveugles*, May

Paris, Galerie Joyant, *La Peinture indépendante*, April–May

Barcelona, *Exposition de peinture française*, May–June

Zurich, Kunsthalle, *Französiche Kunst des XIX und XX Jahrhundert*, 5 October–14 November

Paris, Berger-Levrault, *Le Salon des Armées de la République*

Paris, Galerie Berthe Weill, *Exposition d'ensemble*

1918   Paris, Galerie Goupil et Cie, Manzi et Joyant, *Première exposition de la jeune peinture française*, 6 April–10 May

Paris, Galerie Druet, *Exposition annuelle du deuxième groupe*, 27 May–7 June

Paris, *Le Salon du Temple de guerre*

1919   Paris, Trocadéro, *Musée de l'aéronautique militaire*, 15 January

Paris, Galerie Druet, *Exposition annuelle du deuxième groupe*, 5–16 May

Paris, Grand Palais, *Société du Salon d'Automne*, 1 November–10 December

Paris, Galerie Druet, *Exposition de peinture de M. Jules Flandrin*, 24 November–5 December

1920   Paris, Galerie Druet, *Exposition annuelle du deuxième groupe*, 12–23 April

Paris, Galerie Manzi et Joyant, *Deuxième exposition de la jeune peinture française*, 17 June–4 July

Paris, Galerie Druet, *Exposition d'ensemble*, September

Paris, Galerie Manuel Frères, *L'Enfant*, 11–30 October

Paris, Grand Palais, *Société du Salon d'Automne*, 15 October–12 December

1921   Paris, Galerie Druet, *Exposition annuelle du deuxième groupe*, 18–29 April

Paris, Grand Palais, *Société du Salon d'Automne*, 1 November–20 December

Paris, Galerie Druet, *Exposition de M. Jules Flandrin, aquarelles et dessins*, 21 November–2 December

1922   Paris, Galerie Druet, *Exposition annuelle du deuxième groupe*, 6–17 March

Paris, Galerie Druet, *Exposition de peinture de M. Jules Flandrin*, 20–31 March

Paris, Galerie Bernheim-Jeune, *Cent aquarelles, pastels et dessins*, 3–21 October

Paris, Galerie Devambez, *Exposition des cent dessins*, 9–25 October

Paris, Galerie Barbazanges, *Le Sport dans l'art*, November

Paris, Grand Palais, *Société du Salon d'Automne*, 1 November–17 December

Paris, Galerie Bernheim-Jeune, *Exposition de peinture moderne, groupe I*, 5–15 December

Venice, *XIII. Exposition internationale d'art de la ville de Venise*

1923   Nantes, Musée des Beaux-Arts, *Tableaux contemporains*, January

Stockholm, Liljevalchs Koust Hall, *L'Art français à Stockholm*, February

Paris, Galerie Druet, *Exposition annuelle du deuxième groupe*, 16–27 April

Paris, Musée Galliera, *Cartons de tapisserie pour Aubusson*, April

Paris, Galerie Marcel Bernheim, *Études et pastels de femmes*, June

Paris, Terrasse du bord de l'eau, *Salon des Tuileries*, May

Grenoble, *Le Salon de l'effort, Groupe d'action d'art*, 30 June–30 July

Paris, Galerie Devambez, *Paravents et panneaux décoratifs*, November

Paris, Grand Palais, *Société du Salon d'Automne*, 1 November–16 December

Paris, R.G. Michel, *Exposition permanente de dessins, eaux-fortes et lithographies*

1924 Paris, Galerie Druet, *Exposition annuelle du deuxième groupe*, 24 March–4 April

Paris, Société des amis du Luxembourg, *Première exposition des collectionneurs*, 10 March–10 April

Paris, Galerie Barbazanges, *Quatrième exposition de la jeune peinture française*, 2–19 April

Venice, *XIV. Exposition internationale des beaux-arts*, 27 April–May

Paris, Galerie Druet, *Exposition de peinture de M. Jules Flandrin*, 5–16 May

Paris, Palais de Bois (Porte Maillot), *Salon des Tuileries*, May

Paris, Café de la Rotonde, *Exposition d'ensemble*, August

Paris, Grand Palais, *Société du Salon d'Automne*, 1 November–14 December

Paris, Galerie Druet, *Oeuvres récentes*, 24 December 1924–9 January 1925

1925 Paris, Galerie Druet, *Exposition annuelle du premier groupe*, 1–15 January

Paris, Galerie Druet, *Exposition annuelle du deuxième groupe*, 23 March–3 April

Beauvais, Hôtel de Ville, *Les Peintres de la fleur*, 25 April–12 October

Paris, Galerie Barbazanges, *Cinquième exposition de la jeune peinture française*, April

Paris, Palais de Bois (Porte Maillot), *Salon des Tuileries*, May

Grenoble, Galerie St. Louis, *Exposition Jules Flandrin*, May

Lyon, *Salon du Sud-Est*, 6–30 June

Paris, Galerie Druet, *Exposition de 25 peintres contemporains*, 21 June–30 September

Paris, Terrasse du bord de l'eau, *Société du Salon d'Automne*, 26 September–2 November

Paris, Palais de marbre, Mercier frères, *Exposition de paysage contemporain*, 21 November–5 December

Grenoble, *Exposition de peinture et de sculpture*

Paris, Office du gouvernement général de l'Indochine, *Exposition des artistes Dauphinois*

1926 Paris, Galerie Druet, *Exposition annuelle du premier groupe*, 25 January–5 February

Grenoble, Galerie St. Louis, *Exposition Jules Flandrin*, January

Paris, Galerie Druet, *Salon des peintres de la mer*, January

Paris, Grand Palais, *Trente ans d'art Indépendant*, 20 February–21 March

Paris, Galerie Druet, *Exposition d'ensemble*, 6–16 April

Paris, Galerie Granoff, *Exposition d'ensemble*, 19 April–19 May

Lyon, *Salon du Sud-Est*, 8 May–June

Venice, Palais de l'Exposition, *XV. Exposition internationale de la ville de Venise*, May

Paris, Palais de Bois, *Salon des Tuileries*, May

Paris, Grand Palais, *Société du Salon d'Automne*, 5 November–19 December

1927 Paris, Galerie Druet, *Exposition annuelle du premier groupe*, January

Paris, Galerie Druet, *Exposition de peinture de M. Jules Flandrin*, 7–18 March

Paris, Galerie Druet, *Exposition du deuxième groupe*, 4–15 April

Lyon, *Salon du Sud-Est*, 7 May–12 June

Belfort, Société Belfortaise des Beaux-Arts, *Peinture contemporaine*, 14 June–3 July

Grenoble, Société des amis des arts, *Salon de Grenoble*, 16 June–16 July

Paris, Palais de Bois, *Salon des Tuileries*

Paris, Galerie Druet, *Exposition d'ensemble*, 15–30 September

Paris, Grand Palais, *Société du Salon d'Automne*, 5 November–18 December

Paris, 15 avenue Montaigne, *Salon de l'Escalier*, November

Grenoble, Galerie St. Louis, *Exposition Jules Flandrin*, 22 December 1927–10 January 1928

Grenoble, *Salon de Grenoble, Vème exposition d'art de l'effort*, 22 December 1927–30 January 1928

Paris, Galerie Druet, *Oeuvres récentes*, 26 December 1927–6 January 1928

Paris, Palais de Bois, *Salon des Tuileries*

1928 Brussels, Galerie Giroud, *La Peinture française*, January

Paris, Galerie Druet, *Exposition annuelle du deuxième groupe*, April

Venice, Palais de l'Exposition, *XVI. Exposition internationale de la ville de Venise*, April–May

Le Havre, Musée des Beaux-Arts, *L'Art moderne au Havre*, May

Paris, Galerie Marguerite-Henry, *Fleurs*, May

Paris, Palais de Bois, *Salon des Tuileries*, July

Antibes, *Exposition d'art moderne*, August

Paris, Grand Palais, *Société du Salon d'Automne*, 4 November–16 December

Paris, *Société du Salon d'Automne, Exposition du Jubilé*, 4 November–16 December

Paris, Galerie Druet, *Exposition d'ensemble*, 24 December 1928–4 January 1929

Nice, *XXXIV Salon, Société des Beaux-Arts de Nice*

1929 Paris, Salle de la Renaissance, 11 rue Royale, *Exposition d'oeuvres des XIXèmes et XXèmes siècles*, 15–31 January

Paris, Galerie Druet, *Exposition annuelle du deuxième groupe*, 18 March–5 April

Paris, Galerie Druet, *Exposition de peinture de M. Jules Flandrin*, 24 March–4 April

Lyon, *Salon du Sud-Est*, 20 April–27 May

Paris, Palais des Exposition, *Salon des Tuileries*, June–July

Paris, Galerie Druet, *Exposition d'ensemble*, 7–18 October

Grenoble, Galerie St. Louis, *Exposition Jules Flandrin*

Grenoble, Galerie St. Louis, Musée Carrand-Jongkind, *Rétrospective Jules Flandrin*

1930 Paris, Galerie Druet, *Exposition d'ensemble*, 1–31 March

Paris, Galerie Jean Charpentier, *Peintres actuels*, May 1930

Bristol, Royal West of England Academy, *French Modern Art Exhibition*, 31 May–14 June

Grenoble, Société des amis de Grenoble, *Salon de Grenoble*, 1–31 June

Paris, Galerie Druet, *Aspects de Paris*, 8 June–25 July

Paris, Galerie Druet, *Nus*, 10–30 June

Paris, Cours de la Reine (place de l'Alma),

Salon des Tuileries, June–July

Paris, Grand Palais, *Société du Salon d'Automne*, 1 November–14 December

Venice, *XVII. Exposition Biennale internationale d'art de la ville de Venise*

1931 Grenoble, Galerie St. Louis, *Exposition Jules Flandrin*, 23 January–6 February

Paris, Galerie Bernheim, *Salon de la folle enchère*, 7–20 February

Paris, Galerie Druet, *Exposition annuelle du deuxième groupe*, 9–20 March

Paris, Galerie d'art du Bucheron, *Le Dauphiné vu par les artistes*, 10 March–10 April

Paris, Galerie Druet, *Aspects de Paris*, 8 June–25 July

Paris, *Salon des Tuileries*, June 1931

Grenoble, *Salon de Grenoble, Hommage à Jules Flandrin*, 31 July–30 August

Paris, Grand Palais, *Société du Salon d'Automne*, 1 November–13 December

1932 Grenoble, Galerie St. Louis, *Exposition Jules Flandrin*, January

Paris, Galerie Druet, *Exposition de peinture de M. Jules Flandrin*, 29 February–18 March

Paris, Galerie Druet, *Exposition du troisième groupe*, April

Paris, Galerie d'Art Braun, *De Matisse à Segonzac*, 2–21 May

Paris, *Salon des Tuileries*, May

Grenoble, *Salon de Grenoble, VIIIème exposition d'art de l'effort*, 12 August–10 September

Venice, *XVIII. Exposition internationale de la ville de Venise*

Paris, Grand Palais, *Société du Salon d'Automne*, 1 November–11 December

Grenoble, Société des amis des arts, *XXVIème Salon officiel de Grenoble*, 1–31 October

1933 Paris, Galerie Druet, *Exposition annuelle du deuxième groupe*, April

Grenoble, Galerie St. Louis, *Dessins de Jules Flandrin, Rome, Naples et Florence*, 8 May 1933

Paris, Grand Palais, *Société du Salon d'Automne*, November

Paris, *Salon des Tuileries*

1934 Paris, Galerie Druet, *Exposition annuelle du deuxième groupe*, February–March

Lyon, *Salon du Sud-Est*, 14 April–27 May

1935   Paris, Grand Palais, *Société du Salon d'Automne*, 1 November–2 December

Paris, *Salon des Tuileries*

1935   Paris, Galerie Guy Stein, *Qui fera mon portrait?* February 1935

Paris, Galerie Druet, *Exposition annuelle du deuxième groupe*, February–March

Paris, *Société des Tuileries*, May

Venice, *Exposition du Quarantenaire de la Biennale*, May–June

Paris, Grand Palais, *Société du Salon d'Automne*, 1 November–8 December

Grenoble, 7 rue Montorge, *Exposition d'art chrétien*

1936   Lyon, Galerie des Jacobins, *Exposition Jules Flandrin*, 13–29 January

Paris, Galerie Druet, *Exposition annuelle du deuxième groupe*, 20 April–1 May

Lyon, *Salon du Sud-Est*, 25 April–1 June

Paris, *Salon des Tuileries*

1937   Paris, Galerie Druet, *Exposition annuelle du deuxième groupe*, 22 March–2 April

Paris, Petit Palais, *Les Maîtres de l'art Indépendant, 1895–1937*, June–October

Paris, Galerie Druet, *Exposition Jules Flandrin*, 20–31 December

1938   Paris, Galerie Druet, *Exposition annuelle du deuxième groupe*, March–April

1939   New York, *Exposition internationale*

1940   Grenoble, Galerie Fénoglio, *Jules Flandrin et Henriette Deloras*, 29 August–15 September

1941   Grenoble, Galerie Radio-France, *Jules Flandrin, I. Vicat, Gilioli, M. Lancelon*, May

1942   Grenoble, Galerie Radio-France, *Exposition Jules Flandrin*, February

Oran, Galerie M. Pozzalo, *Exposition Jules Flandrin*, 21 November–5 December

Paris, *Salon des Tuileries*

1943   Grenoble, Galerie Gay, *Exposition de peintres contemporains – Dauphiné et Lyonnais*, September

1945   Grenoble, Galerie de la Librairie Fautrières, *Exposition, études et toiles à caractère religieux*, 31 October–10 November

Grenoble, Galerie St. Louis, *Exposition, toiles profanes*

1946   Grenoble, Salon d'art des Galeries Modernes, *Exposition de peinture Dauphinoise*, 9–30 November

1947   Cannes, Salon de l'Hôtel Gray d'Albion, *Le Musée de Grenoble présente l'art vivant et l'École de Paris*

1949   Grenoble, Lycée Champollion, *Exposition 600 ans d'art Dauphinois*, August

Grenoble, Galerie St. Louis, *Rétrospective Jules Flandrin*, November

1953   Paris, Grand Palais, *Société du Salon d'Automne*, 4–29 November

1960   Grenoble, Société des amis des arts, *Salon d'Hiver*

1963   Grenoble, Galerie Hébert, *E. Berger, H. Deloras, E. Drivier, J. Flandrin, L. Gaillard, E. Gilioli, M. Giraud, H. Gröll, L. Mainssieux, L. Morel, J. Marval, D. Verbanesco, Y. Vicat*, December

1969   La Tronche, Fondation Hébert-d'Ukerman, *Hommage à Jules Flandrin*, 6–29 June

1972   Grenoble, Musée de Grenoble, *Hommage à Jules Flandrin*, 20 April–5 June

1975   Corenc, La Condamine, Mairie de Corenc, *Quelques peintres autour de Corenc*, 13 November–12 December

1978   Grenoble, Galerie Vaujany, *Jules Flandrin*, 3–31 October

1984   Grenoble, espace Achard, *Des réussites graphiques en Dauphiné au début du XXème siècle*, 24 May–30 June

1985   Le Touvet, Château du Touvet, *La Vallée du Grésivaudan vue par les peintres Dauphinois du XIXème au XXème siècle*, 9 June–1 September

1987   Paris, Musée d'Art moderne de la Ville de Paris, *Paris 1937, l'art indépendant*, 12 June–30 August

La Tronche, Musée Hébert, *Jacqueline Marval*, 24 September–31 October

1988   London, Crane Kalman Gallery, *Unfashionable Artists*, 17 March–16 April

1992   Saint-Antoine, Musée Jean Vinay, *Jean Vinay et les peintres Dauphinois de son temps*, 20 September–30 November

2000   Paris, Musée d'Orsay, *Nijinsky, 1889–1950*, 23 October 2000–18 February 2001